Churches, Communities, and Children:

Italian Immigrants in the Archdiocese of New York, 1880–1945

Churches, Communities, and Children:

Italian Immigrants in the Archdiocese of New York, 1880–1945

Mary Elizabeth Brown
CMS
1995

The Center for Migration Studies is an educational, non-profit institute founded in New York in 1964 to encourage and facilitate the study of sociological, demographic, economic, historical, legislative and pastoral aspects of human migration, refugee movements, and ethnic group relations everywhere.

The opinions expressed in this text are those of the author.

CHURCHES, COMMUNITIES, AND CHILDREN:
ITALIAN IMMIGRANTS IN THE
ARCHDIOCESE OF NEW YORK, 1880–1945

First Edition

Copyright © 1995 by
The Center for Migration Studies

CENTER FOR MIGRATION STUDIES
209 Flagg Place, Staten Island, New York 10304-1199

Library of Congress Cataloging-in-Publication Data
Brown, Mary Elizabeth.
    Churches, communities, and children: Italian immigrants in the Archdiocese of New York, 1880–1945/Mary Elizabeth Brown.
        p. cm.
    Includes bibliographical references and index.
    ISBN 0-934733-56-2 (c). – ISBN 0-934733-57-0 (p)
    1. Italian Americans – New York (N.Y.) – History.   2. Catholics – New York (N.Y.) – History.   3. Italian Americans – New York (N.Y.) – History – Religion.   4. New York (N.Y.) – History – 1898–1951.   5. New York (N.Y.) – History – 1865–1898.   6. New York (N.Y.) – Church history.   7. Catholic Church.   Archdiocese of New York (N.Y.)   I. Title.
F128.9.I8B76   1995   94-42461
974.7'100451 – dc20   CIP

Printed in the United States of America

Contents

Introduction and Acknowledgments

New York's Italian Catholics have more than repaid all the attention I gave them over the past few years. They have taught me a great deal about their own ethnic and religious group, about American ethnicity and religion in general, about the society which received the mass migration of the early twentieth century, and even a little about foreign affairs.

This monograph follows a combination of chronological and topical organization. Chapter one sets the scene, describing the experience the Archdiocese of New York had with ethnic Catholics prior to the beginning of Italian mass migration. Much of the writing about American Italian Catholicism has been shaped by a debate about the "Italian problem;" Chapter two gives the history of that debate and raises the question of the importance of gender in understanding nineteenth-century religious practice. Chapter three takes up the first generation of Italian Catholics in New York from the 1880s to the 1900s, and introduces the notion that these parishes, commonly considered to have been founded to help the immigrants conserve their heritage, presented the Italians with the irony of preserving their heritage using American organizing and fundraising techniques. Chapter four highlights the importance of the American-born and -raised generation in accelerating the tendency to use Italian parishes as vehicles for introducing American methods of pastoral care into Italian communities, especially after 1900. Chapter five introduces the thesis that the Italians assimilated toward a moving target, and describes how in the 1910s and 1920s the Archdiocese of New York altered its organization in response to the presence of an increasingly diverse Catholic community. Chapter six takes up the second generation of Italian Catholics in New York, and demonstrates how in the period 1920–1940 the American Italian clergy and laity altered their parishes to suit the type of religious practice to which they had become accustomed. Chapter seven sorts out the conflict between Catholic loyalty, Italian nationalism, and American patriotism which shaped the process of Italian immigrant assimilation from the beginning of World War I to the beginning of the Cold War. Chapter eight takes up the third generation of Italian Catholics in New York, and describes that community as it was on the eve of Vatican II.

In acknowledging all the assistance given in the course of this project, I will start with my family, partly because they do always come first and partly because after I'm through with them there might not be room for anyone else. They are: Lucian G. Brown, Helen L. Brown, B.J. Brown Devlin, Philip M. Devlin, Brendan Philip Devlin, Clare Rose Devlin, Tom Brown, Josie Brown, Lucian Arthur Brown, Chris Borgman, John Borgman, Stephen Wesley Borgman, Lauren Colleen Borgman, Gerard Brown, Laurie Baker, and Margie Brown.

During the time I used it, the Center for Migration Studies had two librarians, Ohla della Cava and Diana J. Zimmerman, both of whom were very helpful. The Archives of the Archdiocese of New York, and its archivist, Sister Marguerita Smith, had less material available. The Reverend Cletus Dello Iacono, O.F.M., Archivist of the Province of the Immaculate Conception, showed me his newspaper clippings, photocopied his parish histories, and lent me his history of the province. Brother Eugene J. Dowling, S.J., located material for me in the Archives of the New York Province of the Society of Jesus just before entering the hospital for what turned out to be a fatal illness. The Reverend Louis A. Mounteer, S.J., thereafter gave me access to the archives. The pastors and secretaries at Saint Patrick's Old Cathedral, the Church of the Transfiguration, the Church of the Nativity, and the Church of Our Lady of Mount Carmel (White Plains) let me use their sacramental records. The Very Reverend Anthony M. Corigliano, C.S.S., and Mr. John J. Prentzel of the Diocese of Wilmington, Delaware, provided photocopies for me. The Most Reverend Joseph M. Pernicone was a living archive, whom I was privileged to speak with before his death.

While I was still struggling to complete the first draft, three scholars finished theirs: the Reverend Stephen M. Di Giovanni, Professor Robert A. Orsi, now of the University of Indiana, and Professor Margaret M. McGuinness of Cabrini College. They kindly shared their research with me, and Bob Orsi has been collegial in a number of other ways.

Professor James P. Shenton of Columbia University was a good advisor who left me alone for the research and initial writing, then stepped in to straighten out the first draft's form and content. Besides Professors Shenton and Orsi, three other readers served on the dissertation committee: Professors John A. Garraty and Randy Ballmar of Columbia University, and Professor Robert A.

McCaughey, of Columbia University and Barnard College. Lydio Tomasi suggested I submit the manuscript to the Center for Migration Studies press; thanks are also due to the two anonymous critics who read the manuscript. Anastasia Mather of the Center for Migration Studies helped ready the manuscript for publication.

While this manuscript was in preparation, portions of it appeared elsewhere in scholarly journals, namely *The Catholic Historical Review* LXXIII:2 (1987), 195–210; *U.S. Catholic Historian* VI:4 (Fall, 1987), 281–300; *Mid-America* LXXI:3 (1989), 137–152; and *Immigration to New York* (Philadelphia: The Balche Institute Press [A New York Historical Society Book], 1991), 109–125. Thanks are due to Monsignor Robert Trisco, Christopher Kauffman, and William Galush, editors of the journals, for permission to use the material again.

I can only wish I could thank all the people who wrote the records I read. I was most struck by how privileged historians are when I was reading through the Jesuits' records on their Italian parishes. The records hadn't been touched in years, and there were pages and pages of reports, requests, complaints, comments, descriptions of parish activities, plans for future parish events – a whole world of people going about their business at the beginning of this century, unaware of the changes that led to my reading their mail at the century's close. I am grateful for the unintentional favor of sharing their lives with me. It is hoped that the readers will find that all this assistance has been given in a worthwhile cause.

Abbreviations Used in the Text and End Notes

AANY	Archives of the Archdiocese of New York.
CMS IAR	Center for Migration Studies, Italian Americans and Religion Collection.
CMS NCWC	Center for Migration Studies, National Catholic Welfare Conference Collection.
CMS OLP	Center for Migration Studies, Our Lady of Pompei Collection.
CMS Saint Joachim	Center for Migration Studies, Saint Joachim Collection.
CMS Saint Joseph	Center for Migration Studies, Saint Joseph Collection.
C.P.S.	Congregation of Saint Paul, or Paulists.
C.S.	Congregation of Saint Charles, or Scalabrinians.
C.S.S.	Stigmatine Fathers and Brothers.
C.S.V.	Clerics of Saint Viator.
M.P.F.	*Maestre Pie Filippini*, or Religious Teachers Filippini.
M.S.C.	Missionaries of the Sacred Heart, or Cabrini Sisters.
M.Z.S.H.	Missionary Zelatrices of the Sacred Heart, an early name for the Apostles of the Sacred Heart of Jesus.
NCWC	National Catholic Welfare Conference, predecessor of the National Catholic Conference.

NYSJ	New York Province of the Society of Jesus.
O.F.M.	Order of Friars Minor, or Franciscans.
O.F.M. Cap.	Capuchin Friars.
O.S.A.	Augustinians.
P.S.M.	Pious Society of Missionaries, an early name for the Society of the Catholic Apostolate.
P.S.S.C.	Pious Society of Saint Charles, an early name for the Congregation of Saint Charles.
S.A.C.	Society of the Catholic Apostolate, or Pallottines.
S.D.B.	Salesians of Saint John Bosco, or Salesians.
S.J.	Society of Jesus, or Jesuits.

1

The Archdiocese of New York before the Great Italian Migration

On Sunday, May 25, 1879, the Archdiocese of New York blessed its new Saint Patrick's Cathedral with as much pomp and circumstance as Catholic New York could muster. John Cardinal McCloskey, Archbishop of New York, presided over the five-hour service, assisted by 6 archbishops, 36 bishops, 150 diocesan clergy, 2 choirs, and 24 acolytes. Beginning at 10:00 a.m., a procession wound around the church on the corner of Fifth Avenue and 50th Street, showering holy water on the building. The high mass featured a two-hour sermon by Buffalo's Bishop Stephen Vincent Ryan. Seven thousand Catholics and non-Catholics filled the pews and aisles.[1] It was an impressive display of how far the Catholic community, which began construction on the cathedral in 1853, had come.

The year proved significant in a more subtle way. In 1879, 5,791 Italians arrived in the United States. The next year, their number more than doubled, to 12,354. The Italian mass migration had begun. Between 1880 and 1900 tens of thousands of Italians migrated to the United States each year. Between 1900 and 1914, hundreds of thousands came.[2] Most entered through New York Harbor. Many made New York City their first home in America. Providing for their spiritual and charitable needs was largely the archdiocese's responsibility.

To understand how the archdiocese approached the Italian immigrant ministry, one must understand how it saw itself and its mission. What follows is a brief

[1] *The New York Times*, 26 May 1879, 5:1.

[2] United States Department of Commerce, Bureau of the Census, *Historical Statistics of the United States, Colonial Times to 1970*, 2 volumes (Washington, D.C.: Government Printing Office, 1975), I:105–106.

introduction to the Archdiocese of New York's history and structure, and some idea of what New York Catholic life was like on the eve of the Italian migration.

Archdiocesan Organization

Rome carved the Diocese of New York out of the Diocese of Baltimore in 1808. Two factors already present at that point helped determine the course of New York Catholic history for the rest of the nineteenth century. One was the diocese's legal status within Catholicism. According to Rome, the United States was mission territory; it remained so until 1908. Therefore, it was governed by canon law which did not apply to other dioceses.[3]

Bishops of missionary dioceses wielded more power than those of regular dioceses. Canon law called the parishes they erected "missions," and the pastors "rectors." (Because "mission" has other meanings, and because contemporaries called them "parishes," "parishes" they will be here.) Missions and rectors did not have the rights which canon law said parishes and pastors had; they were subject to the bishop's will. Arbitrary rule had disadvantages, but permitted flexibility in authorizing parishes and assigning clergy.

A second influential factor was the necessity of building an organization practically *ex nihil*. When the diocese was created, Canada and New Jersey formed its northern and southern borders. Its first bishop, R. Luke Concanen, an Irish Dominican living in Rome, was consecrated in 1808 and died in 1810 without having been able to book passage to his diocese. The Napoleonic Wars delayed naming his successor. Rome finally consecrated another Irish Dominican, John Connolly, in 1814; he inherited 15,000 Catholics, 4 priests, and 2 churches: Saint Peter's on Barclay Street and the yet-to-be-opened Saint Patrick's Cathedral, then on Mott Street. Connolly died in 1826. The third bishop, John DuBois, a Sulpician and a French Revolution refugee, came to New York late in life, and had the further misfortune not to get along with the Irish laity already active there.[4]

In 1838, DuBois received as coadjutor John Hughes, who had immigrated from Ireland but was educated in the United States. DuBois died in 1842, and Hughes served as New York's ordinary until his own death in 1864. His tenure coincided

[3]*The Official Catholic Directory* gives the founding dates for New York parishes. For archdiocesan histories, see John Talbot Smith, *The Catholic Church in New York: A History of the New York Diocese From its Establishment in 1808 to the Present Time*, two volumes (New York: Locke and Hall, 1905), and Florence Cohalen, *A Popular History of the Archdiocese of New York* (Yonkers, New York: United States Catholic Historical Society, 1983).

[4]Richard Shaw, *John DuBois: Founding Father* (Younkers, New York: United States Catholic Historical Society, 1983).

with a wave of Irish and German immigration so huge that by 1850 Catholics outnumbered any single Protestant denomination in the United States. The immigrants, plus Hughes's aggressive personality, forced the diocese to expand. In 1840, New York opened three new churches; thereafter, it averaged one annually until 1918. By the 1850s, it had grown so populous that it was divided into the Archdiocese of New York and a number of suffragan sees, which altogether made up the Province of New York. One of these new dioceses was Brooklyn, erected in 1853.[5]

During Hughes's episcopacy, the archdiocese defined its parishes' status under American law. Through the 1830s, parish properties were owned by corporations established by lay trustees, who were elected from among the pew-renters. All sorts of problems developed between trustees and clergy, and then between trustees and bishops. Hughes could not eliminate corporate ownership, which was part of state law. He did arrange to have corporate ownership of Catholic Church property vested in himself, and to organize each parish so each had its own board of trustees, but the bishop and the pastor were always two of the four people on the board. (Laymen were always the other two.) This ended the disturbances involving the trustees, and also forced the laity from one of their few responsible ecclesiastical positions.[6]

Hughes helped shaped American Catholic-Protestant relationships for the next century. Antebellum non-Catholics harbored an ideological bias against Catholicism as an unreasonable religion presided over by an autocratic pope. The arrival of thousands of impoverished, unskilled, illiterate German and Irish immigrants added class and national antipathies to ideological anti-Catholicism. New York's private philanthropic school system's anti-Catholicism sparked the development of separate public and parochial school systems.[7] The struggle over schooling taught New York Catholics two lessons. First, since Protestants suspected Catholicism was incompatible with American patriotism, Catholics had to become more patriotic than their critics. Second, behind every Protestant philanthropy lay a plot to lure Catholics, youth especially, away from their faith, and so Catholics had to

[5]Richard Shaw, *Dagger John: The Unquiet Life and Times of Archbishop John Hughes of New York* (New York: Paulist Press, 1977).

[6]Patrick J. Dignan, *A History of the Legal Incorporation of Catholic Church Property int he United States, 1784–1932* (Washington, D.C.: Catholic University of America Press, 1933), and Patrick W. Carey, *People, Priests, and Prelates: Ecclesiastical Democracy and the Tensions of Trusteeism* (Notre Dame: University of Notre Dame Press, 1987).

[7]Diane Ravitch, *The Great School Wars: New York City, 1805–1973: A History of the Public Schools as Battlefield of Social Change* (New York: Basic Books, 1974), 3–78.

build not only their own grammar schools, but colleges, hospitals, orphanages, and other eleemosynary institutions.[8]

Upon Hughes's death, John McCloskey became the first New York ordinary born in the United States (in Brooklyn). Under him, the archdiocese became more noticeable as an institution in the city and as a diocese in the Church. Among the last episcopal events at Saint Patrick's Old Cathedral on Mott Street was his elevation to the cardinalate in 1875.[9] The new cathedral's 1879 blessing has already been described.

So far, this has been a history from the hierarchy's point of view, measured in increasing numbers of parishes and institutions. By taking the laity's point of view, one can also see the increasing complexity of the organization of individual parishes.

A "Typical" Gilded-Age Parish

Although parish history may have been the earliest type of American Catholic history, there are still problems with generalizing about it. Few good parish histories exist, and, to be fair, few parishes possess the necessary records. Most of the anecdotal information here comes from Saint Brigid's, a parish with good published materials from the late nineteenth century; reference will be made to other parishes as necessary.

Saint Brigid's location was typical. By 1880, the archdiocese had 49 Manhattan parishes, half of them below 14th Street. Saint Brigid's is in the East Village, facing Tompkins Square Park. Like the other parishes, Saint Brigid's was a territorial unit with geographic boundaries. Catholics were assigned to attend and support parishes on the basis of where they lived. There were exceptions to this rule, some recognized by canon law, and others sanctioned by common practice.

Saint Brigid's was also typical in that parish life centered on the rector. This may reflect a bias in the sources: mostly the clergy's records have survived. However, this impression is supported by the absence of structures or organizations allowed laity to exercise leadership and responsibility, except under the rector's direction.

Saint Brigid's rector was Patrick F. McSweeney. McSweeney did not have a winning personality that attracted and inspired the faithful; even his brother describe described him as "excessively sensitive, reserved and undemonstrative in

[8]Ray Allen Billington, *The Protestant Crusade, 1800–1860: A Study of the Origins of American Nativism* (New York: MacMillan, 1938).

[9][Stephen J. Hannigan], *Souvenir of the Centennial Celebration of Saint Patrick's Old Cathedral, New York, 1809-1909* (New York: n.p., 1909), unpaginated.

his manner." He was, however, at Saint Brigid's for 30 years, from 1877 to 1907. Sheer longevity guaranteed he made an impression on the parish. Other evidence suggests McSweeney was an active pastor who diligently carried out his duties as he saw them.[10]

The rector's main duty was maintaining the parishioners in their faith. The chief means of doing so were getting them to attend mass and to receive the sacraments. Saint Brigid's offered its congregation ample opportunities for both. The clergy celebrated daily masses at 6:30 a.m., 7:00 a.m. in the summer. The Sunday schedule was 6:30 a.m., 8:00 a.m., 10:00 a.m., and 11:00 a.m., with a special children's mass at 9:00 a.m.[11] The clergy baptized on Sundays from 4:00 to 6:00 p.m., and Sundays and Wednesdays from 7:00 to 9:00 p.m., and one could always fetch them (Saint Brigid's had no telephone) to baptize someone in danger of death. Confessions were heard Saturdays and the days before holy days from 4:00 to 9:30 p.m., Thursdays before First Fridays, 7:00 to 9:00 p.m., and every morning after mass.

The daily and most Sunday services were low masses, at which the celebrant recited the mass *sotto voce* while the congregation followed along quietly in their missals or silently recited other prayers. Saint Brigid's schedule does not mention this, but other churches set aside one mass, usually late Sunday morning, for a high mass, at which a choir, which could include paid singers, sang the parts of the mass while the priest performed the ritual actions and whispered those prayers proper to the clergy's role, and the congregation followed along in their missals, or paralleled the priests' prayers with their own private devotions, aided by prayer books and rosaries.

Not everyone considered such passivity ideal congregational behavior. Alfred Young, a Paulist and hymn writer, complained that stillness hardly suited the events at the altar. National leaders taking the podium, Young wrote, can hardly be heard for the people's enthusiastic greetings. When the sacramental God appeared in the eucharist, though, the people were all down on their haunches, heads bowed over their beads. Contrary to most clergy's opinion, congregations could learn hymns for low mass, the parts of the mass for high mass, and psalms for Vespers or Benediction. A well-trained congregation could replace the expensive and inappropriate choir of hired singers. Young tested his thesis at Saint Brigid's in

[10]Edward F. McSweeney, "A New York Pastor of the Latter Half of the Nineteenth Century," American Catholic Historical Society of Philadelphia *Records and Studies* XIX (1908), 42–58. American Catholic historians may know Patrick McSweeney as the Poughkeepsie Plan's originator and his brother Edward as part of the circle around Edward McGlynn and Richard Burtsell.

[11]*Souvenir of the Consecration Year of Saint Brigid's Church* (New York: Privately printed, 1889), and *Souvenir of the Golden Jubilee of Saint Brigid's Church* (New York: Privately printed, 1899).

1888. In January, he distributed hymn books, held a rehearsal at which he emphasized the importance of lauding God in song, and taught the parishioners two Lenten hymns. He returned for Holy Week, and was so pleased by the congregation's progress that he taught them a third hymn.[12] Young's work is worth mentioning because it was unusual. The reverent hush was the preferred sound from the congregation. McSweeney was an innovator in this regard.

The laity compensated for their silence at mass by their participation in other sorts of worship. During most of the nineteenth century, most parishes sponsored vespers, Catholicism's official, or "liturgical," evening prayer. Parishes also divided parishioners into groups by sex, age, and marital status, and confided each group to the spiritual protection of some saint, or the protection of Jesus or Mary under one of their titles. These groups, or "sodalities," practiced paraliturgical acts of worship, or "devotions."[13]

At Saint Brigid's the Society of the Infant Jesus took in the small children, the Guardian Angel and Children of Mary took girls and unmarried women, the Saint Aloysius and Young Men's Sacred Heart societies were for boys and bachelors, the Rosary Society was for married women, and the Sacred Heart Society for married men. Sodalities were not inter-parish groups, but most parishes' sodalities bore similar names. Saint Aloysius Gonzaga was a patron of youth, and nearly every parish confided its young men to his care. Sodalities met weekly. Priest-moderators led prayers, gave instructions, and acted as chaplains. Members received communion corporately monthly, which meant they also went to confession monthly.

Some parishes organized sodalities by special interest. During his pastorate, McSweeney moved from a temperance to a total abstinence advocate. His parish sponsored a total abstinence union, and "Saint Brigid's Confraternity of the Sacred Thirst for Jesus for the Suppression of Intemperance," whose members forswore liquor either temporarily or permanently, prayed for drunkards' conversions, urged alcoholics to join the total abstinence union, and made First Friday devotions together. Other parishes had other interests. Saint Patrick's Old Cathedral, for example, had a Sodality of the Most Precious Blood for the African Americans in its congregation.

Since 1842, New York's hierarchy had urged parishes to build parochial schools to teach both secular and religious subjects. The 1884 Third Plenary

[12]Alfred Young, "How to Obtain Congregational Singing," Catholic World XLVII (1888), 721–738.

[13]Ann Taves, "'External' Devotions and the Interior Life: Popular Devotional Theologies in Mid-Nineteenth Century America," [University of Notre Dame] Cushwa Center for the Study of American Catholicism Working Paper Series, Series 3, Number 2 (1983).

Council reinforced New York's priorities with a decree that every rector, so far as possible, maintain a school, and all parents, so far as possible, enroll their children. Not all Catholics agreed with this emphasis: Edward McGlynn, rector of Saint Stephen's on East 22nd Street, regarded parochial schools as unnecessary and did not have one.[14] McSweeney was more typical. When he arrived at Saint Brigid's in 1877, the school met in the church basement. In 1879, it moved to a new, debt-free, building.

Catholic bishops in the archdiocese and state made great strides in organizing the parochial school system at the end of the nineteenth century. In 1887, the archdiocese published a *Directory and Course of Instruction*, outlining how to place pupils in grades, and what material to cover in which grade. This took such decisions out of the hands of the myriad religious orders staffing the schools. In 1895, the archdiocese held its first teacher institute; up until then, many religious orders had no teaching training or ongoing education for their members. In 1897, the state hierarchy asked that Catholic school pupils be allowed to take the Regents examinations. In 1900, a state-wide board of education capped a separate, state-wide Catholic school system.[15]

Parishes without parochial school held catechism classes for their youngsters. Contemporaries usually mentioned "Sunday schools" only briefly and considered them inferior temporary measures. One of the most complete, if biased, descriptions, was written by a priest associated with Saint Monica's, an Upper East Side parish opened in 1879. Saint Monica's catechized about 500 children annually, all of them, in all the grades, in one large auditorium. Since it had no parochial school, it relied on lay volunteers, who were usually a week ahead of the students in the catechism books and who relied on the pedagogical method of last resort, rote memorization. Not until 1892 did a curate assigned to manage the catechism program introduce written examinations to screen prospective teachers.[16]

A rector's second responsibility after maintaining the faith was maintaining the parish plant. At Saint Brigid's, the plant consisted of a church, rectory, and school. Saint Brigid's records did not mention a convent, but other parishes had them. A staff of curates, brothers, sisters, lay teachers, sacristans, sextons, organists, and

[14]McGlynn has no modern biography; see Robert Emmet Curran, S.J., *Michael Augustine Corrigan and the Shaping of Conservative Catholicism in America, 1878–1902* (New York: Arno, 1978).

[15]M. Patricia Ann Reilly, O.P., "The Administration of Parish Schools in the Archdiocese of New York, 1800–1900," United States Catholic Historical Society *Records and Studies* XLIV (1956), 45–83.

[16]George A. Kelly, *The Story of Saint Monica's Parish, New York City, 1879–1954* (New York: Monica Press, 1954), 38.

choristers awaited stipends or salaries. Bills regularly came in from the bank which extended the mortgage, the gas, light, and water companies, and the manufacturers who produced hosts and votive candles. Besides collecting funds for themselves parishes participated in the Church-wide Peter's pence collection, the American hierarchy's collection for the missions to Negroes and Indians, and the archdiocesan collection for the orphan asylum. In 1889, Saint Brigid's budget balanced at $28,787.25, and it was what one might call a middle-class parish. In short, rectors such as McSweeney had to be accountants, building managers, and contractors as well as pastors.

Saint Brigid's sustained itself principally through pew rents and Sunday collections. The handbook instructed each family to rent a pew and pay for it "QUARTERLY IN ADVANCE." Those who did not rent pews paid a nickel a seat at the 6:30 mass and a dime a seat at the 8:00, 10:00, and 11:00 masses. Children sat free at their 9:00 mass, but adults paid a dime. One could avoid paying pew or seat rent only by standing behind the pews at the church entrance. The parish handbook also directed parishioners to put some money into the collection plate, and reminded them that an offering of a dime represented "little more than ONE CENT A DAY set aside for God's Church and Schools." Sodalities celebrated special occasions with corporate offerings.

Saint Brigid's relied on fundraisers less than other parishes did. When it did have a fundraiser, careful planning maximized the income therefrom. Saint Brigid's scheduled the fund raiser to coincide with a special anniversary or important event, which by itself might attract the devout. Then it added some sort of entertainment, usually a dramatic production. Parishioners themselves acted in the dramas and did the other necessary work, thus saving the parish labor costs. Parishioners were also the main paying audience, and the main purchasers of space in the souvenir program. New York's provincial council regulated such fundraisers because they opened up all sorts of possibilities for misbehavior. Once, when one Lower East Side parish announced a dance, the neighboring rector mounted his pulpit to warn his parish girls against "promiscuous" balls, such as the one promised by the advertisement.[17]

A third possible source of income was the "stole fees" which Catholics offered the priests who officiated at baptisms, weddings, and funerals. Whether this was income to priest or parish depended on whether the clergy were archdiocesan or members of religious communities. Archdiocesan clergy did not take the same vow of poverty as members of religious communities, and thus could have some personal funds. Since Saint Brigid's budget does not mention stole fees as income to the

[17]Thomas F. Lynch to Michael A. Corrigan, New York, 16 May 1886, AANY microfilm roll #9.

parish, McSweeney and his curates may have kept their stole fees for personal use. Members of religious communities, though, took vows of poverty which prevented them from expending any money on their own. They turned over their stole fees to their superiors and then requested spending money as needed, or split their stole fees with the parish.[18]

A rector's third obligation was to disburse charity. Charity literally began at home in nineteenth-century New York parishes. Each had a Saint Vincent de Paul Society, men organized to dispense funds collected from among the better-off parishioners to benefit the poorer ones. If the New York Association for Improving the Condition of the Poor received word of a needy Catholic family, it notified the appropriate parish Saint Vincent de Paul Society, and a Saint Vincent de Paul man (they were usually men) investigated its claims. If family circumstances warranted such intervention, Saint Vincent de Paul offered emergency help (rent money, grocery or fuel vouchers, clothing) and moral encouragement.

Diocesan-wide collections or assessments from each parish funded welfare institutions which served the whole diocese. Particular ethnic groups founded and benefited from some non-parochial institutions. For example, German-American clergy led a national campaign to raise money for Leo House, a German immigrant traveler's aid shelter.[19] Wealthy Catholics such as Thomas Fortune Ryan donated generously to build churches and cathedrals.[20] European-based organizations, such as the Society for the Propagation of the Faith (in Lyons) also took an interest in American Catholic needs.

The rector's final responsibility was to preserve the congregation's Catholic heritage. In the nineteenth century, as we shall see, many people considered the faith to be inseparable from its cultural context. At Saint Brigid's, that meant its Irish context. Saint Brigid's handbook proudly announced that the parish, founded in 1849, was the first one for English-speaking Catholics in its part of the city. The first rector immigrated from Ireland. The second was born in Manchester, but of Irish parents, and retained enough Irish sentiment to serve as chaplain of New York's 69th, or "Meagher's Irish Brigade," in the Civil War. McSweeney, the third rector, was born in County Cork in 1839, and immigrated with his father ten years later. When he became rector, the parish's name was

[18]*The Village Bells* (Spring 1984), 2.

[19]Colman J. Barry, O.S.B., *The Catholic Church and German Americans* (Milwaukee: Bruce Publishing Company, 1953), 104.

[20][Francis Joseph Magri], *The Catholic Church in the City and Diocese of Richmond* (Richmond: Whittet and Shepperson, 1906), 9.

spelled Brigi*t*. McSweeney discovered the parish's patroness, the fifth-century foundress of Ireland's first women's community, had spelled her name Brigi*d*. He had the parish's name legally changed to avoid confusion with another, Swedish, saint. McSweeney used Irish patriotism to encourage his congregation in its faith. Some of his colleagues participated in Irish politics. For example, Edward McGlynn, Saint Stephen's rector, lectured on Irish land reform and organized an American Land League to support the Irish one.[21]

National pride was not confined to the Irish. All nations cherished their particular Catholic history, and most tended to regard themselves as the only truly devout Catholics. For example, the German Capuchins at Our Lady Queen of Angels in East Harlem were unimpressed by their neighboring Hungarians' religiosity. "They called themselves Catholics, but never came to church save for baptism and to marry. Nothing came of the efforts made for them."[22]

The published sources give an impression of busy parishioners actively involved in parish life. It is difficult to tell at this distance whether this impression was accurate or hopeful. There are some hints that if it was accurate, it was a struggle to maintain.

One indication of struggle is in the literature itself. The fact that the "Rules and Regulations of Saint Brigid's Parish" existed in printed form indicated not everyone knew them. The parish handbook spelled out instructions extremely carefully. Sometimes this was necessary: the handbook contained directions for preparing the dying for the last rites, a bit of Catholic knowledge one hopes no one needed often enough to repay memorization. On the other hand, the handbook enjoined parishioners not to bring babies for baptism outside of the scheduled hours, not to ask the clergy to make sick calls at times they were likely to be busy, and to be on time for services. The instructions for funerals, for example, state that funerals were always scheduled for 10:00 a.m. and started at 10:00 a.m., whether or not the funeral party had arrived at the church. Someone must have needed lessons in punctuality.

Another indication of struggle is the size of the churches. Gilded Age Lower East Side pastors counted parishioners in the tens of thousands.[23] No church in

[21]Eric Foner, "Class, Ethnicity, and Radicalism in the Gilded Age: The Land League and Irish-America," in *Politics and Ideology in the Age of the Civil War* (New York: Oxford, 1980), 150–200.

[22]Austin DuBois, O.F.M. Cap., *Golden Jubilee of the Church of Our Lady Queen of Angels* (New York: Privately published, 1936), 82.

[23]In 1879, Saint James on Oliver Street may have had 18,000 parishioners; Oscar Handlin, *Al Smith and his America* (Boston: Little, Brown, 1958), 11. In 1889, Saint Patrick's Old Cathedral's rector counted 14,000; Hannigan, *Centennial*.

this area sufficed to hold all those people. Unless Catholics distributed themselves evenly among the Sunday masses, some could be squeezed out.[24]

A third indication of struggle comes from the area's economic situation. The Lower East Side was already the city's slum showplace, and that could not but affect parish life. Saint Brigid's, for example, fronted one of the area's few open spaces, where boys fought rowdy snowball wars and adults held labor protests.[25] When he first came to Saint Brigid's, McSweeney interested himself in "recovering" Tompkins Square for a park, and restoring some middle-class respectability to the area.[26]

However, McSweeney could do nothing about employment opportunities, on which the middle-class image ultimately rested. Until the Civil War, Saint Brigid's men usually worked on the East River's dry docks. When ship construction declined, they switched to building and transportation route construction. They then followed the transit lines they had erected to better housing elsewhere in the city. Other parishes had similar struggles. Transfiguration parish acquired its permanent church on Mott Street in 1853. Even then Five Points, two blocks south of the church, was a notorious slum. One block south of the church lay Mulberry Bend, on which Jacob Riis lavished so much righteous indignation in *How the Other Half Lives.*

Saint Patrick's Old Cathedral also illustrates the Lower East Side's instability. When it opened in 1815, the cathedral sat on the city's outskirts. Gradually houses engulfed it; then the houses turned to tenements. In 1866, fire destroyed the church's exterior. Because the new cathedral's construction was underway, the old one was repaired with a serviceable but plain exterior. The cathedral's transfer coincided with the arrival of warehouses in SoHo. The conversion of a residential area into a commercial one sent many Irish parishioners in search of new housing.[27]

It is important to note that Saint Patrick's retained its Irish associations after 1879, even though some of the Irish had moved into the middle class. There were two reasons why. First was its history as the cathedral. Second was its rector's

[24]Jay P. Dolan, *The Immigrant Church: New York's Irish and German Catholics, 1815–1865* (Baltimore: The Johns Hopkins University Press, 1975), 51, makes the same argument for antebellum New York Catholicism.

[25]For snowballs, *see* Jacob A. Riis, *Children of the Tenements* (New York: MacMillan, 1904), 159. For labor protests, *see* "Defeat of the Communists," New York *Times*, 14 January 1874, 2:3.

[26]Patrick D. O'Flaherty, "The History of Saint Brigid's Parish in the City of New York under the Administration of the Rev. Patrick F. McSweeney, 1877–1907," (Master's Thesis, Fordham University, 1952), 41–42.

[27]Smith, *The Catholic Church in New York*, 471.

longevity. John F. Kearney was born above Centre Street Market, a few blocks from Saint Patrick's, in 1838. He attended its parochial school as a boy. He left the parish to study for the priesthood, but, upon his ordination in 1866, returned to it as a curate. He was appointed rector in 1879, and held the position until his death in 1923.[28] There are no indications Kearney was an energetic or aggressive leader of either Irish or Catholics. The only accessible records from his hand are baptismal and marriage register entries. Yet his tenure assured that Saint Patrick's would be an "Irish" parish in name even after its population changed.

Variations on a Theme

Saint Peter's, New York's first parish, ministered to a heterogeneous congregation, including the aristocratic Episcopalian convert Elizabeth Ann Bayley Seton and the African-Haitian ex-slave and hairdresser Pierre Toussaint. As population increased and parishes multiplied, Catholics sorted themselves into congregations based on various social distinctions, the most important being ethnicity. Because of their preponderance, the "typical" parish was Irish, but there were others.

Germans began arrived in New York at about the same time as the Irish. At first, they attended mass with everyone else, even though they could not understand English-language sermons. When a German-speaking priest came to Manhattan, he gathered a congregation about him, and Bishop John DuBois authorized the opening of a German parish, Saint Nicholas, in 1833. In canon law, it was a regular parish, drawing support from the people living within its geographical borders. However, Saint Nicholas's boundaries coincided with those of the German neighborhood. Also, there was no way to control border-crossing on Sunday mornings, and no reason to: priests and people preferred the laity to be at services where their languages were spoken their liturgical sensibilities respected. In 1840, Du Bois authorized a second, French, parish, Saint Vincent de Paul. In 1842, the Diocese of New York recognized "national parishes," with linguistic rather geographic boundaries.[29]

In the 1880s, under pressure from Midwestern Germans, the Vatican clarified its position on national parishes. In 1887, it determined that two parishes could indeed occupy the same space, that parishes established for national groups could have irremovable rectors (protection against episcopal authority's arbitrary exercises of power); and that children belonged to their parents' parish so long as they

[28]*The New York Times*, 12 April 1923, 19:5.

[29]Dolan, *Immigrant Church*, 71-72, and Shaw, *Dagger John*, 178-179, 221-222, and 324-325.

lived with them, but could affiliate with either national or territorial parishes upon leaving home.[30] This, though, is getting ahead of the story.

The "typical" New York parish was, and is, staffed by "secular" or "archdiocesan" priests. These are ordained specifically for service in a particular diocese (though transfers are possible), and owe their loyalty to its bishop. New York's early diocesan clergy were often immigrants themselves: Transfiguration's first rector was Cuban.[31] They studied for the priesthood in a number of places, the most prestigious being the North American College in Rome. As the diocese matured it recruited clergy among native boys and in 1896 opened Saint Joseph's Seminary, a permanent place to train local clergy.[32]

Some parishes were, and are, staffed by "religious order" clergy, which differ from secular clergy in that they take vows binding them to their superiors and communities. The secular and religious clergy's different loyalties and priorities often led to conflict in the nineteenth century, and they seldom served in the same parish.[33] Usually, religious orders got their own parishes.

There was a correlation between religious orders and national parishes. Perhaps seminarians or priests could learn the languages of incoming immigrants, but language was not the only issue. National parishes required pastors sensitive to immigrants' approach to Catholicism and sympathetic to people in transit between two cultures. Bishops assigned national parishes to religious orders because the orders could in turn assign clergy with these qualifications. Religious orders accepted the responsibility because a presence in a parish was one way to recruit vocations among young men. In the Archdiocese of New York, the pattern of using religious orders for national parishes was established before the Italians arrived. The French Fathers of Mercy helped found Saint Vincent de Paul in 1823. The German Redemptorists founded Most Holy Redeemer in 1844.

The differences between regular and national parishes, and between secular and religious clergy were the most obvious variations on the themes of parish life. There was a subtle third variation. Despite the moral and pragmatic values of

[30]Barry, *The Catholic Church and German Americans*, 71.

[31]Joseph and Helen McCadden, *Father Valera: Torch Bearer from Cuba* (New York: United States Catholic Historical Society, 1969).

[32]Arthur J. Scanlan, *Saint Joseph's Seminary, Dunwoodie, New York, 1896-1921* (New York: United States Catholic Historical Society, 1922).

[33]John P. Marschall, C.S.V., "Diocesan and Religious Clergy: The History of a Relationship, 1789–1969," in John Tracy Ellis, ed., *The Catholic Priest in the United States: Historical Investigations* (Collegeville, Minnesota: Saint John's University Press, 1971), 385–421.

peace and harmony, nineteenth-century New York Catholics were a tumultuous lot. Conflict between parishioners and clergy over the trusteeship of churches has already been mentioned. Such conflicts ended when Hughes became bishop, but others took their place.

The Catholic loyalty on which the Irish prided themselves was hardly innate. American Catholics accused the early Irish immigrants of ignorance of their faith and laxity of practice.[34] Native-born middle-class New Yorkers noted the preponderance of Irish Catholics among the hooligans vandalizing, looting, and attacking African Americans in the 1863 New York City draft riots. Authorities thought the rioters might listen to their archbishop, and persuaded Hughes to address the crowds. However, Hughes was ill, could move no farther than his bedroom balcony, and could not be heard when he spoke. Rain and the arrival of troops from Gettysburg, not the archbishop, quelled the disturbance.[35]

At German Saint Nicholas, a dispute between those who thought the trustees should hold the balance of power in pastoral affairs and those who thought the pastor should resulted in a rapid turnover in the clergy, until Archbishop Hughes invited the Redemptorists to open Most Holy Redeemer a short distance away. A similar split at the Capuchin Franciscan's German Saint John the Baptist on West 31st Street led to the erection of the Franciscans' Saint Francis, also on West 31st Street. At Saint Alphonsus on West Broadway, the congregation was divided into factions of English- and German-speaking faithful.[36]

In other cases, no public quarrel marred the peace, but the possibility for one existed. There was, for example, the case of Saint Brigid's next door neighbor Saint Ann's, which opened in 1852. Saint Ann's was both within walking distance and a world away: Saint Brigid's fronted working-class Tompkins Square while middle-class Saint Ann's stood near Astor Place until 1870, when it moved to a quiet residential area on East Twelfth Street. Saint Brigid's pastors were all of Irish background, Saint Ann's were mostly converts from Episcopalianism.[37] The differences were subtle, but obvious enough to the Catholics who walked past each other to worship.

[34]Dolan, *The Immigrant Church*, 57.

[35]Adrian Cook, *Armies of the Streets: The New York City Draft Riots of 1863* (Lexington, Kentucky: University Press of Kentucky, 1974).

[36]Dolan, *The Immigrant Church*, 87–98.

[37]Henry J. Browne, *Saint Ann's on East Twelfth Street, New York City, 1852-1952* (New York: Privately published, 1952).

The Italian Variation

Prior to the Civil War, there were not enough Italians to be an issue. As late as 1865, the state census counted only 955 New York City residents born in Italy. (Since their American-born offspring were counted as American, the whole community was probably larger.)[38] The most prominent immigrants were the opera singers, musicians, art and language tutors, artisans, and purveyors of luxury items which found markets among New York's middle class and wealthy, and the revolutionaries, such as Giuseppe Garibaldi, who had been exiled or who had found it expedient to leave Italy for a while. Garibaldi's revolutionary program included revolt against organized religion. Few of the best-known merchants and professionals, even if they were themselves practicing Catholics, interested themselves in becoming Catholic lay leaders.[39]

At the level of locally recognized *prominenti*, some did take up the role of Catholic lay leader. Victor Greene, in his monograph on the nature of ethnic leadership, has highlighted the career of Luigi Fugazy. Fugazy came from Liguria ahead of the mass migration. His most accessible English-language title was "banker," but he served as a kind of general *padrone*, or intermediary between Italians seeking work or help with financial or travel arrangements (for example, converting dollars into lire and remitting savings to relatives in Italy, or purchasing tickets for relatives coming to the United States). As part of his role as community leader, he supported the development of Italian parishes.[40]

The immigrants of most concern here, though, were those noticeable to people such as philanthropist Charles Loring Brace, who left a description of them in his autobiography.[41] Like the Irish, who came from a particular county, or the Germans, who came from specific German-speaking principalities, the Italians had a precise homeland. Brace called them Ligurians, and their first parish history even more exact in stating that their ancestors came from the Fontabuona Valley.[42]

[38]Ira Rosenwaike, *Population History of New York City* (Syracuse, New York: Syracuse University Press, 1972), 67.

[39]Howard R. Marraro, "Italians in New York in the Eighteen-Fifties," *New York History* XXX (1949), 181–203, 276–303.

[40]Victor R. Greene, *American Immigrant Leaders, 1800–1910: Marginality and Identity* (Baltimore: The Johns Hopkins University Press, 1987).

[41]Charles Loring Brace, *The Dangerous Classes of New York and Twenty Years' Work Among Them* (New York: Wynkoop and Hallenbeck, 1880, reprint ed.: Montclair, New Jersey: Patterson Smith, 1978), 195–199.

[42]New York *Catholic News*, 7 October 1916, 1.

In Italy they were itinerant workers who travelled to the country side for the planting and harvest seasons and spent the winters haunting the cities, looking for odd jobs, and begging. According to Brace, about the same time the hand-held organ's invention opened new employment possibilities, Liguria's stagnant economy forced the poor workers further afield to London and New York. The Italian organ-grinder and monkey quickly became stereotypical, but the Ligurians also brought children whose parents, unable to support them in school or find work for them at home, had indentured them. Far from home and family, outdoors in all sorts of weather, unschooled, often visibly suffering from neglect and abuse, the little beggars did excite onlookers' pity. However, as historians Rudolph Vecoli and John Zucchi have shown, rather than increase their donations to the street musicians, Americans denounced the Italian parents for sacrificing their off-spring's best interests, and attempted to halt the traffic in children.[43]

Brace recalled that the Ligurians, though "not fanatics in religion . . . still clung with tenacity to the infallibility of their priests." In 1855, Brace and an Italian Protestant named A.E. Cerqua opened a school for Italians in the Five Points area. Brace recalled that an Italian priest named Rebeccio opposed the school on the grounds that its teachers really intended to convert the students to Protestant-ism. Rebeccio took up a neighborhood collection to fund an Italian Catholic school. He then disappeared, "and it was only after months that he was heard of in affluent circumstances in Italy."

Brace's anecdote cannot be verified, although the Italians' first parish history agreed with him that a sizeable community existed by 1855, and that the Italian secular priests who emigrated "did not have much success" among their compa-triots. However, the first parish history might have made that judgment about the clergy with a different priest, Antonio Sanguinetti, in mind. Sanguinetti arrived in New York in October 1857. He arranged to use Saint Vincent de Paul parish's church, then on Canal Street, for Italian services. When Saint Vincent's relocated to West 23rd Street, the Italians began raising money for their own parish, which apparently was incorporated in 1859. Sanguinetti, though, ran afoul of the Italian community's factions. One group wanted a church, another a hospital, and the priest, whom one American colleague characterized as a bit of a bungler, failed to reconcile the groups. When he bought new gates for the altar rail at the Canal Street church, a portion of the congregation disagreed with how he had spent their

---

[43]Rudolph John Vecoli, "Chicago's Italians prior to World War One: A Study of Their Social and Economic Adjustment" (unpublished Ph.D. dissertation, University of Wisconsin, 1963), and John E. Zucchi, *The Little Slaves of the Harp: Italian Child Street Musicians in Nineteenth-Century Paris, London, and New York* (Montreal: McGill-Queen's University Press [McGill-Queen's Studies in Ethnic History], 1992).

money and attacked him. Archbishop Hughes failed to support him against his congregation, whereupon Sanguinetti left New York for Rome to enlist Vatican officials in supporting him against Hughes. Hughes forestalled his efforts by writing to the Vatican with his side of the story. Presumably, the Austro-Italian War of 1859, the American Civil War, and Hughes's death put an end to the story.[44]

Meanwhile, Italian clergy had come to the nearby Diocese of Buffalo. In 1847, when John Timon became the diocese's first bishop, Nicholas Devereux, a wealthy Catholic in the area, donated $5,000 and a farm to establish a religious order in northern New York. Devereux requested clergy from Saint Isadore's an Irish Franciscan seminary in Rome, but the seminary had no clergy to spare, and passed the request to the Franciscan Minister General, who promised to send friars displaced by the Italian revolutions. In June, 1855, Panfilio Pierbattista da Magliano and three colleagues arrived in Buffalo to organize Saint Bonaventure's.[45] In 1866, Archbishop John McCloskey invited Leone Pacilio to leave Saint Bonaventure's and take up parish work in New York.

The parish's name, Saint Anthony of Padua, could have been chosen for any number of reasons. Apparently, Sanguinetti intended to name his church for Saint Anthony.[46] In keeping the name, the Franciscans honored one of their own. Although born in Lisbon, Anthony achieved his greatest fame as a preacher in northern Italy. Although he was called "of Padua," Anthony's cult appealed to non-Italians as well.

This last was significant because Saint Anthony's was not just for Italians. McCloskey gave it permission to minister to all Italians, wherever they resided, but he also give it geographic boundaries. An early parish history ascribed McCloskey's decision to his awareness of the Italians' poverty and their inability to support their own church.

From its beginning, Saint Anthony's resembled its more thoroughly Irish neighbors. In 1868, rector Gioacchino Guerrini da Monte-Fegatese established the first sodalities, the Daughters of Mary and Guardian Angels. In 1869, he organized the parish temperance and mutual benefit societies, the Catholic

[44]Silvano M. Tomasi, C.S., *Piety and Power: The Role of the Italian Parishes in the New York Metropolitan Area, 1880–1930* (New York: Center for Migration Studies, 1975), 68–71.

[45]Cletus Della Iacona, O.F.M., "A History of the Franciscan Province of the Immaculate Conception, New York, U.S.A." (typescript, 1959), 11–18.

[46]The archdiocesan records lists Saint Anthony of Padua as being first incorporated in 1859, and again in 1866.

Knights, sodalities of Saint Anthony,Mount Carmel, the Rosary, and the Sacred Heart, a sodality to pray for the souls in purgatory, and a Saint Vincent de Paul Society. Of these, the names of the first members of the Saint Vincent de Paul Society have survived: three Italians, one German, and seven others with nondescript or Irish names. Saint Vincent de Paul's first two presidents, whose terms spanned the years 1878 to 1924, were Irish.

Saint Anthony's first three rectors lasted about two years each. The fourth, Giacomo Titta, served from 1870 to 1877, and the fifth, Anacleto de Angelis, from 1877 to 1889 and again from 1895 to 1902. Their personal qualities are more obscure than those of Saint Brigid's McSweeney. The parish histories do not describe Titta. A 1924 history memorialized de Angelis, in Italian as "that zealous and pious priest who is even today mourned by the people who had the luck to know his uncommon worth and virtues." As at Saint Brigid's, the position of pastor conveyed an authority that the pastor's own personality might not.

The concrete evidence suggests both pastors showed initiative. In 1872, Titta purchased an old factory on MacDougal Street and renovated it for a school, which opened on September 5 of that year and soon had 500 Irish and Italian children. Titta engaged the Franciscan Sisters of Allegheny as teachers. Panfilio da Magliano had founded this community, but its members were insufficiently fluent in Italian to teach in that language: a laywoman taught the Italian children their parents' language.

In 1882, de Angelis braved a fierce snowstorm to be the only bidder at an auction for a group of lots on Sullivan Street. The church was built in the Romanesque style more familiar in Italy than the Gothic style of northern European and many New York churches. The church is still standing, although its site is deceptive. Houston Street's widening gave it a prominent corner lot; when it was first built it was a huge edifice looming over a crowd of huddling tenements. Redecoration done in the early 1960s is also deceptive, but it does bring out the size of the interior. The impressions of great height and immense space were fully intended. The parishioners were poor immigrants and laboring people, but they honored God and testified to their own faith with the most magnificent structure they could afford.[47]

Saint Anthony's Gilded Age decorations gave clues as to the kind of congregation that worshipped there. The church's nineteenth-century character was established by its statue of Saint Margaret Mary before the Sacred Heart, a popular devotion. A statue of Saint Bonaventure writing his life of Saint Francis

[47]Ellen Skerret, "The Irish Parish in Chicago, 1880–1930," [University of Notre Dame] Cushwa Center for the Study of American Catholicism Working Papers, Series IX, No. 2 (typescript 1981), 6.

of Assisi indicated its Franciscan associations. The Irish had statues of Saint Brigid and Saint Patrick. The Italians had a trio consisting of the young Virgin Mary with her parents Joachim and Anne. The new church's dedication, which took place June 10, 1888, conformed to archdiocesan standards: the same bishop preached at both this ceremony and Saint Patrick's dedication.[48]

Like Saint Brigid's, Saint Anthony's adhered to a crowded mass schedule. The upper church offered Sunday mass at 6:00 a.m., 7:00 a.m., 8:00 a.m., 9:00 a.m., and 11:00 a.m., with an English sermon at 9:00 and an Italian *discurso* at 11:00. The basement chapel offered mass at 6:00 a.m., 9:00 a.m., and 10:30 a.m, with 9:00 being reserved for Sunday school children. The schedule maximized the opportunities both of the congregation to attend mass and of the many Franciscans staying at the friary to say mass.

The mass schedule noted that the basement 6:00 a.m. mass could be attended without paying pew rent, implying that people paid for seats at the other masses, as they did at Saint Brigid's. Also like Saint Brigid's, Saint Anthony's passed the basket at collection time and took up special collections. The records of the 1901 Grand Envelope Collection survive. They show Saint Anthony's received $669: one donation of $100, one of $25, one of $15, three of $10, and 529 in sums of $5.00 or less.[49]

Like the parishes established under the lay trustee system, Saint Nicholas, Most Holy Redeemer, Saint John the Baptist, Saint Francis of Assisi, Saint Alphonsus, and probably other parishes whose records have been lost and whose histories have not been written, Saint Anthony's had its share of conflict. The earliest evidence of dissension is an 1875 letter from Pietro Soldini, secretary of the Society of Saint Anthony. The letter complained that the Franciscans excoriated their Italian parishioners from the pulpit and even on sick calls. They permitted every nationality to frequent the church, so that Saint Anthony's was in danger of losing its Italian character. The problem seemed to be that other nationalities donated more to Saint Anthony's than the Italians did, and so received a greater share of the Franciscans' attention, while the Italians who did not contribute so much were scorned.[50]

[48]*Programme of the Solemn Dedication of the New Church of Saint Anthony of Padua* (pamphlet, 1888), AANY, Saint Anthony of Padua (Sullivan Street) folder.

[49]*Grand Envelope Collection for Decorating Again* (pamphlet, September 15, 1901), CMS:IAR:Box 6, Miscellaneous Programs and Invitations folder.

[50]Pietro Soldini to Arate Cesare, New York, 26 April 1875, CMS:IAR:Box 1, Saint Anthony folder.

Compared only to other Gilded Age New York City Roman Catholic parishes, Saint Anthony's seems normal. It differed from the norms in that it was not only a territorial parish but a national one, ministering to a specific language group. It was staffed not by secular clergy, but by a religious order. It had its conflicts, but so did many other parishes.

Two differences set the situation at Saint Anthony's apart. First, archdiocesan authorities did not compare Saint Anthony's with its neighbors. They put the Italians in the context of what they knew about nineteenth century Italy, and this perspective gave them additional cause for alarm. Second, historians did not compare Saint Anthony's with its contemporaries. They saw it as the first parish dedicated to the pastoral care of what became "the Italian problem."

2

Opinions on Italian Catholics

The Italian peninsula contained considerable religious diversity. Jewish communities developed during the Middle Ages and a native Protestant population, the Waldensians, antedated Martin Luther. Across the Adriatic lived Italian Albanian Greek Catholics, who spoke Italian, acknowledged the papacy, and worshipped in the Orthodox manner.[1] In America, some Italians converted to various Protestant denominations, and became important ministers in Italian neighborhoods.[2] Radical political ideologies served as analyses of religion's role in modern life. The nineteenth century, though, dismissed these details. American Catholics considered Italy a solidly Catholic country and Italy's migrants a "problem."

It is most productive to approach the "Italian problem" as an historical construct. The linkage of "Italian" and "problem" appeared in American Catholic writing during the mass migration. Since the 1940s, historians have identified the values which biased the original observations. However, attempts to penetrate the sources' predispositions to explain what the Italians were "really" like reveal as much about historians and their times as they do about the Italians. Contemporary historiography may suggest new ways of understanding the Italian immigrants – or may substitute new biases for old.

Historiography

Henry J. Browne, a scholar and priest of Irish American descent, published Italian immigrant Catholicism's first history in 1946. Even then, Browne stressed the significance for the living of his work among the dead. He titled his article "The

[1]Andrew J. Shipman, "Our Italian Greek Catholics," in Condé B. Pallen, ed., A Memorial of Andrew J. Shipman: His Life and Writings (New York: Encyclopedia Press, Inc., 1916)., 106–120.

[2]John B. Bisceglia, Italian Evangelical Pioneers (Kansas City, Missouri: Brown-White-Lowell Press, Inc., 1948).

'Italian Problem' in the Catholic Church of the United States, 1880–1900," and explained he chose those dates to make his work more historical than sociological. For, "who will say when this situation ceased to be troublesome, or if it really has been fully remedied?"[3]

Browne listed the traits which made American Catholics consider the Italians a problem: they didn't attend mass, didn't receive the sacraments, didn't support the church financially, didn't patronize parochial schools, didn't respect the clergy or contribute to their numbers, and didn't realize they should have been doing better at all these things. He also enumerated possible reasons why the Italians presented difficulties: work interfered with religious obligations and poverty reduced church contributions; poorly educated immigrants knew neither how to defend their faith against challenges from other faiths or from modern philosophies nor how to practice it without constant clerical guidance; in Italy the churches had been standing for centuries and were maintained by wealthy benefactors, poor preparation for conditions in the United States; the Irish dominating American Catholicism discriminated against them; few Italian clergy accompanied the migrants and those that did were of dubious quality; and the Italians in United States had few churches. In short, the Italians lacked resources: experiential, financial, and human. The solution to the problem lay in American supervision of Italian pastoral care. First, American territorial parishes' pastors brought in Italian clergy from religious orders and established "annex congregations" meeting on their church premises separately from the English-speaking congregation. Then diocesan ordinaries authorized "national parishes" and recruited religious orders to staff them.

Browne based his article on printed materials in English, Italian, and Latin, and on material in diocesan archives. Although more sensitive to "racial antipathies" than his sources' writers had been, he still followed his sources' interpretations: defining the Italians as a "problem," claiming that they themselves contributed to this problem, and accepting the annex congregations and national parishes as American Catholic inventions that solved the problem. Later researchers and bibliographers have compiled a lengthy bibliography of published and unpublished sources which support Browne's major points so long as one remembers that this was how Americans *saw* the Italians as much as how they really were. Later historians continued to read their new-found documents in the way Browne established, although they increasingly questioned the values which led Browne's sources, and Browne himself, to their conclusions.

[3]Henry J. Browne, "The 'Italian Problem' in the Catholic Church of the Untied States, 1880-1900," United States Catholic Historical Society *Records and Studies* XXXV (1946), 46–72; quote p. 46.

Three years after Browne's article appeared, Italian-born American Giovanni Schiavo published his two-volume *Italian-American History*. He titled his second volume *The Italian Contribution to the Catholic Church in America*. Whereas Browne saw anti-Italian prejudice as a contributing factor to the "Italian problem," Schiavo saw prejudice as the main cause. Accepting Browne's definition of a practicing Catholic (attending mass, frequenting the sacraments, contributing to the ranks of the clergy), Schiavo marshalled the evidence to indicate the Italians met it. In Schiavo's writings, it was the laity who got the American clergy to attend to their needs with annex congregations and their own parishes. It was Italy who supplied pastorally-minded clergy and women religious who, in the case of Mother Cabrini, became accepted as *bona fide* saints. It is a thousand-page refutation the very length and organization of which still acknowledges the strength of the "Italian problem" interpretation.

The Journal of Social History gave the "Italian problem" its largest audience outside of Italian and Catholic circles when in 1969 it published Rudolph J. Vecoli's essay on "Prelates and Peasants." Vecoli placed what had previously been seen as an ecclesiastical issue in a social and economic context. He emphasized the immigrants' *mezzogiorno* origins and cited the scholarship which indicated that even in the nineteenth and early twentieth centuries, pre-Christian paganism shaped southern Italian Catholicism. He also discussed the influence of Italian landholding patterns, in which a few large landlords, including the Catholic Church, owned vast territories and exploited the peasants, driving many to radical politics. Irish discrimination, narrow visions of proper Catholic practice, and anti-radicalism added to what were really the Italians' burdens rather than an "Italian problem."[4] Between them, Browne's and Schiavo's writings create a dichotomy. Did the Italians constitute a problem, or a contribution to American Catholicism? In one way, Vecoli's writings go beyond dichotomies to explore the multiplicity of roles religion played in historical situations. Later writers have left aside the anticlerical thinkers whom Vecoli saw as part of Italian immigrant community life. They have concentrated on his description of Italian folk religion, and have used it to pose a new dichotomy. Were the Italians good Catholics or not?

The importance of perspective in interpreting Italian Catholicism can be seen in two books that appeared in the 1970s and 1980s, both written by scholars and clergy of Italian descent doing case studies of New York Italian Catholicism. Silvano Tomasi received his doctorate in sociology from Fordham University in

[4]Rudolph J. Vecoli, "Prelates and Peasants: Italian Immigrants and the Catholic Church," *Journal of Social History* II (1969), 217–267.

1972, when interest in white American ethnicity peaked. He emphasized the Italians' distinctive sense of the sacred, and presented Italian laity and clergy as taking active roles in preserving their ethnic religiosity and controlling the pace at which they adapted to new ways.[5] Stephen Michael Di Giovanni received his doctorate in history from Rome's Gregorian University in 1983. He posited that the Vatican expected the American hierarchy to offer the Italians the special assistance these "needy and religiously indifferent" Italians needed.[6] Finances and language limitations inhibited American ability to provide such extra care. Di Giovanni credited the Americans, specifically Archbishop Michael Augustine Corrigan, with doing their best in this difficult situation, providing the type of pastoral care which helped support the Italians in their faith.

During the 1980s one issue facing American Catholicism was the extent of hierarchical involvement in what were seen as political questions and the extent to which Catholic individuals incorporated hierarchical moral teaching in the performance of their public responsibilities. In 1986, Joseph A. Varacalli made the "Italian Problem" a symbol for the issue of compliance with the magisterium. Although recognizing the problems prejudice posed, Varacalli listed the principle reason for the "Italian problem" as "the immigrant's ultimate allegiance to the mostly non-Catholic culture of south Italy." The Italians became a metaphor for all people who called themselves Catholic while differing with the hierarchy. He cited as an example a recent exchange between two Catholics in high places: John Cardinal O'Connor of New York, who deplored what he saw as Catholic public officials betraying their faith by upholding permissive abortion legislation, and New York State Governor Mario Cuomo, who defended what he saw as his sworn obligation to obey the laws as they stood.[7]

Given that people writing about Italian Catholicism observed it through their own lenses, the first question to ask is: what caused these observers to see what they saw? Two factors besides the Italians themselves animated American Catholic discussion. One was the abstract question of the role Catholicism ought to play in the United States. The other was the practical question of parochial management.

[5]Tomasi, *Piety and Power.*

[6]Stephen Michael Di Giovanni, "Michael Augustine Corrigan and the Italian Immigrants: The Relationship Between the Church and the Italians in the Archdiocese of New York, 1885–1902" (Ph.D. dissertation, Gregorian Pontifical University [Rome], 1983); quote p. 470.

[7]Joseph A. Varacalli, "The Changing Nature of the 'Italian Problem' in the Catholic Church of the United States," *Faith and Reason* XII:1 (1986), 38–73. Had the "Italian problem" and the O'Connor-Cuomo exchange been truly analogous, the governor might have ignored the archbishop instead of presenting a careful defense.

American Problems: Catholicism in the United States and the World

American Catholics suffered from an inferiority complex. Revolutionary heroes regarded the papacy as the best example of sort of government the United States should not have. Ante-bellum evangelical revivalists considered Catholicism antithetical to true American religion. In 1848, when Pius IX condemned the liberal revolutions sweeping Europe, the American revolutionary heritage confronted the Catholic conservative present.[8]

Yet American Catholics looked toward a bright future. By the 1880s, they had their own list of accomplishments. As we saw in the last chapter, Catholicism grew throughout the nineteenth century, and without the usual government supports. As Europe's urban, industrial working classes became alienated from Catholicism, the American hierarchy labored to prove that in the United States the Church was the worker's friend.[9] Some American Catholic leaders attributed these developments to the general freedom from European traditions. They especially praised the separation of church and state, which supposedly freed Catholicism from entangling alliances with governments seen as supporting the wealthy elite against the ordinary worker.

An issue which has long stimulated American Catholic historiography is the degree to which some Catholics championed American arrangements as a unique contribution to the universal Church. There is a long bibliography on the 1890s "Americanist heresy."[10] Of importance here is how the advocacy of "Americanism" intersects with the treatment of immigrants.

If Americans indeed intended to develop a specifically American Catholicism, the mere fact of immigration hindered this goal. Non-Catholic Americans could be as anti-immigrant as they were anti-Catholic. The fact that at least through the 1890s many immigrants were Catholic did not help bishops in their quest for complete acceptance of their faith. The immigrants' social and economic class further impeded efforts to bring Catholicism into the mainstream of American life.[11]

[8][Isaac T. Hecker], "The Outlook in Italy," *Catholic World* XXVI (October 1877), 1–21. *See also* Sandra Yocum Mize, "Defending Roman Loyalties and Republican Values: The 1848 Italian Revolution in American Catholic Apologetics," *Church History* LX:4 (December 1991), 480–492.

[9]Henry J. Browne, *The Catholic Church and the Knights of Labor* (Washington, D.C.: Catholic University Press, 1949).

[10]For just one useful book, see Thomas T. McAvoy, C.S.C., *The Americanist Heresy in Roman Catholicism, 1895-1900* (Notre Dame: University of Notre Dame Press, 1963).

[11]John Higham, *Strangers in the Land: Patterns of American Nativism, 1860–1925* (New Brunswick: Rutgers University Press, 1955).

As we saw in the previous chapter, the ante-bellum Irish were not considered an asset. By the 1880s, the Irish had achieved enough respectability to complain about the Italians.

As early as 1896, the Reverend Francis Howard congratulated American Catholicism for Americanizing the immigrants, defining "Americanization" as leading immigrants to adopt English, accept the United States' system of government, and favor middle-class social mores.[12] Americanizing immigrants furthered two causes. For those interested in making Catholicism acceptably American, here was a service to the republic that led to such recognition. If anyone truly was interested in an American contribution to universal Catholicism, American Catholic unity was needed to accomplish that goal as well.

These twin goals clashed with the goals of other forces within Catholicism. The two forces of interest here were European Catholics involved in immigrant care and the papacy.

Peter Paul Cahensly's name eventually came to stand for European involvement in Catholic immigrant pastoral care. Cahensly, a German layman, helped to found the Saint Raphael Society for the Protection of German Emigrants to provide for German Catholics' material and spiritual welfare during their journeys and after they settled in their new homes. This Saint Raphael became a model for similar organizations founded by Catholics from other European nations.[13]

Giovanni Battista Scalabrini played a role in Italy similar to Cahensly's in Germany. Scalabrini, bishop of the Diocese of Piacenza in northwest Italy, dated his interest in immigrants to the day he walked through the Milan railway station and saw the people waiting for the train, heading off to places about which they knew nothing except that work was available. Scalabrini was instrumental in founding several organizations to assist his compatriots: an Italian Saint Raphael Society, and a men's religious community which he called the Pious Society of Saint Charles but which was better known as the Scalabrinians. He also supported women's communities such as the Sisters of Saint Charles, the Missionary Zelatrices of the Sacred Heart and Frances Cabrini's Missionaries of the Sacred Heart.[14]

On December 9 and 10, 1890, delegates from various national Saint Raphaels met in Lucerne, Switzerland, to discuss problems of migrants bound for the

[12]Francis Howard, "The Church and Social Reform," *Catholic World* LXIII (1896), 286–293.

[13]*The* book on this subject is Barry, *The Catholic Church and German Americans.* The organizations all took the name Saint Raphael after the angel who accompanied Tobias on his journey, and whom the Church recognized as the patron saint of travellers.

[14]Marco Caliaro and Mario Francesconi, *John Baptist Scalabrini, Apostle to Emigrants,* trans. Alba I. Zizzamia (New York: Center for Migration Studies, 1977).

United States. They nominated Cahensly and the Marquis Giovanni-Battista Volpe-Landi, the Italian Saint Raphael Society president, to give to Pope Leo XIII a "memorial" consisting of suggestions made at this meeting. Volpe-Landi was called home, but Cahensly presented the memorial on April 16, 1891.

The memorial's business portion began by charging that since their migration to the United States, 10 million souls had fallen away from Catholicism. Suggestions to prevent further losses included national parishes for each ethnic group; the administration of such parishes by clergy who spoke the necessary languages; parochial schools teaching "the mother tongue as well as the language and history of the adopted country;" benevolent organizations that bound together immigrants from the same country; and European seminaries to train European clergy for the American mission. The most controversial proposal was the appointing of bishops along national lines, giving each ethnic groups its episcopal representative to protect its interests.

Cahensly and Volpe-Landi also prepared a French-language pamphlet supporting the memorial. The pamphlet is most interesting for its definition of Americanization, a definition made easier to understand by the French language's way of distinguishing reflexive verbs. The pamphlet used the word *s'americaniser*, literally, to Americanize one's self. This was defined as becoming an American citizen. Good citizens were defined as accepting the Constitution as fundamental law. However, the Constitution purportedly recognized each emigrant people's right to conserve its religion, language, and national character:

> *To americanize*, then, is first and foremost to accept and respect that right which the Constitution accords to the different people who live under its tutelage, and who, in their *diversity*, form the American nation.[15]

D'Americaniser, on the other hand, meant to force immigrants to forget their mother tongues and father lands. Forcible Americanization was anti-American, contravened the Constitution, and opposed the essence of the American nation. So impressed were Cahensly and Volpe-Landi with the diversity possible under the Constitution's unifying mantle that they urged federalism as a model for Catholicism. Representative bishops could lead their respective ethnic groups to their full potential in any nation. The best example was what had happened when Irish immigrants around the world had their own bishops:

> Who sustained and maintained heroic Ireland in spite of many centuries of persecution from a number of nations? Its bishops! . . . Who made of the Irish

---

[15] P. P. Cahensly and J. B. Volpe-Landi, 8. The pamphlet is in AANY, microfilm reel #14. The title page is either missing or was not microfilmed.

immigrants in the United States and Australia a people so generous, so strong, so worth of admiration? Their national bishops!

Certainly, other nations ought to have the same opportunity.

American Catholic bishops and writers condemned the memorial. The reaction of Archibishop Corrigan of New York is relevant here. Corrigan's letter to Cahensly began by refuting the notion that Americans welcomed diversity:

> . . . one of the great drawbacks to the progress of our holy faith is the taunt continually cast up to us that we are *aliens*, and the Catholic Church is a *foreign institution*. The prejudice is unjust; but nevertheless it has a most real existence, and we are continually obliged to show that we Catholics are not opposed to the institutions of this country; that we are not subjects of a foreign potentate; and are sincerely attached to the land of our birth and adoption.[16]

Corrigan's lament about the lack of "progress of our holy faith" signifies that he thought Catholicism ought to progress, but not toward increased heterogeneity. In another letter, Corrigan explained further: "If the Church of God wishes to make true progress among us, it cannot depend exclusively upon European immigration, but must fix deeply its roots elsewhere than this alone. Therefore, the Church will be neither Irish, nor will it be German, but American, and even more, Roman. . . ."[17] The idea was Catholicism had to position itself to convert Americans. Since it was going to convert Ameicans, it could not be un-American itself, and if it was going to attract Americans, it could not be identified with some other nationality.

Corrigan's wish that Catholicism be "Roman" reflected Rome's own desires, but the Vatican fit the immigrants into its plan for exercising leadership in a different way than Corrigan did. Although the Vatican had no well-publicized statement of general principles regarding immigration until Pius XII's 1952 apostolic constitution *Exsul Familia*, that document had an ancestry in Vatican efforts to direct the spiritual care of particular groups of nineteenth- and twentieth-century immigrants.[18] Of these groups, the Italians were especially significant.

[16]Michael Augustine Corrigan to Peter Paul Cahensly, New York, 22 July 1891, CMS IAR Series I, Box 1, Miscellaneous Correspondence regarding Saint Raphaelsverein folder.

[17]Corrigan to Giovanni Cardinal Simeoni, New York, 17 December 1886. Quoted in Di Giovanni, "Corrigan and the Italian Immigrants," 67.

[18]Giulivo Tessarolo, P.S.S.C., ed., *The Church's Magna Charta for Migrants* (New York: Saint Charles Seminary, 1962). See also Velasio De Paolis, C. S., *The Pastoral Care of Migrants in the Teaching and in the Directives of the Church*, translated by Thomas F. Carlesimo, C.S. (New York: CMS [Center for Migration Studies Occasional Papers: Pastoral Series #1], 1983); and Marchetto, Ezio, C.S., *The Catholic Church and the Phenomenon of Migration: An Overview* (New York: CMS [Center for Migration Studies Occasional Papers: Pastoral Series #10], 1989).

The most relevant Vatican document regarding the Italians is Leo XIII's apostolic letter 1888 *Quam Aerumnesa*.[19] Di Giovanni places the letter in the context of a complex political struggle.[20] In Italy, the liberal national government claimed responsibility for immigrants as a way of extending control over them. In the United States, American bishops were developing their definition of the "Italian problem," a definition which blamed the problem in part on the quality of pastoral care in Italy. In the urban industrialized nations of Europe and the Americas, the old attachment to a universal Christendom declined as new attachments to particular nations strengthened their hold on the masses. Di Giovanni considers ingenious the way the document phrased the reasons for papal concern for Italian immigrants. Leo held the Italian immigrants close to his heart because they had "sprung from the same soil as ourselves." However, without mentioning by name any government that might disagree with him, he asserted his right to concern himself with the preservation of the Italians' faith in their journeys and in the their new homes.

Leo's pastoral concern had two elements. *Quam Aerumnesa* discussed the temporal element first. Like Scalabrini in his writings and like Corrigan in private letters, Leo deplored the frauds perpetrated upon immigrants and the exploitation of their labor.[21] He did not, however, suggest a ministry to awaken the moral sensibilities of those who took unfair advantage of immigrants. More seriously, he did not suggest any structural changes to eradicate systemic sources of exploitation. Rather, he passed quickly to the second, spiritual, element of Italian immigrant pastoral care. He announced he had approved of Bishop Scalabrini's plan for a community of men religious dedicated to the Italian immigrant ministry. Without discussing the theoretical questions of whether language saves faith, or whether immigrants ought to remain loyal to their national origins or become loyal to their new national homes, Leo pointed out the advantages of Italian-speaking clergy in helping Italians with baptism, marriage, the last rites, the other sacraments, religious education, and spiritual encouragement. The ability to speak Italian did not depend on being brought up on the peninsula. Leo recommended that Italian youths living abroad who had a vocation for religious life consider joining Scalabrini's congregation.

[19]English translation in John Tracy Ellis, ed., *Documents of American Catholic History* (Milwaukee: Bruce Publishing Co., 1956), 482–485.

[20]Di Giovanni, "Corrigan and the Italian Immigrants," 115–119.

[21]For Scalabrini's writings, see Giovanni Battista Scalabrini, *L'Emigrazione Italiana in America*, fifth printing (Piacenza, Tipografia dell'Amico del Popolo, 1888; reprinted in *Studio Emigrazione* V [1968], 199–230), For Corrigan, see Michael Augustine Corrigan to Thomas Becker, New York, 16 December 1884. Archives of the Diocese of Wilmington.

When the Lucerne Memorial came before him, with its accompanying essay on *s'americaniser* and *d'americaniser*, Leo did not act upon its suggestions. Thus he made the Roman position clear. Rome was willing to provide spiritual assistance in the vernacular, whatever language that was at the moment. It insisted neither on maintaining homeland ties via language nor on instant adaptation to the new country.

Di Giovanni suggested that Leo's willingness to accommodate Italians on the issue of language was at variance with American needs. American priests who encountered Italians in their parishes might not have been Americanists, but they felt they could afford neither Cahenslyism's efforts to maintain the immigrants' European-style practice of the faith nor Leo's plans to give the Italians pastoral care in their preferred language. They feared not only that the Italians would not survive in the harsh conditions of parish life, but that the Italians might impede the parish's ability to survive as well.

The View from the Parish

Americans used another phrase for Italian Catholics besides "problem." They sometimes described the Italians as possessing a "simple faith." There was no one definition of simple faith, but a 1923 article illuminated the concept most clearly as follows. " . . . [T]he religious education of Italians, which was sufficient for a deeply Catholic country like Italy, was defective in a country widely dominated by all kinds of sects hostile to the Catholic Church," that is, the United States.[22] Advocates of simple faith ignored the political theories that supported Italy's liberal national government and fueled its radical politics, and argued that until migration Italians had been able to rely on affection, emotion, or sentiment to persevere in their religion, but what had worked in Italy wouldn't work in the United States.

Simple faith predominated in southern Italy. In an 1888 *Catholic World* article, Bernard Lynch thought New York City's Genoese and Lombards, both northern Italians, "a fairly instructed people."[23] Southerners were another matter. Thomas Lynch, pastor of Manhattan's Transfiguration, where his brother Bernard did his research, complained specifically that "These Neapolitan men stand up in

[22]Aurelio Palmieri, O.S.A. "The contribution of the Italian Catholic Clergy to the United States," in C.E. McGuire, ed., *Catholic Builders of the Nation: A Symposium on the Catholic Contribution to the Civilization of the United States* (Boston: Continental Press, Inc., 1923), volume II, pp. 128–149; quote page 128.

[23]Bernard J. Lynch, "The Italians in New York," *Catholic World* XLVII (1888), 67–73.

[illegible] rows in the back part of the basement [to avoid paying pew rent], and about every tenth man gives a cent on his plate."[24]

Simple faith had much to recommend. Of the American Catholic writers surveyed, only Bernard Lynch accused the Italians of any major sins (he thought them avaricious). Denis Lynch, S.J., no known relation to Bernard or Thomas, enumerated Italian virtues: "The Italian is not intemperate, he is not immoral; and, notwithstanding the fame of his imaginary stiletto, he is not sanguinary."[25] "An Old Missionary," who had served Italians in western mining camps, agreed. The Italians were thrifty, sober, and despite their reputation for carrying knives, the Old Missionary never saw a fatal stabbing among the Italians on the frontier, though he saw several lethal shootings committed by those of Anglo-Saxon descent.[26]

Anyone worried about modern secular values' effects on women's traditional roles could take heart in an anecdote the Jesuit weekly *America* ran in 1931. The story concerned an Italian mother's complaints against her town's public school system. The teachers wore cosmetics. The boys learned nothing (actually, her son learned to play football, but she counted that as nothing.) The girls learned to emulate the teacher. This mother planned to keep her daughter safe at home.[27] Although *America* received numerous letters to the editor regarding other articles on Italians, this one, pitting Italian simple faith and sturdy family values against secularism and cosmetics, evoked no negative comment.

Italian Americans and their supporters tried to explain, and therefore render reasonable and excusable, their compatriots' unattractive religious traits. They blamed the liberal national government for contaminating the simple Italians and leaving them less devout than they naturally were.[28] They described how their Italian experience and American poverty made the Italians parsimonious towards the Church, and promised "When Italians begin to take their place in the great

[24]Lynch to Corrigan, 19 September 1886.

[25]D[enis] Lynch, S.J., "In the Italian Quarter of New York," *The Messenger of the Sacred Heart of Jesus* XXXVI (February 1901), 115–126; quote 115.

[26]An Old Missionary, "Priests for Italian Immigrants," *American Ecclesiastical Review* XX (1889), 513–516.

[27]Jerome Blake, "The Worm that Talked," *America* LXV (1 August 1931), 399–400.

[28]Francis C. Kelley, "The Church and the Immigrant," *Catholic Mind* XIII (1915), 471–484. *See also* Denis Lynch, "In the Italian Quarter," p. 125; and Bernard Lynch, "The Italians in New York," 69. Henry Brann, a New York archdiocesan priest, reversed cause and effect: "Why should a population of over thirty millions of so-called Catholics stand patiently under the laws which oppress religion, and make a victim of their illustrious countryman, the Head of the Church?" *See* Henry A. Brann, "Mr. Cahensly and the Church in the U.S." *Catholic World* LIV (1892), 568–581.

American middle class we may expect that they will more fully recognize the obligation toward their churches."[29] John Tolino, an Italian American priest in South Philadelphia, offered a subtle analysis of supposed Italian anti-clericalism:

> Italians have mentally set up a very strict standard for the priest. They want to be able to look upon him as a true man of God, and spiritually superior to themselves. They want the priest to be kind and considerate, to have a sympathetic understanding of their needs, and to visit them in sickness and sorrow, but . . . they are such simple folk, they are easily shocked by the priest who becomes 'one of them'. . . . Their respect for him is easily lessened or lost.[30]

Tolino offered a similarly acute comment on the "simple faith" approach to the Italians. "When he [the Italian] was not actually despised, he was patronized."[31] While no one else put it this way, everyone agreed with the logical conclusion of that statement: Italians could not be allowed to continue as they were; their simple faith had to be replaced by something more suitable to the American environment.

Those who wrote for the American Catholic periodical press offered three reasons why Italians had to be taught new ways. The first was the danger of Protestant proselytism. In the 1890s, Protestants and Catholics saw themselves as more different than alike. The Catholic press published articles which defined several modern developments as degeneracies, and traced them back to the Reformation, thus linking secularism and Protestantism together, rather than linking all churches together in a struggle against the secular values. Protestants accepted the connection between themselves and modern values, but celebrated it. As one writer explained, Catholicism was a religion which the immigrants would outgrow morally and spiritually.[32]

If one takes the threat of soul-stealing as seriously as nineteenth-century American Catholics did, danger was everywhere. Some writers regarded the Italian immigration as a modern Exodus, from the Egyptian darkness of Rome across the Atlantic to the freedom of the Gospel. They prayed "May American Christendom rise to its opportunities."[33] In New York, the Episcopalians, not

---

[29]Louis Giambastiani, "In the Melting Pot – The Italians," *Extension* VII (1912), 9–10, 20-21; quote p. 10.

[30]John V. Tolino, "The Church in America and the Italian Problem," *Ecclesiastical Review* C (1939), 27.

[31]John V. Tolino, "Solving the Italian Problem," *Ecclesiastical Review* XCIX (1938), 246–256.

[32]Minnie J. Reynolds, "The Italian and his Church at Home," *The Missionary Review of the World* n.s. XX (1907), 607–610.

[33]Frederick H. Wright, "The Italian in America," *The Missionary Review of the World* n.s. XX (March 1907), 196–198; quote p. 198.

usually counted among the evangelical churches, circulated the following solicitation in Italian:

> We invite you to associate yourself with us, we won't ask you about your religion: our church is neither papist nor Protestant, but the Christian Church in America, of the Anglican rite (Episcopalian). The substance is nothing other than Christian charity. It costs nothing. The services are in Italian. We are all Italian brothers and sisters who come together to live better and to be better under the patronage and guidance of the Church in America.[34]

Evangelical denominations used their periodical press to raise interest in the mission to foreigners who came to American cities. Several denominations had outposts in New York's Little Italies. The Baptists built Judson Memorial Church on the south side of the Washington Square Park, to maintain a denominational presence in an Italian neighborhood.[35] The Methodists had a "Church of All Nations," designed to attract not only Italians, but everyone else living near its address at 48 Saint Mark's Place in the heterogeneous East Village. The Presbyterian New York City Mission supported the Reverend Antonio Arrighi, a convert who presided over the (395) Broome Street Tabernacle.[36]

The Catholic press ran numerous articles listing and describing Protestant efforts. Sometimes the articles conveyed a sense that the Catholics had better redouble their efforts or risk losing the Italians.[37] Sometimes they criticized Protestants for soul-stealing.[38] Sometimes they pictured Protestant efforts as failures for despite all the resources devoted to Italians the number of Italian Protestants in the United States remained miniscule.[39] Nevertheless, the frequency with which Catholics brought up the topic indicated they were worried.

[34]C. Stauder, "Report of the Minister in Charge," *The Italian Mission of the Protestant Episcopal Church in the City of New York Yearbook* (New York: Privately published, 1885), 7.

[35]Joan Jacobs Brumberg, *Mission for Life: The Story of the Family of Adoniram Judson, the Dramatic Events of the first American Foreign Mission, and the Course of Evangelical Religion in the Nineteenth Century* (New York: Free Press, 1980).

[36]Stefano L. Testa, "'Strangers from Rome' in Greater New York," *The Missionary Review* XXXI (1908), 216–218. This covers more denominations than just the Presbyterians. For more on the Presbyterians specifically, *see* John McNab, "Bethlehem Chapel: Presbyterians and Italian Americans in New York City," *Journal of Presbyterian History* LV (1977), 145–160.

[37]Thomas F. Meehan, "Evangelizing the Italians," *The Messenger of the Sacred Heart of Jesus* XXXIX (1903), 16–32.

[38]"An Italian P.E. Editorial," *America* XI (30 May 1914), 158–159.

[39]Aurelio Palmieri, O.S.A., "Italian Protestantism in the United States," *Catholic World* CVII (1918), 177–189.

A second reason for Americanizing the Italians lay in parish economics. As described in the last chapter, dioceses expected parishes to support themselves and to contribute to the support of diocesan bureaucracies and diocesan institutions such as orphanages. Late nineteenth-century lower Manhattan parishes found this policy burdensome. Immigrants flooded into their neighborhoods and the parishes incurred debts to build churches and schools. Then the immigrants moved up the social and economic ladder and out to better housing in better neighborhoods, leaving the parishes with debts larger than the remaining parishioners could pay. New immigrants came in but like the Irish and Germans before them they started at the bottom of the economic ladder and did not have much to spare for the parish collection plate. Also like the Irish and Germans, they wanted their own parishes, named for their own saints, and staffed by their own clergy.

American Catholics had complained about German clannishness, exclusiveness, and unwillingness to assimilate because their communities took up collections, petitioned for parishes, and lobbied at the Vatican when their local ordinaries denied them their own churches and clergy. As the number of Italians increased, attitudes toward Germans changed. They became good Catholics, concerned to supply themselves with churches, clergy, parochial schools, and teaching sisters, and held up as models for the Italians to emulate.[40] That the Germans perhaps had some incentive in that they were giving to their own churches, while the Italians were being expected to pick up where others had left off, was overlooked.

Transfiguration is a case in point. Thomas Lynch complained about the ungenerous Neapolitan men. His successor, Thomas McLoughlin, reported an inverse ratio between the increase of Italians and the decrease in Sunday attendance and collection receipts.[41] However, when they collected for themselves, the Italians proved their liberality. In 1886, pastor Lynch discovered that the poor Italian congregation in his basement had $5,000 in savings, presumably for a church of their own. He dispatched a letter to the chancery claiming the entire sum for Transfiguration on the grounds that the Italians had never contributed to adequately to the parish.[42] Even if this the $5,000 represented Italian accommodation to the American situation, it was only a partial accommodation: the Italians had Americanized to the point of giving, but had not developed loyalty to existing, non-Italian, parishes.

[40]Kelley, "The Church and the Immigrant," 471–484.

[41]Thomas P. McLoughlin to Corrigan, New York, 28 August 1901, CMS IAR, Box 1, Transfiguration folder.

[42]Thomas Lynch to Thomas S. Preston, New York, 20 September 1886, CMS IAR, Box 1, Transfiguration folder

A third reason for Americanizing the Italians lay in the parts of their faith they did practice, especially the southerners among them. The most noticeable Italian devotion was the *festa*, or feastday in honor of the home town or provincial patron saint.

An Irish American Paulist, Joseph McSorley, had a chance to observe the 1909 feast of Saint Agatha in its natural setting in Catania, Sicily. Beginning January 29, a triduum, three days of special devotions, prepared the faithful for the celebration. The first two days of the feast emphasized secular entertainments such as band music, horse races, and balloon launchings, but there was also a charitable event, a lottery which awarded as prizes dowries to three poor orphan girls and cash for three poor families of army conscripts. More devotional events appeared on the third day, when a procession of petitioners carried wax models of body parts they wished Saint Agatha to heal, or candles to ask the saint for a favor desired, or to show gratitude for a favor bestowed. The fourth day featured another procession, this time bearing the saint's relic, which reposed in a reliquary of silver and jewels, and was carried beneath a swirl of balloons, banners, and specially prepared paper streamers, a sort of primitive ticker-tape parade. On February 5, the actual feast day, the cardinal said mass and the community closed the affair with a concert and a fireworks display. Besides the details of celebration, McSorley presented the people's mood during the feast. Into their poor, workaday world came light, color, sound, banners, balloons, rich church ornaments, brass bands, and fireworks. They responded by putting on their finest, eating their best, relaxing and enjoying.[43] Other observers made a point which fit in perfectly with American Catholics' stereotype of ignorant Italians, noting how often Italian festival traditions correlated with ancient pagan customs.[44]

Italians celebrated their first American *feste* (the Italian plural) simply. On July 16, 1881, former residents of Polla, relocated to East Harlem, gathered to celebrate their patroness, Our Lady of Mount Carmel. They decided to establish a society to plan next year's festa. By 1882, the society had acquired a "paper image" of the Madonna's statue in Polla, and the number of devotees had grown so that the committee moved the *festa* outdoors, to a tenement courtyard.[45]

Descriptions of turn-of-the-century New York *feste* abound. A particularly detailed one is from Jacob Riis, who in 1899 accompanied Police Commissioner Theodore Roosevelt to Saint Donato's *festa*. Riis and Roosevelt were alerted to

[43]Joseph McSorley, C.S.P., "In Sicily," *Catholic World* LXXXVIII (1909), 653–659, 810–819.

[44]Grace V. Christmas, "May Customs in Italy," *Catholic World* LXXVII (1903), 155–158.

[45]Domenico Pistella, *The Crowning of a Queen*, translated Peter Rofrano (New York: Shrine of Our Lady of Mount Carmel, 1954), 42–43.

the affair by a parade winding its way around the police station, with a statue of Saint Donato, the men of the Saint Donato Society, and a brass band. They followed the procession back to a saloon on Elizabeth Street. The crowd installed Saint Donato on a temporary makeshift altar decorated with candles. Some of the devout approached the altar to say prayers, then joined in the secular amusements. Roosevelt purchased a raffle ticket. To his relief the grand prize, a live sheep, went to someone else.[46]

The Jesuit *Messenger of the Sacred Heart* approved of the *festa* as a manifestation of the Italians' simple faith, and recommended pastors encourage the practice. The Jesuit Nicholas Russo scheduled the opening of his parish, Our Lady of Loreto, for the *festa* of Saint Rocco and invited the local Saint Rocco Society to participate; their procession, with its brass band, attracted a crowd to the church.[47] Other Italian clergy, particularly from the northern areas, apparently forbade *feste* in their parishes.[48] Clergy such as John Tolino complained that the *feste* mortified the more Americanized among the Italians. They also presented a challenge to clerical control, since they were usually sponsored – planned, executed, and the money collected by – lay societies.[49]

As immigration increased, *feste* grew more numerous and elaborate. The processions marched under arches of garlands, flags, Chinese lanterns, and electric lights. The pious brought huge, heavy candles, the height and weight of the person needing a favor, or wax images of body parts they wanted healed. Vendors sold Italian delicacies and inexpensive religious items. Band concerts and fireworks enlivened the evenings. Small children, dressed as angels, swung through the air on ropes, strewing flowers and singing hymns praising the saint of the day.[50] Even when no altars full of candles caught fire and no gunfights marred the celebration, a *festa* was a spectacle, a wonder to non-Catholics, and an embarrassment to Catholics from other cultures.[51] So intense was their discomfiture that except for Our Lady of Mount Carmel it was not until after World War II that other New York Italian Catholic parishes added *feste* to their calendars.

[46]Jacob A. Riis, "Feast-Days in Little Italy," *The Century magazine* LVIIII (1899), 491–499.

[47]Nicholas Russo, S.J., "The Origin and Progress of our Italian Mission in New York," *Woodstock Letters*, 25:135–143.

[48]Caroline Ware, *Greenwich Village, 1920-1930: A Comment on American Civilization in the Post-War Years* (New York: , 1935; reprinted New York: Harper, 1965), 312.

[49]Tolino, "Solving the Italian Problem," 246–256.

[50]"Italian Festivals in New York," (1901), 228–229.

[51]For fire, see *The New York Times*, 16 August 1903, 11:7. for gunfight, see *The New York Times*, 8 May 1922, 19:7.

What Were Americans Seeing?

Three remarks frequently appeared in passing in American observers' published and private writings on Italian Cathoicism. The observers had in their commentary the means to add a new perspective to their subject, a perspective based on the Italian immigrants' demographic characteristics.

The first remark concerned the Italians' geographic mobility. As early as 1884, Archbishop Corrigan explained that "Differing from other immigrants, the Italians do not come here to stay, but always hope and intend to return to their home in Italy."[52] Thomas Lynch complained that "These unmarried Neapolitan men are here today and a thousand miles away next week."[53] In 1891, Our Lady of Mount Carmel's pastor wrote Archbishop Corrigan announcing the discovery of an Italian neighborhood being formed under the Harlem Bridge. He estimated the population at 2,000, but explained that it fluctuated, especially in the summer, when hundreds were "drafted into the country by contractors."[54]

Secular scholars were familiar with these observations. In his study of worldwide Italian migration, Harvard economist Robert Foerster explained that the Italians left their home not because of a disaster akin to the Irish potato famine or the Russian anti-Semitic pogroms, but because of the decline of the nation's economy, particularly in the south.[55] Migration was not an effort to establish one's self elsewhere, but a last-ditch attempt to save what the family had at home. Betty Boyd Caroli figured that 1.5 million of those who migrated to the United States eventually returned permanently to Italy.[56] Neither Foerster nor Caroli mentioned the impact of such transiency on ecclesiastical affairs, but Corrigan was well aware of it: ". . . they take no interest in Church or Religion here: will not contribute a penny for their support."[57]

The migrants' transiency was linked to gender. Between 1881 and 1890, Italian males accounted for 78.9 percent of the total Italian migration to the United States. Between 1891 and 1900, they accounted for 77.2 percent, between 1901 and 1910, 77.1 percent. In the decade that included World War I (which led

[52]Corrigan to Becker.

[53]Lynch to Corrigan, 26 March 1888.

[54]Michael Carmody, P.S.M., to Corrigan, New York, 9 February 1891, AANY microfilm roll #13.

[55]Robert F. Foerster, *The Italian Emigration of our Times* (Cambridge, Massachusetts: Harvard University Press [Harvard Economic Studies], 1924).

[56]Betty Boyd Caroli, *Italian Repatriation from the United States, 1900–1914* (New York: Center for Migration Studies, 1973), v.

[57]Corrigan to Becker.

many families to decide to leave Europe and which led European countries to tighten their regulations governing the migration of potential military personnel), Italian males accounted for 69.4 percent, and between 1921 and 1930, 60.6 percent. Females always accounted for less than half the Italian migration.

The reason for this lopsided migration lay in the intersection of Italian economic needs and sex roles. Women were expected to stay close to home. They contributed to family income either by working in nearby fields or by selling their own farm products, and they managed the money they and their husbands made. Men, though, had the freedom to travel far from home, in deference to their masculinity and because they were expected to bring in money for the household rather than manage it.[58]

The unbalanced migration affected Italian religiosity in the United States, for the Italians also practiced a gender division of religious labor. The men organized the mutual benefit societies. These had two functions. For those whose employers did not offer such benefits or who could not afford commercial policies, mutual benefits societies extended life and health insurance. More importantly here, they planned the annual *festa* for the home town's patron saint. John Tolino described the men's work in South Philadelphia's Little Italy. The men sometimes kept the saint's statue themselves, in a private home or club house rather than in a church. Prior to the feast day, they canvassed the community for money with which to celebrate the feast. The feast's date was set by Catholicism's liturgical calendar, but a lay men's committee visited their pastor to set a time for the mass and to discuss whom to assign to preach. Priests presided over the mass, but the lay men reclaimed their leadership role immediately thereafter. They carried their patron saint's statue on their shoulders in a procession through the streets, pausing to lower the statue for veneration or for monetary offerings. Other men played in the accompanying brass band.[59] Although Tolino made no mention of secular entertainments accompanying the *festa*, in other communities men erected arches along the parade route, set up amusement park rides, ran games of chance, and launched fireworks.

Women had their part in such lay-directed religious practices, as they were the ones who usually knew which saint was especially efficacious for what problem (Saint Anthony of Padua was the one to pray to for the recovery of lost objects,

[58]The summary on the roles individuals played in the southern Italian family structure is Leonard Covello, *The Social Background of the Italo-American School Child: A Study of the Southern Italian Family Mores and Their Effects on the School Situation in Italy and America* (Lieden: E.J. Brill, 1967).

[59]Tolino, "Solving the Italian Problem," 255.

for example). More important here, women linked the family to the official church. As the men readily explained, the women attended mass, made their confessions, and received communion. And it was mass attendance, confession, and communion, not feast days, that interested the American Catholic clergy. Clergy's unpublished comments on Italian frequently mentioned the difference in men's and women's religious behavior. Archbishop Corrigan was distressed to find that "Men of 26 when they come to be married are found never to have made a confession, ignoring its necessity, and pleading that *la donna* will go to confession, and that will suffice."[60] Denis Lynch thought it noteworthy that about 1910 one New York City Italian church counted 2,000 male communicants on holy days.[61] In the 1910s, a group of Italian clergy offered "missions," one or two weeks of preaching, in parishes throughout the archdiocese. Their 1915 report on these events indicate a gender gap. A mission held at Mary, Help of Christians, on East Twelfth Street, induced 900 women to have their confessions heard, but attracted only a few "spiritually cold" men. A mission at Assumption, New Brighton, Staten Island drew 100 women and 70 men. A mission at Saint Joachim's on Roosevelt Street brought in mostly women. Only at Saint Joseph's chapel (precursor to Saint Joseph's on Catherine Street) did men outnumber women.[62]

Observable differences in Italian men's and women's religious behavior continued after World War I. A 1931 *America* article described "types" of Italian Catholics. All the types described were male. One found the United States a land of freedom and so exercised his freedom to stay away from mass, another was alienated from Catholicism because Italian priests weren't respected and because the Church always seemed to be asking the poor for money; and a third did not frequent mass himself because he couldn't understand the sermons' abstract thought, but he made sure his wife and children attended.[63] In 1935 a non-Italian college student reported that for his Italian co-workers at the construction site, religion was largely the "play thing of women and the aged."[64]

A few Catholics based strategies of pastoral care on these gender differences. Italian men, said Bishop Edward M. Dunne of Peoria, should be discouraged

[60]Corrigan to Becker.

[61]D[enis] Lynch, S.J., "The Religious Conditions of Italians in New York," *America* X (21 March 1910), 558–559.

[62]Roberto Biasotti, C.S, "Rapporto morale dell' Italiano di New York, 1 Gennaio 1916." Handwritten copy in AANY, New York Italian Apostolate NYC Folder.

[63]Joseph C. Lagnese, "The Italian Catholic," *America* XL (21 February 1931), 475–476.

[64]M.J. Hillenbrand, "Has the Immigrant Kept the Faith?" *America* LV (23 November 1935), 153–155.

from leaving Italy without their families.[65] A New York Catholic social worker alerted her colleagues to the problems Italian women faced in getting to mass, as they often had no one with whom to leave their young children.[66] More Protestants capitalized on the observation that one Italian wife and mother controlled the religious affiliations of whole families of men and children, and advocated the deployment of female home missionaries to visit Italian women in their homes.[67]

A third demographic characteristic of Italian communities was the presence of rapidly Americanizing children. Even with the high transiency and the preponderance of males, children abounded in urban areas. It might be expected that the presence of children would affect the parents' religiosity. An evangelical revival among ante-bellum native white Protestants coincided with the emergence of the type of family Americans consider middle class: a separation of parental duties such that the father and husband goes out of the household to work while the wife and mother remains at the household and devotes much of her time and attention to the children.[68] A resurgence of interest in religion accompanied the 1950s baby boom. A similar convergence of religion and family occurred when the Moral Majority flourished in the early 1980s, and when politicians mades speeches on "family values" in the 1990s.

Within the smaller community of Italian immigrants, religion and family also intersected. Nicholas Russo, the pastor who used the Saint Rocco *festa* to attract people to Our Lady of Loreto, also found children useful. Upon arriving at his parish on Elizabeth Street, Russo set out on pastoral calls and reported "We were oftentimes received with the coldest indifference; not seldom avoided; at times greeting with insulting remarks." When he managed to convince a few adults to attend church, he asked them to send their children to catechism. " . . .[O]ur mission began to be appreciated; the children especially became so many little apostles, and thanks be to God! continue to be such."[69] Gideon de Vincentis,

---

[65]Edward M. Dunne, "Memoirs of 'Zi Pre,'" *American Ecclesiastical Review* XLIX (1898), 192–203.

[66]Daisy H. Mosley, "The Catholic Social Worker in an Italian District," *Catholic World* CXIV (1922-1923), 618–628.

[67]Philip M. Rose, *The Italians in America* (New York: George H. Doran Company, 1922), 46.

[68]Paul E. Johnson, *A Shopkeeper's Millennium: Society and Revivals in Rochester, New York, 1815–1837* (New York: Hill and Wang, 1978).

[69]Russo, 139.

who worked among Italians in Newark, echoed the theme of children as the apostles to parents.[70]

The children were not just the links between their parents and their local Catholic parish. They were the links between their parents and American Catholicism. As early as 1896, Franciscan priests at Most Precious Blood on Baxter Street found it necessary to use English when hearing children's confessions.[71] American Catholics who wrote for the periodical press urged pastors to take pains with the children.[72] Clergy from Chicago, New York, and Philadelphia reported on how they conducted their children's apostolate.[73]

But Is It Catholicism?

This chapter outlined the "Italian problem" in order to set it in its historical context. Once observers affixed the label in the 1880s, it took on a life of its own. Even historians whose own values led them to reject the label still had to contend with it in their research and analysis.

The original observers did not view the Italians in a historical context. They might mention demographic features, social background, or economic circumstances in passing, but they made it clear these elements should not have altered the Italians' practice of their faith in any fundamental way. Roman Catholicism, being the same in all times and places, imposed the same obligations upon all. As one can see from the Varacalli article, the issue of the proper intersection of the universality of the faith and the uniformity of practice is still a provocative issue.

It is, though, an issue on which the historian must yield to the theologian. This research must turn to other questions, to the stages of development of Italian American Catholicism over the next two generations in New York.

---

[70]Gideon de Vincentis, typescript dated 1903, CMS IAR Series I, Box 4, Archives of the Archdiocese of Newark – Italians in the Diocese of Newark folder.

[71]J.H. Senner, "Immigration from Italy," *North American Review* CLXII (1896), 649–657.

[72]"The Italian Question," *America* XII (19 December 1914), 246.

[73]For Chicago, see W. H. Agnew, S.J., "Pastoral Care of Italian Children in America," *Ecclesiastical Review* LXVIII (1913), 256-267. For New York, see Joseph McSorley, C.S.P., "The Church and the Italian Child: The Situation in New York," *Ecclesiastical Review* LXVIII (1913), 268–282. For Philadelphia, see John V. Tolino, "The Future of the Italian-American Problem," *Ecclesiastical Review* CI (1939), 221–232.

3

The First Generation and the National Parish System

In 1880, when Michael Augustine Corrigan became coadjutor (auxiliary with the right of succession) to John Cardinal McCloskey, the Archdiocese of New York had one Italian parish. In 1902, when Corrigan died, after five years as McCloskey's coadjutor and seventeen as archbishop, there were ten Italian parishes. Corrigan's successor, John Murphy Farley (Cardinal Farley after 1911) was archbishop from 1902 to 1918; he authorized a dozen Italian parishes. Patrick Joseph Hayes (Cardinal Hayes after 1924), archbishop from 1918 to 1938, established eighteen. In 1941, when New York City Works Progress Administration employees counted them for a Federal Writers' Project book, 47 parishes in the City and Archdiocese of New York (Manhattan, Staten Island, and the Bronx) used Italian for at least one sermon on the Sunday Mass schedule.[1] The Italians were the largest group of non-English-speaking Catholics the Archdiocese of New York had until the recent Hispanic migration.

Many of the historians who have written about Italian-American Catholicism have based their studies on parishes staffed by religious order clergy. Silvano Tomasi's *Power and Piety* is a survey of Italian parishes in the New York metropolitan area; the parishes for which he had the most information were staffed by religious orders such as the Franciscans and Scalabrinians. Stephen Michael Di Giovanni's "Michael Augustine Corrigan and the Italian Immigrants" is a case study of one archbishop's approach to Italian pastoral care: all the parishes utilized for the case study were staffed by religious orders. Deanna Paoli Gumina's work on San Franciscan Italians gives attention to the Church of Saints Peter and Paul, a Salesian parish.

The parish founded specifically for Italians and staffed by religious orders was not the only pattern, as we shall see below. However, all Italian parishes had some points in common. All parishes had a beginning. If the parish existed before the

[1] New York City Works Progress Administration, "Inventory of the Church Archives in New York City: Roman Catholic Church, Archdiocese of New York," vol. 2 (typescript, 1941).

Italians came, there was a point at which special arrangements were made for the Italians' pastoral care. If the parish was erected for the Italians, a site had to be chosen. If the clergy had not had a hand in creating the parish, the archbishop had to select clergy. The parish had to have a meeting space, which usually meant renting, buying, or building a church. It had to keep the adults practicing their faith via sodalities and devotional groups. It had to educate its children, with lay teachers or religious order teachers, a Sunday school or a parochial school. The parish had to establish itself among factions within the Italian and Catholic community, and among the non-Italian and non-Catholic segments of the neighborhood.

There was no one way to accomplish any of these tasks. If one reads a number of parish histories, one finds that the outlines are similar, and that the parishes shared similar problems and solutions. But one also finds that the parishioners of each parish regarded their parish as a special extraordinary, and unique place.

Turning Old Parishes to New Uses

Like the immigrants who came before them, Italians migrating to New York sought out inexpensive housing in proximity to employment opportunities. Thus they gravitated toward neighborhoods already associated with struggling ethnic groups. Five Points, identified with the Irish, and Greenwich Village, in which many African Americans lived, were two examples of neighborhoods which became Little Italies. The Italians' first churches, were, as we saw in the case of Saint Vincent de Paul, those established for other ethnic groups.

When Saint Patrick's Old Cathedral was authorized in 1809, it was in such a lightly populated neighborhood that the land around the cathedral was set aside for a cemetery. Even before the Civil War, the single-family townhouses lining Mott and Mulberry Streets had been turned into multi-unit multi-purpose buildings, in which people both lived and worked. A friendly visitor for the New York Association for Improving the Conditions of the Poor inspected the tenements in 1879, the year Saint Patrick's lost its cathedral status, and left this description of Number 5 Jersey Street, within walking distance of the church:

> Jersey Street, at first sight, looks like a pestilence breeding, law breaking colony. A more intimate acquaintance with it, and a few words with one or two white and colored inhabitants, confirmed the first but not the second impression; no more peaceable, thrifty, orderly neighbors could be found than these Italians. They do not beg, are seldom or never arrested for theft, are quiet; though quick to quarrel amongst themselves, are equally ready to forgive. The officer on duty mentioned that this colony, numbering, perhaps two hundred Italian families, can not be matched by any similar number, of corresponding social condition, in New York City, for their law abiding qualities. He seems quite proud of them, but admitted that the business should not be permitted in a densely

thronged district, but did not seem to think that they were excessively dirty. I asked him to accompany me, and we proceeded to the yard of No. 5; here on lines strung across, were thousands of rags hung up to dry; on the ground, piled against the board fences, rags mixed with bones, bottles, and papers; the middle of the yard covered with every imaginable variety of dirt. On asking him what would be the effect of a shower of rain upon this conglomeration, followed by a hot sun, he admitted that it would certainly produce sickness wherever the poison was carried. We then turned to go into the cellars, in which was a large and a small room, opposite the door stood a stove upon which meat was being cooked, to the right stood a bedstead roughly constructed out of boards, in the left hand corner a similar one, the small room contains another; these board bunks were covered with three or four army blankets and would each accommodate four men. There was no other furniture in the room, which was so dark that we could only see by waiting till the eyes became accustomed to the light. There was scarcely standing room for the heaps of bags and rags, and right opposite to them stood a large pile of bones, mostly having meat on them, in various stages of decomposition; these were removed however at the time of my second visit. Notwithstanding the dense tobacco smoke, the smell could be likened only to that of an exhumed body. There were nine men in the room at the time of our visit, but a larger number occupy the room. I met with no sickness excepting one case of whooping cough and a number afflicted with rheumatism; yet, in some of these ragpicker's dens there are, not doubt, the germs of pestilence, only needing heat and moisture for their development.[2]

The problem was not what the stereotype of bachelor housekeeping might lead one to believe. Jacob Riis also visited the Jersey Street rag-pickers, and took a photograph of another household similarly cluttered with huge barrels, buckets, and bales of cloth. In the center of these oversized objects, he posed a woman, wearing a blouse, apron, and skirt, all of different and mismatched patterns, clutching a well-swaddled baby.[3] Even households whose members included those traditionally charged with housekeeping failed to maintain order.

The Italian rag-pickers came to the attention of Saint Patrick's clergy in the early 1870s. John B. Salter, who was stationed at Saint Patrick's from 1873 to 1875, recalled that Jersey Street suffered from a smallpox epidemic in the winter of 1874–1875. The Italians concealed their sick, lest public health officials transfer them to Blackwell's Island's pest house. However, when the sickness was unto death, they sent for a priest. Father Salter answer such a sick call, contracted smallpox, and was himself quarantined, although in a room on the top floor of the rectory rather than in a public pest house.[4]

[2]*Thirty-Sixth Annual Report of the New York Association for Improving the Conditions of the Poor* (New York: Office of the Association, 1879), 63–64.

[3]Jacob A. Riis, *How the Other Half Lives: Studies among the Tenements of New York* (New York: Dover, 1971), 45.

[4][Stephen J. Hannigan], *Souvenir of the Centennial Celebration of Saint Patrick's Old Cathedral, New York, 1809-1909* (New York: n.p., 1909), unpaginated.

Archdiocesan historian John Talbot Smith, writing close to the events, credited Saint Patrick's pastor John F. Kearney with pioneering a system whereby a parish created for a different population came to incorporate the Italians:

> The Italians invaded his parish in such numbers as to drive out the old residents, or rather to accelerate the movement which commerce had already begun in New York. The expansion of the city turned many residential districts to commercial uses, and sent the inhabitants all over the island and into the suburbs. The Italians showed very little interest in religion after their arrival, and acted as if the Catholic Church did not exist in the United States. Father Kearney persuaded them inquire into the matter, then gave them the use of his church for Mass, secured the ministrations of an Italian priest, brought the Italian children to the church school, and after some years, when custom had paved the way, he abolished the distinction of races, and made Italians and natives join in the same services. This work extended over a period of twenty years and showed such results that it was imitated in many other parishes.[5]

Smith claimed that James McGean, rector of Transfiguration on Mott Street, expanded upon Kearney's model. According to Thomas Preston, Corrigan's vicar general, McGean turned over Transfiguration's basement chapel to the Italians and recruited the Franciscans from Saint Anthony of Padua to staff what was in effect a separate congregation. By 1888, McGean had been replaced by another rector, Thomas Lynch, and the separate Italian congregation had been formalized into what Lynch's brother Bernard called, in an article for *Catholic World*, and "annex congregation."[6]

For a time, Manhattan had several Italian annex congregations. There were, however, problems with this arrangement. First, the non-Italian pastors who divided their congregation thus did not always do so out of any commitment to preserving a distinctive ethnic culture. The Reverend Nicholas Russo differed from historian John Talbot Smith in his account of how the separate Italian congregation at Saint Patrick's came to an end:

> The results [of Kearney's method] were far from encouraging. Out of the many thousand Italians living in the neighborhood few availed themselves of the opportunity—so few, indeed, that after several year's trial, the parish priest was disgusted, asked the archbishop to make other provisions for them, and the basement of his church was consequently closed to the Italians. Of course, the willing ones might have gone to hear Mass in the upper church; but, besides being deprived of religious instruction, they were placed in an alternative which was distasteful to them. They had either to pay five cents at the door, like all others, or be refused a seat during Mass. The former attacked their purse, the latter their pride and sensitiveness.[7]

[5] Smith, *The Catholic Church in New York: A History of the New York Diocese From its Establishment in 1808 to the Present Time*, 471.

[6] Bernard J. Lynch, "The Italians in New York," 67–73.

[7] Russo, "The Origin and Progress of our Italian Mission in New York," 136–137.

At least one group of laity also expressed themselves on the issue. Epiphany on East 22nd Street had an Italian annex congregation meeting in its basement. When a committee of Italian men wrote Cardinal Farley in 1914, the annex congregation had been in Epiphany's basement for 15 years. The Italians still did not have full use of the basement; they offered Sunday mass there, but otherwise the "American" congregation had priority. The Italians wanted a church that was available to them all the time. They had already collected the money, and needed only Farley's permission to open a chapel.[8] Saint Sebastian's opened on East 24th Street the next year.

One secular rector who shared his facilities with Italians preferred that missionaries from religious orders minister to the annex congregation. Patrick McSweeney of Saint Brigid's explained to Archbishop Farley that if there were no missionaries, with their own mission house, McSweeney might have to have as many as two Italian secular priests in his own rectory, and "two Italian priests would be too much to endure."[9] Given the differences between secular and religious clergy, the religious clergy who staffed the basement congregations might also have contributed to the eventual transition from annex congregations to separate parishes. Saint Brigid's annex congregation, for example, became the foundation for Mary, Help of Christians, a parish opened by the Salesians in 1908. Transfiguration's annex congregation became the Scalabrinian (1891), then the Franciscan (1894), parish of Most Precious Blood. Transfiguration itself was given over to the care of the Salesians from 1902 to 1950.

Besides the problems with the pastors, there were also parts of New York City where there were no parishes for the Italians to join. The Italians were the Catholic pioneers in places such as the Bronx, where construction firms hired gangs of Italian men to work. Saint Philip Neri in Bedford Park, for example, was organized for the Italians who had come to turn the Jerome Park Racetrack into the Jerome Reservoir.[10]

Founding New Parishes

There could be many claimants to the honor of "founding the parish." In some cases, the laity's role is well documented. Epiphany's annex congregation's

[8]Generoso Valentino, et al., to John Farley, New York, 9 December 1914, CMS IAR Box 1, Italian Colony, East 18th Street to 24th Street (NYC) folder.

[9]Patrick McSweeney to John Murphy Farley, New York, November 23, 1903, AANY Saint Brigid's folder.

[10][William A. Hanley], Golden Jubilee of Saint Philip Neri Church, 1898-1948 (New York: Allied Printing, [1948]), unpaginated.

committee petition to the archbishop for a church has already been mentioned. The committee of men representing Van Nest's (North Bronx) Italians even knew what arguments appealed to American prelates. They wrote Farley, in Italian: "We believe it is useful to note for Your Excellency that here there exists already one American Protestant mission and that another has opened for the Italians. . . ."[11] The Church of Saint Anthony was incorporated that November.[12]

Usually the laity were organized not into *ad hoc* committees but into permanent associations which began by organizing the annual patron saint's *festa* and then had a hand in founding the parish. The committee which sponsored the annual *festa* in honor of Our Lady of Mount Carmel became the nucleus of the parish by that name on East 115th Street. Saint Joachimi on Roosevelt Street was a confederation of serveral societies. Each society made a contract with the parish whereby the parish took custody of the patron saint's statue, the priests committed themselves to saying the feast day mass and funeral masses for deceased members of the mutual benefit society, and the mutual benefit society commiteed itself to pay a certain amount, usually based on the number of society members, for these privileges.[13]

There is one example of an individual layman being the driving force behind a parish. Most Holy Crucifix, which opened on Broome Street in 1925, seems to have been the pet project of Frank Angelo Rizzo. Rizzo was born on the Lower East Side in 1887. He was not so much an Americanized Italian as a Hibernianized one. His obituary noted that among his heroes was Big Tim Sullivan, the area's political boss during Rizzo's youth. Rizzo's undertaking business provided him with the funds for munificent acts of charity, such as distributing 300 clothing baskets at Christmas. Rizzo was Most Holy Crucifix's chief fundraisers, one of its trustees, its sacristan, president of its Holy Name Society, and member of its Knights of Columbus.

In taking the lead in obtaining parishes, men reaffirmed their traditional role as the community's public religious leaders. There is no indication as to how intensely they kept up their interest after the parishes were actually established. Italian missionaries commented on the poor attendance at their churches without reference to gender. The poor attendance alone, though, indicates that once the church was established and the clergy replaced the community men as the public religious leaders, men, for cultural and economic reasons, became less noticeable.

[11] Angelo Rezzano, *et al.*, to Farley, Bronx, May 17, 1908, CMS IAR Box 1, Italian Colony: Van Nest and West Farm folder.

[12] Incorporation Certificate 00971-08C, 31 Chambers Street, Room 703, New York, New York.

[13] CMS Saint Joachim, Box 5, Folders 118 through 131.

New York's archbishop was another claimant to the title of parish founder. The ordinary's permission was always necessary to authorize any parish or to erect any church or chapel. An example of chancery input comes from the Bronx in 1902. In September of that year, the diocesan consultors voted to establish a parish in the Van Nest-Morris Park area, and the archbishop accordingly appointed a pastor, Daniel J. Curley, and a committee of two (Charles Parks of the older Saint Thomas Aquinas parish in the Bronx, and Denis McMahon, then pastor of Nativity on East 2nd Street) to draft a proposal for where to set the new parish's boundaries. In November, the diocesan consultors met again, and voted to fix the boundaries, while Father Curley chose Our Lady of Solace as the new parish's name. Curley also made the final decision as to where to put the church, on the corner of Columbus Avenue and Washington Street. However, neither Curley nor the chancery could make all the decisions by themselves. The Italians in the Van Nest-West Farms area protested that Our Lady of Solace was unsuitable because there was no Italian priest on the staff; the above-mentioned Saint Anthony was established in response to their requests. However, in order to keep some distance between each new church, the chancery placed Saint Anthony's too far north for a portion of the Italian community. Hence Saint Dominic's was established in 1924.[14]

As Our Lady of Solace's story indicates, a third claimant to the title of parish founder was the first pastor, who came from either the diocesan secular clergy or from the religious orders. In the early years of Italian parishes, the religious orders predominated. McCloskey invited the Order of Friars Minor (Franciscans) into the Italian mission; Corrigan invited the Pious Society of the Missions (or Pallottines; now the Society of the Catholic Apostolate) to the New York in 1884, the Missionaries of Saint Charles in 1887, the Society of Jesus (Jesuits) in 1891, and the Salesians of Saint John Bosco in 1898. Farley invited no new men's orders, but in 1922 Hayes introduced the Congregation of the Sacred Stigmata (Stigamatines).

Corrigan also invited the most famous of the women's orders, Mother Frances Xavier Cabrini's Missionaries of the Sacred Heart, into the archdiocese in 1889. The Pallottine Sisters of Charity also came that year. The Religious Teachers Filippine came to the United States in 1910, and took their first school in the City and Archdiocese of New York, Saint Ann's on East 110th Street, in 1926. The Missionary Zelatrices (after 1967, the Apostles) of the Sacred Heart also began their first teaching assignment at Saint Joseph's on Catherine Street in 1926. A number of other orders were not specifically Italian in origin, but worked in the Italian apostolate. In some cases, women religious became the nucleus of a parish.

[14]George E. Tiffany, *Our Lady of Solace Parish, Seventy-Fifth Anniversary* (New York: Privately published, 1977), 5–20.

The Missionaries of the Sacred Heart helped to gather the community and organize the religious education ministry of Saint Rita of Cascia in the South Bronx.[15]

Once admitted to the archdiocese and assigned to one parish, men's orders could expand. At one time or another, the Scalabrinians had five parishes: Saint Joachim on Roosevelt Street, from 1888 to 1958; Resurrection on Centre Street, in 1889; Most Precious Blood on Baxter Street, from 1891 to 1894; Our Lady of Pompei, in Greenwich Village, beginning in 1892; and Saint Joseph's on Catherine Street, beginning in 1925. The Scalabrinians also served as chaplains for New York's branch of the Italian Saint Raphael Society. The Franciscans had the most extensive network. They began with Saint Anthony of Padua, and succeeded the Scalabrinians at Most Precious Blood in 1894. They also staffed Saint Clare at 436 West 36th Street from 1903 to 1940; Saint Sebastian on East 24th Street from 1917 to 1972; and Our Lady of Pity on East 151st Street, starting in 1908. The Salesians had two annex congregations and two parishes: Saint Brigid's from 1898 to 1908; Epiphany from 1899 to 1901; Transfiguration from 1902 to 1950; and Mary, Help of Christians, starting in 1908. The Pallottines had two parishes: Our Lady of Mount Carmel on East 115th Street, starting in 1884; and Saint Ann's on East 112th Street, starting in 1911. The Jesuits had a chapel and a parish: Our Lady of Loreto from 1891 to 1917; and Nativity on Second Avenue at East 2nd Street, starting in 1917.

In at least one case, the order's interest in staffing an Italian parish dovetailed with the interests of one of the order's members. Nicholas Russo was born in 1845 in Ascoli, Foggia. He joined the Jesuits in France in 1862, and they sent him to Woodstock, Maryland, in 1875. In 1877 he was ordained, and spent the next eleven years teaching logic and philosophy at Boston College, serving as vice-rector, and publishing two theological works. In 1888, he became procurator at Saint Francis Xavier on West 16th Street in New York, and also moderator of cases of conscience for the archdiocese; perhaps it was in that capacity that he became acquainted with Archbishop Corrigan. Russo spent 1889 at Georgetown University in Washington, D.C., where he taught philosophy and published a third theological work. In 1890, he returned to New York, to Saint Ignatius Loyola on Park Avenue at East 84th Street. Among his duties at his new assignment was drafting material for Corrigan.[16] Russo's first recorded meeting with his fellow

---

[15]Mary Louise Sullivan, M.S.C., *Mother Cabrini: "Italian Immigrant of the Century"* (New York: CMS, 1992), 156–157.

[16]Nicholas Russo, S.J., to Michael Augustine Corrigan, New York, early 1891?, AANY microfilm reel #14; letter began "I thought I would send you the enclosed before Christmas but was unable to do so." For Russo's biography, see "Father Nicholas Russo," *Woodstock Letters* XXXI (1902), 281–282.

immigrants came in December 1889, when he and a colleague preached a mission at Saint Patrick's Old Cathedral. It was quite a shock. Russo recalled that rector John Kearney "refused us [permission] to give a mission to the Italians in the upper church, for reasons which a priest should feel ashamed to give."[17] Thereafter, Russo involved himself in the Italian ministry, and wrote Corrigan and his Jesuit superiors about starting an Italian chapel.[18] In 1891, he opened Our Lady of Loreto on Elizabeth Street.

In the early years, it was less common for the founding pastor to come from the ranks of the secular clergy. The available pool of clergy divided into two types: non-Italian clergy and Italian immigrant clergy. There is only one case of a non-Italian priest founding a parish for Italians, Daniel Burke.[19] Burke was born in 1858 in New York City, to Irish parents. He was educated in Rome, and ordained there in 1883. He spent an extra year in Rome, earning a doctorate of divinity. When he returned to New York, he taught at Saint Joseph's Seminary and worked as a curate in various Manhattan parishes. In 1898, Corrigan sent him to Bedford Park in the Bronx.[20] Burke seems to have been unaffected by anti-Italian prejudices; as we shall see in the next few paragraphs, he was one of the few rectors who had a good word for his Italian curate. His parish, though, was quasi-Italian at best. He named it for Saint Philip Neri, an Italian but not a popular hero among southern Italians: he was a sixteenth-century Florentine noted for his revival of religious life in Reformation-era Rome. Most of the laity who assisted in setting up the parish had Irish names. Burke needed the money the Irish brought in, and in 1900 he received permission to preach in English (instead of just in Italian), and to enroll non-Italians as parishioners.[21] The Italian mission remained a consideration. When Burke died in 1931, his successor was chosen partly because of his fluency in Italian and interest in Italians' spiritual welfare.

Italian immigrant secular priests were rarely appointed as pastors not because there were not many of them, but because the chancery perceived them as likely to cause scandal. It might be possible to claim the religious order clergy were no more reliable. Di Giovanni's "Michael Augustine Corrigan and the Italian

[17]Russo to Corrigan, New York, 24 October 1891, AANY microfilm reel #14.

[18]Russo to Corrigan, New York, 3 May 1891, AANY microfilm reel #14.

[19]John Edwards, rector of Immaculate Conception on East 14th Street in the 1880s and 1890s, also involved himself in the Italian ministry. Chancery-level personnel will be discussed later.

[20][William A. Hanley], *Golden Jubilee of Saint Philip Neri Church, 1898–1948.*

[21]Daniel Burke to Corrigan, Bronx, 11 October 1900, AANY St. Philip Neri folder.

Immigrants" and Edward C. Stibili's "The St. Raphael Society for the Protection of Italian Immigrants, 1887–1923" give several examples of the problems that arose in parishes and agencies staffed by religious order clergy. The chancery, however, had a series of bad experiences with Italian secular clergy, the most spectacular of which was the Giuseppe Cirringione episode of 1903.

Cirringione first appeared on the records in October, 1893, saying mass for an Italian congregation at Saint Brigid's.[22] He may have preceded Daniel Burke at Bedford Park; Saint Philip Neri's *Golden Jubilee* anniversary booklet puts him first on a chronological list of clergy who had served the parish. Burke valued him highly:

> Last Sunday we had more than 150 Italian communions. Father Maltese and I agree in saying that the credit for this is due almost exclusively to Father Cirringione.[23]

> I have only words of praise for him. He is a very hard, willing and successful worker. He preached an excellent mission recently to the Italians. It was at least twice as successful as anything, which I attempted since I came here. The success was due under God to Father Cirringione's efforts. Since that mission I feel far more encouraged in regard to final success with the Italians than I have felt at any previous time.[24]

Cirringione also preached missions at Saint Brigid's and Immaculate Conception.[25] He left Saint Philip Neri in November, 1902. The next year, he became the first rector of the new Italian church of the Immaculate Conception at Williamsbridge in the Bronx.[26] Up to this point, he was a notably successful Italian priest.

Then, sometime between Friday night, November 13, and Sunday morning, November 15, 1903, Cirringione disappeared. He reappeared the morning of November 16. He was brought to Flower Hospital and then to Saint Vincent's Hospital on West Twelfth Street for treatment of hysteria. His story was that on Friday night he had been kidnapped by four men, who had robbed him of his ebony cane, a watch chain, and a large sum of money, most of which he was holding for his sister's dowry. Several bits of evidence supported Cirringione's story. He was found at First Avenue and 51st Street, far from home. He had rope marks

[22]O'Flaherty 73–74.

[23]Burke to Corrigan, Bronx, 17 April 1900, AANY St. Philip Neri folder.

[24]Burke to Corrigan, Bronx, 5 April 1901, AANY St. Philip Neri folder.

[25]Burke to Corrigan, Bronx, 17 April 1900, AANY St. Philip Neri folder.

[26]Giuseppe Cirringione to John M. Farley, New York, 9 February 1903, CMS IAR Box 1, Italians in Williamsbridge folder.

on his wrist. And, after he was transferred to Saint Vincent's, four men appeared at Flower Hospital, looking for a priest.[27] The plot thickened over the next few days, as a friend of Cirringione's and then the priest's father received letters, in a different hand than the original ones, threatening Cirringione with death if he continued to publicize his kidnapping, the details of which were appearing in all the local papers.[28] Whether because of this or because he sensed trouble with the chancery, Cirringione left for Sicily December 11.[29] On December 2, claiming Cirringione had resigned, Farley appointed Patrick T. Lennon Immaculate Conception's rector.[30] Lennon discovered that Immaculate Conception was in bad financial shape. The rectory alone had three mortgages on it, and was assessed at less than two-thirds of what Cirringione had paid for it. The archbishop's secretary informed Cirringione, still in Palermo, that Immaculate Conception was so badly off that no Italian priest was thought able to take it, and no American priest wanted it. Between the evidence of mismanagement and the excitement caused by his disappearance, the archdiocese did not want Cirringione back.[31]

Other Italian secular clergy entrusted with parishes did the best they could under difficult circumstances. Sometime in 1900, Carlo Ferina came to the South Bronx to take charge of a parish named in honor of Saint Rita of Cascia. He found a storefront next to a saloon on East 149th Street and Courtlandt Avenue, and began saying mass in November.[32] He characterized his new parishioners as "a poor Christian people and wants so much the compassion." (Ferina learned to write English on the job.) He feared the etiquette they observed at mass scandalized other Catholics: they received Communion the way the clergy did, sitting, rather than kneeling, before and after.[33] They attended mass erratically. The first Sunday of November, Ferina had 120 people, mostly children. Two weeks later, he had seventeen adults "and children." Their giving habits were uniformly poor.

[27] The New York Times, 17 November 1903, 5:4.

[28] The New York Times, 20 November 1903, 7:4; and 21 November 1903, 6:4.

[29] The New York Times, 11 December 1903, 16:6.

[30] The New York Times, 2 December 1903, 6:2.

[31] James V. Livio to Giuseppe Cirringione, New York, 2 February 1904, CMS IAR Box 1, Italians in Williamsbridge folder.

[32] Carlo Ferina to Corrigan, Bronx, undated, AANY St. Rita of Cascia folder.

[33] Ferina to Corrigan, Bronx, January 21, 1901, AANY St. Rita of Cascia folder.

The congregation of 120 gave a total of $2.00.[34] By July 1901, Ferina estimated he had 5,000 Italians in his area, but it was a highly transient population, and a trolley line was threatening to divide the colony along Morris Avenue and cut the population in half.[35] As it was, only 500 Italians came to church; only 150 came to Saint Rita's (which sat 200), while the rest went to a German Catholic church. Their contribution record was dismal. During the first seven months of 1901, the offering ranged from $4.08 to $12.63.[36]

In order to keep his parish going, Ferina tried to prevent "his" Italians from going anywhere else. When he heard that some South Bronx parents had brought their infants to Our Lady of Mount Carmel on East 115th Street to be baptized, he wrote both Mount Carmel's rector and Corrigan to complain.[37] Ferina also tried to attract English-speaking Catholics to his parish. This Corrigan forbade: Saint Rita's was for Italians, and other Catholics were supposed to go elsewhere.[38] Ferina then petitioned for generous parish borders that included both Americans and Italians.[39]

The chancery inspectors who reported to Corrigan on Saint Rita's in 1901 did not think generous borders were the answer. They counted only 1,000 Italians in the area. Saint Rita's congregation was only 20 percent Italian. The Italians seemed uninterested in the church, and the rector spoke English too poorly to qualify as rector of a regular parish. The inspectors recommended allowing the nearby German church to absorb the English-speaking people, while Ferina concentrated on getting the Italian children into school.[40] It would be another generation before a large number of Italian clergy were charged with the responsibilities of a pastor.

Parish Finances

The Italians were the despair of debt-haunted rectors. Mention has been made of Thomas McLouglin's experience with increasing number of Italians and declining

[34]Ferina to Corrigan, Bronx, November 1900?, AANY St. Rita of Cascia folder.

[35]Ferina to Corrigan, Bronx, 25 July 1901, AANY St. Rita of Cascia folder.

[36]Ferina to Corrigan, Bronx, 23 July 1901, AANY St. Rita of Cascia folder.

[37]Ferina to Corrigan, Bronx, 25 July 1901, AANY St. Rita of Cascia folder.

[38]Ferina to Corrigan, Bronx, 5 March 1901, AANY St. Rita of Cascia folder.

[39]Ferina to Corrigan, Bronx, 6 July 1901, AANY St. Rita of Cascia folder.

[40]"Report on Saint Rita's Mission," New York, 1901?, AANY St. Rita of Cascia folder.

collections at Transfiguration on Mott Street.[41] The Italian clergy, as one can see by Ferina's statistics, had no better luck.

Journalists explained that Italians gave so little because they were so poor, and because they were unaccustomed to the American system of congregationally supported parishes.[42] New York City rectors were not so much concerned with why the Italians did not donate as they were with how to get them to start contributing. National parishes were established partly with the idea that "if the Italians had a church of their own, they might feel interested in it, patronize it, perhaps support it."[43] The theory did not test out, and rectors turned to other ways of coping.

The Italian pastors quickly learned to emulate the non-Italian clergy in insisting on territorial borders even for Italian parishes, for the borders gave them a particular group of people to target for collections. The above-mentioned Saint Anthony's on Commonwealth Avenue quickly found that while there were enough Italians to get a parish, there might not be enough in the area to maintain it. According to Pasquale Maltese, Saint Anthony's second pastor, the solution lay in parish boundaries that incorporated English-speaking Catholics. In making his case to the cardinal, Maltese sounded like a non-Italian priest complaining about Italians: "There are many english [sic] speaking of German, French and even Irish parentage who never entered the door of a Catholic church. Their children must be attended to – and those poor people neglected for many years must be cultivated."[44]

Another method was to supplement parish income with benefactors outside the parish. Religious orders that had been established a long time in the United States usually had patrons who could be tapped for patronage. Our Lady of Loreto was supported not by its Sicilian parishioners but by friends of the various Jesuit rectors.[45] Annie Leary, who was over a long life a donor to many archdiocesan charities, supported Our Lady of Pompei from about 1895 to about 1905, and also subsidized the Cabrini's Missionaries of the Sacred Heart in their efforts to

[41]Thomas P. McLoughlin to Corrigan, New York, 28 August 1901, CMS IAR Box 1, Transfiguration folder.

[42]Louis M. Giambastini, "Into the Melting Pot – the Italians," 9–10, 20-21.

[43]Nicholas Russo, S.J., "The Origin and Progress of our Italian Mission in New York," 136.

[44]Pasquale Maltese to Farley, Bronx, 17 January 1913, AANY St. Anthony's (Commonwealth Ave.) folder.

[45]Russo was embarrassed when a friend began collecting before Russo had been given permission to raise money for Loreto, and even got a donation from Corrigan. Russo to Corrigan, New York, 1891?, AANY microfilm reel #14.

run a school in Greenwich Village.[46] Corrigan and Farley gave from their personal funds to Italian parishes.[47]

The archbishops also gave permission for collections to be taken up on behalf of the Italians. Saint Sebastian's on East 24th Street was partially funded this way.[48] Collections, though, were not always successful, as one rector informed the archbishop: "The contributions of my very few people toward outside charities are negligible unless perhaps an appeal be made for Irish relief. Indians, Negroes, and Italians are not popular in these parts."[49]

A second way to raise funds was by charging for services and devotional aids. Rules against simony prohibited pastors from charging for the performance of the sacraments. However, as we saw in Chapter 1, it was possible to charge for specific kinds of funeral masses. Parishes also charged for votive candles, holy pictures, and other devotional objects. Income from these sources, though, was not guaranteed. In 1901, Corrigan gave Saint Rita of Cascia a relic of the saint, who had been canonized the year before.[50] Later that year, the church became the American shrine.[51] Father Ferina laid in a supply of holy pictures to attract devotees.[52] The cult caught on quickly among the English-speaking, but the Italians remained aloof.

Pasquale Lombardo of Saint Lucy's on Mace Avenue earned money for his church by writing and translating Italian prayer books and by selling votive candles. St. Lucy's parish anniversary book remembered him as an aggressive salesman: "How many of us can still remember Monsignor personally selling devotional candles to all who came to visit, in order to make money for our church and school?"[53]

[46]Mary Elizabeth Brown, *From Italian Villages to Greenwich Village: Our Lady of Pompei, 1892-1992* (New York: Center for Migration Studies, 1992), pp. 21, 24–25, and 32.

[47]"Cronaca della Casa di Santa Brigida in New York City," entry for 11 February 1911. Copy in CMS IAR Box 6, Saint Brigid's, NYC, folder.

[48]*New York Catholic News*, 30 December 1916, p. 6, and 24 March 1917, p. 2.

[49]Henry J. Browne, *Saint Ann's on East Twelfth Street, New York City, 1852-1952*, 41.

[50]Ferina to Corrigan, Bronx, 25 October 1901, ANNY St. Rita of Cascia folder.

[51]*Saint Rita of Cascia Shrine Church* (South Hackensack, New Jersey: Custombook, 1975), no pagination.

[52]Ferina to Corrigan, Bronx, November 1900, ANNY St. Rita of Cascia folder.

[53]*Saint Lucy's Church, Bronx, New York* (New York: Privately printed, 1977), 13.

No parish, though, sponsored a *festa* to raise money. That privilege was still the laity's. The parish was part of the *festa* of Our Lady of Mount Carmel in East Harlem: the feast's focal point was a statue which usually stood in the church's basement (it was moved to the upper church in the 1920s), the procession ended at the church, and the priests said mass for the occasion.[54] However, a lay committee organized the affair and handled the funds. Reporters speculated that the snipers who put three bullets through one pastor's bedroom window were retaliating for the pastor's attempt to get his congregation to forgo their annual Saint Rocco *festa* in favor of building a new church.[55]

A third way to raise money was to hold social events and charge admission. Secular and ecclesiastical forces limited the kinds of social events parishes could sponsor. In the early twentieth century, laws against gambling precluded games of chance.[56] Under Cardinal Farley, the archdiocese prohibited balls, with their opportunities for immoral dance styles.[57] Professionals' performances were censored or prohibited.[58]

Our Lady of Pompei in Greenwich Village, preserved extensive records of its experiences with fundraisers. The parish opened in 1892 as the chapel of the Saint Raphael Society for the Protection of Italian Immigrants. At that time, it occupied one room of the society's headquarters, which were in a house at 113 Waverly Place. In 1895, the chapel took a step toward becoming an independent parish, and moved to a former African American Methodist church at 214 Sullivan Street. At this point, the parish men organized such affairs as picnics, to which parishioners paid a quarter admission.[59]

In 1898, Pompei moved again, this time to 210 Bleecker Street, the building it occupied until 1926. It also acquired a new priest, Antonio Demo, P.S.S.C., who in 1899 became pastor, a position he occupied until 1933, to the great benefit of parish stability. Demo tapped groups of parishioners interested in various types of fundraising. In 1901 a Church Aid Society sponsored a variety show, complete

[54]Dominic Pistella, *The Crowning of a Queen*, 62.

[55]"Attenatato contro un Prete," *Opinione*, 14 April 1908, CMS:IAR Box 5, Miscellaneous Clippings, third folder.

[56]Anthony Comstock to Antonio Demo, New York, 15 February 1912, CMS OLP Box 2, Folder 13.

[57]John Cardinal Farley, circular letter, New York, 14 June 1916, CMS OLP Box 8 Folder 91.

[58]Father Provincial to Dominic Cirigliano, New York, 19 July 1929, NYSJ Nativity 1922–1932.

[59]Sunday announcement, 8 July 1900, CMS OLP Box 28, Folder 309.

with singers, comedians, and circus-type acts. The presence on the program of a "Hebrew comedian" and a banjoist may testify to the Italians' appreciation of the Jews and African Americans living within walking distance, but more likely it indicated that Pompei was trying to attract an audience larger than just the parishioners. At least one of the people on the program probably donated her talents: Mrs. Luigi Fugazy, wife of the prominent Greenwich Village Italian-American businessman who chaired the event.[60]

Probably as early as the 1900s, Pompei had parishioners who organized entire dramatic performances rather than variety shows. The parish records include several programs which were undated but which must have been for events before 1907, because it was about that year that Pompei stopped using other church's space and finished the basement of the church at 210 Sullivan Street so that it could hold events there.[61] The early programs consisted of two plays. The first was a serious drama or melodrama. Some of these had titles such as *L'Eroismo di una Figlia di Maria*, which indicated a play focusing on morality. (It is also possible the plays were chosen because the dramatic group had the right numbers of male and female performers for the script.) The second was always a farce. Besides raising funds, parish dramas performed other functions as well; we will return to them in the next chapter.

Other parishes tried other ways of raising money. The Italian congregation in the basement at Saint Brigid's tried a bazaar.[62] Our Lady of Pity in the Bronx sponsored a Saint Patrick's "entertainment" to attract donations from outside the parish.[63]

If a parish had difficulty raising money, the other option was to try to reduce expenses. The most effective way to do so was to forgo large expenditures. Transfiguration's annex congregation stayed in its basement until it had the money – and the clerical leadership – to start building Most Precious Blood. Congregations gathered in places that could be leased inexpensively; it could not have cost Saint Philip Neri parish much to use the defunct Jerome Park Racetrack clubhouse for its first masses. Parishes that built their own churches minimized expenses: Nicholas Russo purchased a lot with two tenements, then altered the two tenements for Our Lady of Loreto rather than tear them down and build a church.

[60]Program dated [30 May] 1900, CMS OLP Box 12, Folder 144.

[61]Program for *Primo Trattenimento Drammatico*, CMS OLP Box 12, Folder 144. There are several undated programs in the same box.

[62]"Cronaca della Casa di Santa Brigida," entry for October 1917.

[63]*New York Catholic News*, 17 March 1917, p. 17.

Few Italian parishes conducted parochial schools in the late nineteenth and early twentieth centuries. Of those that did, some were, like Saint Anthony of Padua, already well-established, or, like Transfiguration, able to use a school which had been built for another ethnic group. Others cut expenses ruthlessly. Nicholas Russo divided the basement of Our Lady of Loreto into six classrooms for two hundred children. Russo recalled that "Much was said against our keeping the children in dark rooms, without much ventilation, using only gaslight. . . ."[64]

Emiliano Kirner at Our Lady of Mount Carmel in East Harlem economized in a particularly tragic way. According to newspaper reports, Kirner had built six churches before Mount Carmel, and therefore felt able to dispense with a professional builder for Mount Carmel's parochial school. Under his direction, laborers erected east and west walls. They were putting up the crossbeams when the walls buckled and fell, crushing Kirner and seventeen workers in the ruins. Five men died instantly; Kirner died the next day from his wounds.[65]

Fostering Devotional and Sacramental Life

Italian parish historians often explained that their churches were built because the immigrants "desired to worship God in their own beautiful language and to retain the noble tradition they carried from their native country."[66] The clergy ministering to Italian parishes, who have provided the most extensive records, indicate that something more complex was going on. The clergy used Italian customs to draw the Italians to American norms regarding the practice of their common Catholic faith.

When parishes first opened, the clergy often used popular devotions to attract the people. Mention has already been made of Nicholas Russo's use of the Saint Rocco *festa* to attract a crowd to the first mass at Our Lady of Loreto. "The opening day was pronounced a success," Russo later recalled, "but I could not help looking forward with dread to the following Sunday."[67] Emiliano Kirner went a step further. When he came to East Harlem in 1884, he purchased from the Our Lady of Mount Carmel Society the statue which the organization had

[64]Russo, "Our Italian Mission," 141.

[65]*The New York Times* 18 October 1887, 1:1–2; 20 October 1887, 8:1; and 22 October 1887, 3:3.

[66][Joseph Lumia] *Golden Jubilee: Our Lady of Mount Carmel Church, Poughkeepsie, New York* (New York: Privately printed, 1960), unpaginated.

[67]Russo, "Our Italian Mission," 137–138.

been using for its *festa*. He then set up the statue in the basement chapel and put the society under ecclesiastical authority, as a sort of sodality.[68] The *festa* then became part of the parish's calendar.

Other pastors were not so successful. Felix Morelli of Saint Joachim's on Roosevelt Street signed a contract with immigrants from Potenza regarding their statue of Saint Rocco. Morelli agreed to keep the statue in the church, to say the annual *festa* mass, and to say funeral masses for deceased members of Saint Rocco's mutual benefit society. In return, the society agreed to pay a sum to the church. A dispute broke out, and an unhappy member of the Saint Rocco Society went to court, received legal custody of the statue, and took Saint Rocco to his place of business, a funeral parlor, for safe keeping. The women of the parish, accustomed to being able to visit the saint in the church to pray and ask for favors, objected so strenuously that Father Morelli went to court and had legal custody of the statue restored to him. A delegation of parish women, accompanied the marshal to the funeral parlor, served the undertaker the legal papers, reclaimed the statue, and bore Saint Rocco in joyous procession back to the church.[69]

Italians had a basis in their experience for understanding the sodalities which were part of American Catholic parish life. John Briggs has studied the men's mutual benefit societies, which not only provided insurance, but brought the men together to organize the home town patron saint's annual *festa*. Women in Italy may not have participated in the mutual benefit aspect of such societies, but they had devotional societies: one of the earliest societies at Our Lady of Pompei in Greenwich Village consisted of a group of women immigrants from San Stefano, who re-established their devotion to Our Lady of Guadalupe in their new home.[70]

Usually each sodality had its assigned Sunday when all the members sat together in the church and received communion as a group. This meant each sodality had its unofficial Saturday for confession as well. Pastors also found other ways to encourage reception of the sacraments. Vincenzo Jannuzzi, P.S.S.C., at Saint Joachim's on Roosevelt Street, instituted a requirement that all persons who presented themselves as sponsors for candidates for confirmation (Italians regarded it as an honor to be asked to serve as sponsor) had to go to confession and receive communion before the confirmation ceremony.[71]

[68]Pistella, *The Crowning of a Queen*, 62.

[69]*New York Evening Post*, July 19, 1906.

[70]Di Giovanni, "Corrigan and the Immigrants," 493.

[71]Vincenzo Jannuzzi, P.S.S.C., to Farley, New York, 21 June 1916, AANY Saint Joachim, Manhattan, folder.

Sensitive pastors accommodated Italian customs as much as possible, since it was more important that the Italians receive the sacraments than that they do it the American way. When Archbishop Corrigan presided over the first confirmation at Our Lady of Mount Carmel in East Harlem, he confirmed 1,638 persons, one-third of them infants. Americans confirmed school-age children, but southern Italians confirmed soon after baptism, and Emiliano Kirner thought it wise for once to follow *mezzogiorno* practice.[72] Thirty years later, Kirner's successors still accommodated the Italian customs. In 1921, pastor Henry Mazzatesta, P.S.M., wrote Archbishop Hayes, asking if the date for confirmation could be moved: it was scheduled for a Friday, a day on which meat was forbidden, but the Italians usually celebrated confirmation with a big meal, including meat. The date was moved.[73]

Left to their own devices, Italians themselves changed familiar customs that no longer fit in the new environment. When Our Lady of Pompei in Greenwich Village first opened, the congregation remained after each Sunday mass to recite prayers for the dead. This was the custom in the southern Italian towns from which some of them came, but it was neither American practice nor part of the official liturgy, and eventually the ritual was dropped *con soddisfazione di tutti*. Likewise, Italians also adopted the American customs they found useful. Again, Our Lady of Pompei's experience is instructive. "The American custom is that every Sunday and feastday mass, the celebrant ascends the pulpit, after the Gospel, for the reading of the announcements of the week. . . ."[74]

Some elements of Italian Catholicism were hard to change or to make a conscious effort to keep because they were hard to pin down. Carolyn Ware, a social scientist who studied Greenwich Village in the 1920s reported about Pompei that "informality during Mass was strongly reminiscent of the comings and goings in the churches in Italy and was in sharp contrast to the strictness with which the Irish priests maintained silence and order."[75]

[72]Unidentified newspaper clipping dated 26 August 1885, AANY Our Lady of Mount Carmel, Manhattan, folder.

[73]Joseph P. Dineen to Henry Mazzatesta, P.S.M., New York, 25 April 1921, AANY Our Lady of Mount Carmel, Manhattan, folder.

[74]Constantino Sassi, P.S.S.C., *Parrocchia della Madonna di Pompei in New York: Notizie Storiche dei Primi Cinquant'anni dalla sua Fondazione, 1892–1942* (Rome: Tipografia Santa Lucia, 1946), 54.

[75]Caroline Ware, *Greenwich Village, 1920–1930: A comment on American Civilization in the Post-War Years*, 313.

Sources of Conflict and Sources of Unity

During Sunday mass, Catholics recite a profession of faith which includes the line "I believe in one holy catholic and apostolic church." One might say the universality of Catholicism had to be an article of faith, rather than knowledge derived from experience, for New York's first generation of Italian immigrants. There were so many centrifugal forces, some working to pull apart the Italian community, others to pull the Italian Catholics away from their co-religionists.

The proliferation of Italian parishes testified to continued *campanilismo*, an Italian word popular among scholars and meaning a feeling of solidarity extending only to those who lived within the sound of one's own church bell. The result of this sensibility meant that sometimes Italian parishes existed within walking distance of each other. For example, the Italians of the Fontanabuona Valley in the interior of Liguria established Saint Anthony of Padua, while the Italians of Genoa on the seacoast of Liguria established Our Lady of Pompei. For a brief time in the late 1890s both parishes had churches on Sullivan Street, and they were always within walking distance of each other. Our Lady of Loreto was not an *Italian* parish but a *Sicilian* one, and was listed as such in *The Catholic Directory*. One parish managed to combine two communities, but at the price of an unwieldy formal name: Saint Sebastian and Our Lady of Piano di Campa (usually called Saint Sebastian's).[76]

Italian men's religious orders also competed with each other to promote their work. The Franciscans never forgave the Scalabrinians for taking their annex congregation at Transfiguration, with its bank account, and then bringing the congregation to bankruptcy by building Most Precious Blood.[77]

Men's and women's religious orders also crossed swords. Although Bishop Scalabrini was instrumental in bringing Mother Cabrini to the United States, she eventually came to distrust the Missionaries of Saint Charles, and her Missionaries of the Sacred Heart did not long work in Scalabrinian parishes in New York City. The most extreme case was that of the Pallottine fathers and sisters at Our Lady of Mount Carmel in East Harlem. After Emiliano Kirner's death, the Pallottines assigned an Anglo-Irish missionary, Michael Carmody, as pastor. The parish also had English and Italian Pallottine Sisters of Charity. Carmody tried to force the sisters' superiors to remove them from Mount Carmel by sending the sisters on vacation and then locking them out of their convent so that when they returned to town, they had to trudge from East Harlem to the archbishop's house in midtown,

[76]*New York Catholic News*, 13 October 1917, 1.

[77]Mauro Roberti, O.F.M., "La Piu' Antica Chiesa Italiana di New York City," *Corriere d'America*, April 10, 1936.

luggage in tow, to find a place to stay. Matters grew so heated that the Pallottine priests sent a vicar general to mediate the dispute between Carmody and the sisters, and, ultimately, to recall Carmody.[78]

Anti-Italian prejudice continued strong at least until the 1920s, as can be seen in the story of Holy Rosary on East 119th Street. Holy Rosary had been founded at the same time as and within walking distance of Our Lady of Mount Carmel, circumstantial evidence that one parish was for the Italians and one for the Irish of the neighborhood. In the fall of 1914, Cardinal Farley assigned an Italian-American curate, Gaetano Arcese, to Holy Rosary.[79] Under Arcese, the Italians split into an annex congregation. By 1918, the Italian and non-Italian clergy had separate rectories.[80] In January 1925, Cardinal Hayes promoted Holy Rosary's pastor to the more prestigious East Harlem parish of Saint Paul, and made Arcese pastor of Holy Rosary.[81] The non-Italian portion of the parish reacted as though Hayes had given the church to the Protestants, and wrote about how they had helped build Holy Rosary only to be "forced to hand it over to a foreign element."[82] One women wrote the cardinal, "when you think of our beautiful church turned over to them, and we turned out of the House of God that we helped to build, one wonders whether there is justice anywhere."[83] Non-Italian clergy opposed Italian religious orders for reasons of both ethnic and ecclesiastical loyalty. When the Scalabrinians took the Italians out of his church basement of their new parish of the most Precious Blood, Thomas Lynch of Transfiguration watched them closely, and reported on them to the archbishop. The Scalabrinians permitted the Italians to continue their feste, even walking in procession with them and letting them use the church in their celebrations.[84] They also let the Italians observe the anniversary of the fall of Rome without so much as a word on the temporal power of the papacy.[85]

[78]Correspondence between Michael Carmody, P.S.M. and Corrigan on AANY microfilm reel #13.

[79]*New York Catholic News*, 9 October 1943, 7.

[80]Gaetano Arcese to Dineen, New York, 8 January 1919, AANY Holy Rosary folder.

[81]Arcese to Patrick Cardinal Hayes, New York, 26 January 1925, AANY Holy Rosary folder.

[82]Edwin M. Fay to Hayes, New York, 26 January 1924 [sic – should be 1925], AANY Holy Rosary folder.

[83]Ida V. Collins to Hayes, New York, 25 January 1925, AANY Holy Rosary folder. *See also* William O'Rourke to Hayes, New York, 26 January 1925, *ibid.*

[84]Thomas Lynch to Corrigan, New York, 10 August 1892, AANY microfilm reel #14.

[85]Lynch to Corrigan, New York, 12 October 1891, AANY microfilm reel #13.

The Italians fought against such discrimination, sometimes literally. In 1892, an Italian parishioner at Our Lady of Mount Carmel in East Harlem gave one of the non-Italian Pallottine priests a black eye, the last blow in a long "race war" between Irish and Italians there.[86] Parishioners at Our Lady of Pity in the South Bronx, who had no official voice when in 1921 their pastor was transferred, vented their feelings in ominous letters to the archbishop and in riots.[87] The religious orders were less physical, but showed a similar concern for their own interests. When the archdiocese contemplated giving Saint Brigid's to Italian archdiocesan clergy, the Salesians' superior warned the chancery that if that happened, the Salesians would consider their position at nearby Mary, Help of Christians, untenable, and would ask to be relieved.[88]

One final problem was the assumption that the Italians were united in their Catholicism when in fact they were not, as one letter to Cardinal Hayes testified. The writer's purpose was to seek assistance in purchasing the required white outfit for his child's confirmation. What was interesting was that, although the writer evidently took his child's upcoming confirmation seriously, and although apparently his wife and all his children attended church, the writer himself began his letter to cardinal with the information that he was an atheist.[89]

There were also occasional problems with criminals. Giuseppe Cirringione was the most extreme example of Mafia-style threats against clergy and churches. The Salesians in Saint Brigid's basement recorded receiving a note threatening them with dynamite, but nothing came of it.[90] Saint Patrick's Old Cathedral received a similar note in 1909 when it held a funeral for parishioner Joseph Petrosino, a New York Police Department detective gunned down while in Palermo checking the records of criminals who had supposedly migrated to the United States.[91]

Few forces worked for unity in the early days of the national parishes. Parishes functioned autonomously, with little guidance from the archdiocese. The archdiocese had little bureaucracy, more than it had under Archbishop Hughes, but less

[86]*The New York Times*, 29 August 1892, 8:1.

[87]Nicholas Spallone to Hayes, New York, 1 and 14 October 1921, AANY Our Lady of Pity, Bronx, folder; and *The New York Times*, 21 December 1921, 16:1; and 25 February 1922, 6:1.

[88]Ernesto Coppo, S.D.B., to Farley, New York, 30 November 1915, CMS IAR, Box 1, Transfiguration folder.

[89]J. Francis McIntyre to Marchegiani, New York, 29 May 1934, CMS OLP Box 9, Folder 104.

[90]"Cronaca della Casa di Santa Brigida," entry for 8 December 1907.

[91]*The New York Times*, 12 April 1923, 19:5

than it was to have under Cardinal Hayes. Archbishop Corrigan had one chancery-level assistant for Italian affairs, Monsignor Gherardo Ferrante. Ferrante was born in 1853 in Frosinone, in central Italy, and in 1891 accepted Corrigan's invitation to migrate to New York. He became the chancery's "Italian secretary;" one of his duties was to supervise Italian women's religious orders and handle their finances. Over the years, as the archdiocese became more bureaucratized, he performed other duties as well.[92] By the time of Ferrante's death in 1921, the Italian national parishes and the chancery had evolved far beyond what they had been in the 1890s; that is the subject of another chapter.

In concluding this chapter, one can point of the irony of the national parish system. The Italians hoped, and the non-Italians feared, that national parishes allowed the Italians to maintain their own customs and language. However, in order to have national parishes, the Italians had to adopt some American ways. In Italy, Catholicism was as part of the total culture; in New York, a specific institution, the parish, was charged with maintaining the faith. In Italy, especially in southern Italy, lay men played an important role in organizing community *feste*, and lay women played an important role in mediating between their families and the Church; in New York, both lay men and lay women had the same duties, and one of those duties was to follow the clergy's leadership. And, even though outsiders were generous, had the Italians not adopted American attitudes toward parish finance, there would have been no Italian parishes.

The Italian national parishes contained within them their own antithesis, rapidly Americanizing children. Even as the first generation was getting settled and organizing national parishes, those parishes were introducing new, non-Italian customs to hold the children to the faith.

[92]"La Guida del Clero Italiano di New York," *Il Carroccio* II (1915), p. 76-77; *Il Carroccio* XIII (1921), 683; and *The New York Times*, 6 May 1921, 13:4.

4

"The Adoption of the Tactics of the Enemy"

In 1903, the Jesuit devotional magazine The Messenger of the Sacred Heart of Jesus published a survey of the Archdiocese of New York's Italian Catholic ministry by lay Catholic journalist Thomas F. Meehan. Meehan counted 133,100 Italian Catholics in the archdiocese, most of them on Manhattan. They were served by 52 clergy, representing the archdiocese and four religious orders, in eighteen parishes, two chapels, and seven annex congregations. Six parochial schools taught 3,317 pupils. Another 5,770 students attended Sunday schools.

All of which sounded tremendous until Meehan described what the Protestants were doing. The Woman's Branch of the New York City Mission and Tract Society taught sewing, a popular accomplishment among Italian girls. The New York City Baptist Mission Society invited children to its summer Sunday school camps. The Children's Aid society, a secular organization dominated by Protestants, had an Italian school. Meehan feared that these techniques of fun and games might succeed in converting the younger generation of Italian Catholics. He then challenged his audience:

> To my mind – it may be a crude lay opinion . . . we need a more effective, general and practical system of Catholic organization, the abandonment of many old time methods . . . and the adoption of the tactics of the enemy. We may scoff at 'settlement work' and the kindred varieties of modern profession-ally trained philanthropists but their disastrous results stare us in the face on all sides. And what do we offer in their place as a practical substitute?[1]

With these words, Meehan introduced a new possible solution to the "Italian problem," the use of Progressive means – settlement houses, nurseries, kindergar-tens, summer camps, and youth recreational work – for Catholic ends. This was a controversial idea, and even though Catholics took it up, some did so with misgivings, outlined in the next section.

[1] Thomas F. Meehan, "Evangelizing the Italians," The Messenger of the Sacred Heart of Jesus XXIX (1903), 16-32; quote on p. 32.

American Catholics, Protestants, and Progressives

American Catholics placed the Progressive Era in the larger context of the long history of American Protestant-Catholic rivalry. The earliest part of that quarrel of concern here is the career of Charles Loring Brace. Brace has already been introduced as the founder of New York's first Italian school. He also worked with Irish and German youth, many of whom were also Catholic. Brace considered himself unbiased; it was the Catholic clergy and laity who rebuffed his benevolent efforts and regarded them as a cover for proselytism. However, Brace's actions were easy to misinterpret. Ideally, he wanted to send destitute children to foster parents in the countryside to have the sort of childhood which produced prosperous and stable adults. When that proved impossible, he instituted schools and newsboys' lodging houses to train children not only in job skills, but also in the habits of industry, thrift, and temperance that allowed them to lead more middle-class lives. Neither method provided for the children's study or practice of their parents' faith. Early experience with philanthropists such as Brace taught Catholics to link secular and Protestant charity and to distrust both.

Other Protestants explicitly emphasized conversion, and regarded the Italian migration as a second Exodus, a crossing of the Atlantic away from the Egyptian darkness of papist superstition into the light of the Gospel. Such Protestants were of two types. Most were American, but a significant minority were Italian. Very few were Waldensians, the only native Italian Protestant church. Most had converted in America. They were important because they were used as role models, sent as missionaries to Italian Catholic areas and encouraged to write their memoirs in the hopes that other Italians might follow their example.[2]

Evangelizing the Italians was a patriotic as well as a religious duty. Catholicism, governed by a hierarchy whose authority was accepted on faith rather than reason was considered an insufficient moral basis for democracy and self-government. American Protestants prayed "may American Christendom rise to its opportunities."[3] Antonio Arrighi, himself born in Italy, gave a nativist-sounding reason for evangelization:

> . . . we believe there are three plain reasons for prosecuting the work of the Broome Street Tabernacle. The first is a purely patriotic reason. The presence in the midst of the national body politic of an undigested mass must be extremely hurtful, threatening finally the very life of the body. I said undigested, not undigestible, for I am not ready to admit that our American institutions and Christian civilization are not able to digest anything that has yet come to our shores. But against an unrestricted flood of ignorant immigrants many wise voices have been raised, and many strong arguments have been set forth by

[2]John B. Bisceglia, *Italian Evangelical Pioneers.*

[3]The quote is from Frederick H. Wright, "The Italian in America," 196–198.

statesmen and writers in our magazines and reviews. The problem is not easily settled. As the gates have been closed, to some extent , on the Pacific coast against an undesirable Chinese immigration, so, it would seem that it was high time for a judicious closing of the gates on the Atlantic coast. The supreme value of our public schools, especially in a city like this, is their amalgamating influence. They bring together and Americanize the children of foreign-born parents. Should we now close the gates, the future of our institutions would be assured at the end of twenty years by means of the schools but where, in the meantime, shall we be if we permit the parents of these children, with their oftentimes hostile notions regarding our institutions, to remain amongst us untaught and un-Americanized?

The second reason, response to Jesus' command to preach to all nations, and the third, the salvation of souls, merited two short sentences each.[4]

To evangelize the Italians, New York's Protestant denominations hired Italian converts and built or rented churches in Italian neighborhoods. The churches engaged in traditional Protestant activities: worship, Sunday school, and the distribution of bibles, hymnals, and tracts. Although Baptists, Methodists, and Presbyterians participated in the effort, the Episcopalians were in the best position. Their liturgy was closest to the Catholics' and their history allowed them to de-emphasize Protestant-Catholic conflict. Chapter two quoted from an advertisement from an Episcopalian congregation taking advantage of that coincidence.[5]

Catholics watched Protestant activities carefully. They accused Protestants of using charity as a lure, of drawing families to services and Sunday schools with offers of material assistance.[6] They combed Protestant prayerbooks for examples of the insertion of Catholic-sounding prayers that deceived the simple.[7] They exposed instances of non-liturgical Protestant churches adapting their services to what they thought was an Italian taste for more solemn and splendid worship.[8] They quoted Protestant statistics on churches and converts, mostly for the purposes of pointing out inconsistences and inaccuracies, and comparing the poor results with the effort, the expense, and the number of souls yet to be won.[9] Although

[4][Antonio Arrighi] Italian Evangelical Church, *Sixty-Ninth Annual Report* (New York: Privately printed, 1895), 41–42.

[5]*The Italian Mission of the Protestant Episcopal Church in the City of New York Yearbook* (New York: Privately published, 1885), 7.

[6]Lawrence Franklin, "The Italian in America: What He Has Been, What He Shall Be," *Catholic World* LXXI (1900), 70.

[7]Dominic Cirigliano, S.J., "Protestant Activities in our Parishes," *Woodstock Letters* LXVIX (1920), 229-231, 340–341.

[8]Francis Beattie, "The Waldensian and Protestant Episcopal Entente," *America* XXI (1919), 273–275.

[9]Aurelio Palmieri, O.S.A., "Italian Protestantism in the United States," 177–189.

Catholics discounted Protestant claims of success, they worried about the Protestant threat, especially to vulnerable children.

Catholic concern increased in the 1890s, when a renewed philanthropy joined traditional evangelism. Not all Progressive philanthropists emphasized their Protestant background, but the point here is that Catholics did so. For Catholics, the symbol of the new Protestant benevolence was the settlement house, but there were other innovations as well. Many settlement houses had day care nurseries or kindergartens which benefited both working mothers and the children whose homes were deprived of playmates, space, and equipment. Professionally-trained social workers hired by private and public welfare agencies also organized summer camps, and worked out a modern system for replacing orphanages and infant asylums with foster care placement. Youth recreation encompassed a variety of programs: organized sports teams, equipment and space for free play, arts-and-crafts classes, or drama or music lessons.

Catholic response to innovative charity may be divided into three types. One was represented by the Paulist monthly Catholic World, which had a reputation for an open-minded approach to liberal American developments. Even Catholic World raised objections to the new charities. According to the articles it published, settlement workers thought poverty was eradicable, by one of two methods. In the first method, the settlement "uplifted" the poor, inculcating habits of thrift and industry which enabled them to become as middle class as the settlement workers. In the second method, settlements studied and recommended changes in the social structure which ended poverty. Catholic World journalists argued that the gospel aphorism "the poor you will always have with you" was meant more literally. Poverty was not a personal fault to be eliminated nor did it indicate societal malfunction except insofar as the wealthy failed in their obligation to relieve extreme want. Poverty played a part in salvation, protecting the poor from the temptations which came with riches and teaching them humility, and enabling the wealthy to practice the virtue of charity.[10] Even those contributors who advocated using settlements as models stressed the need to use only those philosophical and charitable innovations compatible with Catholic teaching.[11]

Other writers did not engage Progressive philanthropy intellectually. Cardinal Hayes accused the innovative charities of playing the traditional role of luring Catholics away from their faith, and called for American Catholics to emulate the Protestants not out of any respect for the innate qualities of their new forms of

[10]John J. O'Shea, "After the Manner of St. Francis," Catholic World LXII (1895), 377–383; and Francis Howard, "The Church and Social Reform," 286–293.

[11]Joseph McSorley, C.S.P., "The Catholic Layman and Social Reform," Catholic World XCII (1910), 187–195.

charity, but so that Catholics could receive the aid they needed without endangering their faith.[12] This was not entirely a figment of Catholic imagination. The Italian-American educator Leonard Covello left an account of how he began going to read and play at Miss Ann C. Ruddy's Home Garden and ended up considering himself a Protestant.[13]

A third response came on the neighborhood level, where parishes saw non-Catholic social service in action. Almost all parishes responded to non-Catholic initiatives in some way. The Jesuits working among the Italians on the Lower East Side left a record not only of actions taken, but of reasons for those actions, and it is to their story that we now turn.

Nicholas Russo, S.J., 1891–1902: A Traditional Approach

Nicholas Russo and his chapel of Our Lady of Loreto have already been introduced.[14] Letters from Russo to Archbishop Corrigan indicate that one motivating force in opening the chapel was that Saint Patrick's Old Cathedral's rector, John F. Kearney, had asked that other arrangements be made for the Italians in his basement.[15] However, the Italian Mission of the Protestant Episcopal Church, at Grace Church on Broadway and East 12th Street, thought Loreto had been opened to counter their activities and accused him of preaching against them.[16]

When Russo first came to the Lower East Side, he found the west Sicilians in the area unresponsive: "We were oftentimes received with coldest indifference; not seldom avoided, at times greeted with insulting remarks." Russo first reached the adults through the children. He asked the parents to send their offspring to catechism in the afternoons, which they did. The youngsters then "became so

[12]Patrick J. Hayes, "The Immigrant Problem," *Extension* XVIII (1923), 13–14, 57.

[13]Leonard Covello, *The Heart is the Teacher* (New York: McGraw-Hill, 1958), 145.

[14]Material on the Jesuits at Our Lady of Loreto and at Nativity previously appeared in "The Making of Italian-American Catholics: Jesuit Work on the Lower East Side, New York, 1890s–1950s," *Catholic Historical Review* LXXIII (April 1987), 195–210; and in "'The Adoption of the Tactics of the Enemy': The Care of Italian Immigrant Youth in the Archdiocese of New York During the Progressive Era,." In William Pencak, *et al.*, editors, *Immigration to New York* (Philadelphia: The Balch Institute Press [A New-York Historical Society Book], 1991), 109–125.

[15]Nicholas Russo, S.J., to Corrigan, New York, 22 February 1898, CMS IAR Box 1 Our Lady of Loreto folder.

[16]*Annual Report of the Italian Mission of the Protestant Episcopal Church in the City of New York, 1892* (New York: n.p, [1892]?), 18.

many little apostles," and, like their mothers in the mezzogiorno, the link between their parents and official Catholicism.[17]

Like Hayes, Russo was anxious to "rescue all my children from the grasp of the Protestants." Russo's first efforts in parochial education were described in Chapter three. He observed that Italian parents supported the school because they found in it an ally: under public school tutelage, "the children were becoming less respectful and obedient and more independent." Fortunately for the students, the two tenements adjoining Loreto went on the market, and the Jesuits purchased them (for $35,000) and had them altered for a school. The youngsters moved out of the church basement and into the schoolhouse in October 1895.

Another way to rescue the children from the Protestants was to start sodalities for them. Among these sodalities was the Saint Aloysius Club, which was organized in 1892 or 1893. The Saint Aloysius Club accepted boys who had made their first communion (between seven and ten years old) but who had not yet turned 14. Like other sodalities it met for prayers, spiritual instruction, and its patron saint's feastday.[18] Many of the trappings of sodality membership strengthened camaraderie among the boys. In the early 1890s, club members wore distinctive badges and sashes on festive occasions at church, and special caps outdoors. They had their own banner, under which they marched in processions. They also had their own club officers.

Russo encouraged the club's social and recreational aspects. Until 1899, he met with the boys himself every Saturday morning from ten to twelve. He turned two of the basement classrooms into clubrooms, and furnished them with chess, checkers, and tiddley-winks games. He coached the boys in dramatics, wrote them plays, taught them carpentry, and threw them parties.[19] The musically inclined joined the club band, which had its own uniforms and "costly brass instruments," and which could have been called on to play in processions. At its peak, the club reached 120 boys.[20]

When some of the boys got too old for the Saint Aloysius Club, Russo organized a second group. The Loreto Club was intended for young men of 19 or 20. Two more of the basement classrooms were turned into clubrooms for it. Although

[17]This and the next paragraph rely Russo, "Our Italian Mission," 139–141.

[18]This and the next paragraph rely on "A Short History of the Mission of Our Lady of Loreto, New York," *Woodstock Letters* XLVI (1917), 185.

[19]"Father Nicholas Russo," *Woodstock Letters* XXXI (1903), 284.

[20]"Short History," 185.

Russo met the youths nightly, club government was left up to them, allowing them some opportunity for individual responsibility while tying them to the Church.[21]

By 1899, the work at Loreto had grown so much that Russo delegated responsibility for the Saint Aloysius Club to a curate, Joseph Gennaro. Gennaro added light-blue sailor-suit uniforms and a pianola to the club's attractions.[22] But when Russo died on April 1, 1902, the boys' apostolate was still recognizable as a traditional Catholic response to a traditional fear of Protestant and secular forces.[23] The youth ministry took a different turn under Russo's successor.

William H. Walsh, S.J., 1903–1919: Progressive Pastor

William H. Walsh was born in New York City on January 7, 1855. He entered the Jesuits January 30, 1975. He seems to have spent most of his priestly life in New York State. His assignment just before Loreto was at the Jesuit novitiate Saint Andrew-on-Hudson in Poughkeepsie.[24]

Unlike Russo, Walsh revealed no special affinity for the Italian apostolate. He found the Italians "unresponsive to religious influence, distrustful of the church, and careless about the great obligations, Mass, Easter Communion, Friday abstinence." The youngsters' catechetical training was behind that of American children: "Scarcely one or two out of some odd twenty [boys] knows the Our Father, the Hail Mary, and the Apostles' Creed, yet they range from ten to fourteen years of age."[25]

Walsh did have a special interest in youth, particularly young men. In some ways, this was entirely traditional. The Jesuits have a historic mission to educate youth. By the time Walsh came to Loreto, the Jesuits had transplanted that tradition to New York.[26] Walsh, though, was more intense than most Jesuits. He had a unique devotion to the Boy Jesus, the Savior as youngster and adolescent.[27]

[21]"Father Nicholas Russo," 284.

[22]"Short History," 185-186.

[23]*New York Times*, 2 April 1902, 9:7.

[24]Rufo Mendezabal, S.J., *Catalogus Defunctorum in Renata Societate Iesu ab a. 1814 ad a. 1970* (Rome: Curiam P. Gen., 1972), #23,447.

[25]"Our Church for Italians," *Woodstock Letters* XXXIV (1905), 448–449.

[26]Christa R. Klein, "Jesuits and Boyhood in Victorian New York," *U.S. Catholic Historian* VII:4 (Fall 1988), 375–391.

[27]"William H. Walsh, S.J., to Father Provincial, Poughkeepsie, New York, 17 March 1942, NYSJ 1933–1947 folder.

In terms of this interest, Loreto was a good place for him. If Russo is to be believed, girls and boys were among its most active parishioners.

Soon after he came to Loreto, Walsh made some changes in the parochial school. Until he came, most parents sent their children to Loreto's school only until they made their first confession and communion. Then the parents transferred their offspring to public school, thinking they would learn English better. Walsh encouraged the parents to keep their children in parochial school. In 1904, he introduced three sisters of the Community of Jesus and Mary to teach in the Girls' Department. By 1917, the Girls' Department had 15 teachers.[28]

In 1905, Walsh brought in a French lay woman, Miss Louise Rossi, as principal of the Boys' Department. He kept in touch with the boys who graduated from Loreto, some of whom went on to Saint Francis Xavier preparatory school and to Fordham University. The "College Boys" attended mass at Loreto in the morning, studied there in the afternoon and early evening, and said the rosary with Walsh at night.

In 1905, when, in accordance with Pius X's motu proprio on the subject, male choirs replaced female ones, the choir became another vehicle of boy ministry. The choristers attended Loreto's school, took voice lessons from Miss Rossi, studied in the study hall, played in the courtyard, and said prayers with Walsh before going home to bed.

Walsh rearranged Russo's boys' clubs to suit his interest in adolescents. Boys between the age of first communion and 14 were organized into a sodality under the patronage of Saint Stanislas. Older adolescents stayed in the Saint Aloysius Club. Walsh was moderator of both clubs, but the Saint Aloysius Club was the more active. It had its own amateur theatricals, debates, choral society (organized in 1912), and newsletter (organized in 1910).

In the early twentieth century, the Jesuits' historic mandate to work with young people had not broadened to incorporate young women. American Catholics segregated church activities by sex. Italians also practiced strict sex segregation. For all these reasons, Loreto's girls' work was the province of the Children of Mary of Manhattanville, alumnae of the prestigious finishing school run by the Religious of the Sacred Heart of Jesus.

The Children of Mary began their work in 1905, renting rooms in which to teach Loreto girls manual arts. At about the same time, Walsh began teaching catechism in a former barber shop east of the Bowery from Loreto. Walsh could not persuade the parents to let their children come to Loreto: the Bowery was a wide, curving street with four sets of trolley tracks down its center, difficult enough

---

[28]The next few paragraphs rely on "Short History," 179–187.

for adults to cross. So, in 1908, Walsh took steps to bring Loreto to the children. He purchased a house across the Bowery on Christie Street, and rented it to the Children of Mary for a settlement. The women named their house in honor of Madeleine Sophie Barat, foundress of the Religious of the Sacred Heart.[29]

Barat began as a catechetical center. By 1912, it taught 60 boys Tuesdays and Thursdays, and 75 girls Mondays and Wednesdays. A priest heard confessions at the settlement Saturday afternoons. A live-in matron (unlike other settlements, Barat's volunteers did not live on the premises) chaperoned the children at mass on Sunday. Barat also provided space for boys' and girls' sodalities and celebrated with breakfasts and luncheons religious events such as the children's first communions and Madeleine Sophie Barat's feastday.

In 1912, Barat moved from religious to social welfare by adding a "kindergarten," or day care center for working mothers. The kindergarten was supposed to operate from 9:00 a.m. to 3:00 p.m., but mothers dropped off their pre-school children as early as 7:00 a.m. The experience with the kindergarten revealed such a pressing need for day care that in 1915 Walsh purchased a second building adjoining the first and rented it to the Barat women for a "nursery" for even younger children. The nursery soon had 32 toddler and eighteen infant "guests" each day.[30]

The youth work dearest to Walsh's heart, though, was the summer camp. Concerned about Protestant summer camp's effects on Catholic youth, Walsh began renting hotels for the summer to provide an alternative. A wealthy man offered to buy him a hotel in Monroe, Orange County, New York. The man was ruined in the 1907 crash, but Walsh went ahead with the purchase, using Jesuit funds.[31] At Monroe, the boys had luxuries they did not have on the Lower East Side, beginning with 65 acres of play space. There was also a ball field, swimming pool, and, for rainy days, a movie projector.[32]

While the Italian ministry at Loreto reached east across the Bowery, that at the Church of the Nativity, east of the Bowery on Second Avenue and 2nd Street, lagged. Nativity's pastor once referred to the Italians as "about the worst Catholics who ever came to this country," and, although he did try to attract them to the

[29]*The Year Book of the Barat Settlement House* (New York: Privately printed, 1913), 6–7.

[30]*The Year Book of the Barat Settlement and Day Nursery* (New York: Privately printed, 1915), 15.

[31]"Report of Father Zwinge," typescript, Woodstock, Maryland, 22 January 1913, NYSJ Loreto-Nativity folder. Father Zwinge was the provincial procurator.

[32]"Short History," 181.

parish, he thought his efforts were unsuccessful.[33] The Jesuits at Loreto thought the parish was in poor financial shape, dependent upon entertainments and fundraisers.[34]

In 1917, Walsh submitted a long memorandum to Monsignor Joseph Mooney, explaining how the Jesuits' work at Loreto was diminishing while opportunities east of the Bowery were increasing and asking that the archdiocese buy Loreto and give the Jesuits permission to move east.[35] In a second memorandum, he mentioned specifically the possibility of the Jesuits taking over Nativity.[36] On May 11, 1917, Cardinal Farley formally made the transfer, swapping the Jesuits Loreto for Nativity.[37] However, the archdiocese did not send Loreto a secular priest until 1919. For two years, Walsh was pastor of Loreto's chapel and school, Nativity, the Barat Settlement and Day Nursery, and the Monroe summer camp.

Walsh collapsed in July 1919. Although he recovered and lived to be 90, he never returned to Nativity. Instead, he turned to an unsuccessful effort to promote his devotion to the cult of the Boy Jesus. He died at Saint Andrew-on-Hudson on August 4, 1945.

Daniel J. Quinn, S.J., 1919–1922: Critic

Daniel J. Quinn was born May 12, 1864, in New York City.[38] He began preparing for the archdiocesan priesthood and switched to the Jesuits while studying at Innsbruck, Austria. In 1893 he began his academic career, teaching at Boston College. He was ordained in 1899. His highest appointment was as rector at Saint John's (now Fordham University), from 1907 to 1911. From 1911 to 1919, he led men's retreats, weeks or weekends of quiet, contemplative prayer, and spiritual talks. Walsh's sudden release from his duties at Nativity necessitated sending someone right away.

[33]B[ernard] J. Reilly to Farley, New York, 4 March 1917, CMS IAR, Box 1, Nativity folder.

[34]Dominic Cirigliano, S.J., "Jottings on the History of Nativity Church in Preparation for the Centenary Celebration, 1942," typescript NYSJ History of Nativity, 1842-1917 folder, 37.

[35]"Father Walsh's Memorandum Concerning the Present Condition of the Mission of Our Lady of Loreto," typescript, January 22, 1917, NYSJ Loreto-Nativity folder.

[36]"Short Statement of Father Walsh to the Cardinal's Committee," typescript, 16 February 1917, NYSJ Loreto-Nativity folder.

[37]"Church of the Nativity Transferred to Our Fathers," *Woodstock Letters* XLVI (1917), 411-412.

[38]"Obituary: Father Daniel J. Quinn, S.J., 1864-1940," *Woodstock Letters* LXIX (1940), 359-373.

Three months after his arrival at his new assignment. Quinn wrote his provincial superior: "I am not a reformer or an iconoclast. My experience here has shocked me beyond my powers of telling."[39] Quinn hardly knew where to begin to describe the disastrous conditions he found at Loreto and Nativity, and spent the next three years trying to explain to his provincial superior what had gone wrong.

Loreto was in bad shape physically. Quinn toured its school and, "mortified at what I saw," refused to open it for the 1919–1920 term. It turned out that almost nothing had been spent on upkeep for the chapel and school.

At least, so Quinn thought. It was difficult to know for sure. There were no books. The yearly financial report was unintelligible. All that was clear was a series of loans and mortgages on Loreto, the Barat Settlement, the summer house at Monroe, and a house adjoining Nativity's rectory which Walsh bought to provide office space for the summer camp. There were also debts going back to Russo's tenure.

The clergy also posed problems. Two young Italian-American priests left soon after Quinn arrived. The remaining two were elderly and ill. The staff's final member was reliable and capable but not Italian. Although Quinn felt the need for an Italian curate (it is not clear how well he spoke Italian), he did not see the need for an Italian parish. The neighborhood around Nativity was Jewish.

Animosity characterized relations between clergy and laity. Nativity's few remaining Irish resented the Jesuits and their Italian ministry. The Barat women complained that Father Walsh had been insufficiently helpful. The Italians seemed indifferent.

Quinn traced all these problems to Walsh's emphasis on the youth ministry, and his alleged neglect of the "essentials" in favor of the "accidentals." Quinn was especially opposed to the summer camp. He had ample opportunity to elaborate his reservations as he and his superiors discussed opening Monroe for the summer of 1920.

Quinn's principle objects were three. First, summer camps were expensive. Monroe was especially so: its isolation increased delivery charges; its playgrounds were in disrepair; and alternative forms of entertainment, such as movies, were costly. Quinn consulted Father Joseph Congedo, who ran a summer camp from his parish of the Sacred Hearts of Jesus and Mary on East 33rd Street, and reported to his provincial superior that Congedo had told him that he could never

[39]The following paragraphs rely on Daniel J. Quinn, S.J., to Father Provincial, New York, 21 September 1919, and 1 and 29 October 1919, NYSJ Loreto-Nativity folder. The quote is from the 1 October letter.

finance Monroe. Even Walsh might find it difficult to do so after the post-World War I inflation.[40]

Second, there was a question as to whether Monroe had ever accomplished its intended purpose, and a question as to whether it was still necessary. Monroe had never fully substituted for Protestant summer camp; boys who spent two weeks in the country with the Catholics went again with the Protestants. By 1920, parents could afford to take their children on summer vacations and outings, and needed neither Protestant nor Catholic camp.

Third, Quinn subscribed to the anti-Progressive school of thought on the nature of poverty:

> All the uplift schemes now so popular are protestantizing and pauperizing in their effects. Better to teach our people and particularly the Italians that the 'way of the Cross' leads to glory. Catholicism and sacrifice are inseparable in thought. In moral and religious fields the same mistake is being made as in educational work, viz., teach the child to sidestep difficulties instead of facing and overcoming them.[41]

Quinn outlined his own theory of pastoral care in another letter to his superiors: "The only results we get are obtained by a quiet and faithful attention to ordinary pastoral duties—solidifying and unifying the congregation, preaching the gospel, and administering the sacraments."[42]

Quinn worked steadily to solidify his congregation, and felt frustrated in every attempt. He invited a guest homilist for Ash Wednesday, 1920, and attendance was so poor that the preacher scolded the few who did come.[43] He went to some trouble to get a priest whom he considered a good Italian curate, but fretted the curate had little to do. He wrote his superior wearily: "These Italians were here before we came and they'll be here when we're gone and nothing short of a miracle of grace will ever bring them to the Church they hate and curse."[44]

It is unfair to suggest Quinn hated his job. He seems to have been baffled by the disorder he found when he first came, and he wrote his share of frustrated letters to his superiors. Other letters reflected bemused tolerance of the difference between himself and the Italians. When Dominic Cirigliano, a parish boy who had entered the Jesuits, returned to Nativity as curate, the parish organized a

[40]Quinn to Father Provincial, New York, 15 April 1920, NYSJ Loreto-Nativity folder.

[41]Quinn to Father Provincial, New York, 9 August 1920, NYSJ Loreto-Nativity folder.

[42]Quinn to Father Provincial, New York, 13 October 1920, NYSJ Loreto-Nativity folder.

[43]Quinn to Father Provincial, New York, 2 March 1920, NYSJ Loreto-Nativity folder.

[44]Quinn to Father Provincial, New York, 13 October 1920, NYSJ Loreto-Nativity folder.

"welcome home night," with other Italian clergy as invited guests, and another welcoming event, a spaghetti dinner night: "The Italians do love excitement."[45] Quinn referred to Cirigliano as "Father Ciri," which was pronounced "Cheery." Shortly after Father Cirigliano arrived, there was some question as to whether Nativity needed a third Italian-speaking priest. In a letter explaining that he did not need further help, Father Quinn radiated contentment:

> Since Father Kleinmeyer left I have taken charge of the boys and young men and find myself getting deeply interested. Everything looks brighter. I am not as content with the girls and young ladies as with the men.
>
> We are all in good health and spirits. Fr. Longo is in retreat at Keyser. I'm trying to get rid of fat.[46]

Ironically, in his efforts to solidify his parish, Quinn relied on one of Walsh's innovations, Barat. Nativity had no parochial school and the Barat women substituted for it by catechizing the children. Quinn once referred cuttingly to the "uplifters from uptown," but he also told his superior "it is our work they are doing," and refused to continue Walsh's practice of charging rent for their Christie Street houses.[47] The settlement house, at least, had proved its usefulness.

Summer camp never provided its usefulness to Quinn, who refused to conduct it. But on this matter, he was out of step with general trends. In 1922, he was transferred to the Gesu' Church in Philadelphia; one of his successor's first acts was to re-open Monroe.[48] Quinn continued in parochial and retreat work until his final illness in 1939 and death in 1940.

Parishes with Italian Pastors

Nativity was unusual in being an Italian parish with non-Italian pastors, but it was not so unusual in its arrangements for pastoral care. Parishes with Italian parishes may not have had quite as many Progressive programs, but almost every parish had something.

Contemporaries complained that Italians showed little interest in parochial schools, and scholars have followed this lead.[49] Parochial schools were so expen-

[45] Quinn to Father Provincial, New York, September 10, 1920, NYSJ Loreto-Nativity folder.

[46] Quinn to Father Provincial, New York, September 22, 1920, NYSJ Loreto-Nativity folder.

[47] "Uplifters" quote from Quinn to Father Provincial, 29 October 1919, NYSJ Loreto-Nativity folder. "It is our work" quote from Quinn to Father Provincial, New York, 21 September 1919.

[48] Patrick F. Quinnan, S.J., to Father Provincial, New York, 10 July 1922, NYSJ, 1922–1932 folder.

[49] James W. Sanders, *The Education of an Urban Minority: Catholics in Chicago, 1833–1965* (New York: Oxford University Press, 1977), 67–71 and 112–115.

sive that many poor parishes could not afford them right away. However, even pastors who were reputed to have trouble with Italians in church accepted Italians in parochial school; as early as 1889, John Kearney reported:

> Italian children are admitted into the parish school without question. We are anxious to receive them. We request the Italian priests to urge their people to send their children to the school. We have now in the school two hundred and fifty (250) bright, intelligent Italian children, and are now trying to arrange with the Brothers of the Christian Schools to provide Italian Brothers. When these are obtained, we shall open classes where Italians will be taught.[50]

When Kearney died in 1923, 3,000 Italian children attended Saint Patrick's parochial school.[51] In the late nineteenth century, Italian children also attended schools set up for them at Our Lady of Mount Carmel on East 115th Street in the 1880s and at Loreto in the 1890s.

Parishes that did not have parochial school had catechism, usually on Sunday. At Immaculate Conception in Williamsbridge, Giuseppe Cirringione (the one who later embarrassed the archdiocese by claiming to have been kidnapped by the Mafia) had his Sunday school organized so that the teachers and pupils attended Sunday mass together at 9:00 a.m., presumably before classes.[52] At Our Lady of Pompei in Greenwich Village, Brother Eliphus Victor of the Christian Brothers supervised unmarried parish lay women who in turn taught the children.[53]

Of the Progressive innovations, youth recreation was most popular. Probably this was because it was an easy need to identify; everyone saw some benefit in keeping children busy with supervised play rather than letting them loose in the dangerous streets, or letting them develop their own delinquent pasttimes. Recreation was also the most flexible, and every parish could have something, mostly sports, for its boys. Saint Anthony of Padua on Sullivan Street built a three-story "settlement" to house its recreational facilities, with a theater, meeting rooms, and club rooms for young men that included a swimming pool, billiards table, two bowling alleys, and what the parish history called, in Italian, "other gymnastic diversions."[54] At nearby Our Lady of Pompei, Father Antonio Demo organized

[50]Hannigan, Centennial, 1809–1909: Saint Patrick's.

[51]The New York Times, 12 April 1923, 19:5.

[52]Cirringione to Farley, Bronx, 9 February, 1903, CMS IAR Box 1, Italians in Williamsbridge folder.

[53]Michael A. Cosenza, Our Lady of Pompei in Greenwich Village (New York: Our Lady of Pompei, 1967), 8.

[54]Note di Cronaca sull' Origine e Progresso della Chiesa di S. Antonio (Naples: Tipografia Pontifica M. D'Auria, 1925), 18.

a basketball team. Ruggero Passeri, O.F.M., pastor of Saint Sebastian's on East 24th Street, organized a baseball team.[55]

Besides sports, Saint Anthony's, Saint Sebastian's, and Pompei sponsored drama groups for their young people. As mentioned in the previous chapter, drama groups doubled as fundraisers. However, they also served specific purposes connected with the youth apostolate. The theater had long been popular in New York's ethnic, working class neighborhoods. In some neighborhoods, the Italian parishes existed side by side with what the archdiocesan hierarchy saw a questionable theater: Out Lady of Loreto on Elizabeth Street was a block away from the Bowery with its burlesque and vaudeville shows, and Saint Anthony of Padua and Our Lady of Pompei in Greenwich Village were within walking distance of the what were then the provocative new dramas of Eugene O'Neill. Every neighborhood had its nickelodeons and movie theaters, and Catholics were suspcicious of this form of entertainment, too. As the Catholics provided sports and summer camps to win youngsters away from Protestants, so they provided drama to win youngsters away from secular amusements.

Pompei preserved programs from numerous drama productions between the 1900s and the 1930s.[56] Some of the plays may have been chosen because the parish drama group had the personnel appropriate for the performance. Others may have been chosen because they contained a moral message. Still others were among the best-known in the European theatre tradtion. Evidence from outside the parish, though, suggests that Pompei fought a valiant but losing value with new forms of entertainment. One progressive reformer took note of the Italian mothers who came to church for evening devotions then wound up their rosary beads, gathered their children, and proceeded to the next event of the evening, taking in the nickelodeon or motion picture show.[57]

Day care was also popular, probably because the need was so apparent in Italian neighborhoods with large numbers of working mothers. Saint Anthony of Padua's parish history preserved a lengthy description of its nursery. The facility occupied the top floor of Saint Anthony's "settlement." The space included a kitchen, a medical room, and a small refectory or dining room. One large room contained 60 little beds and cribs for naptime. A nurse and two sisters from the same order as that which staffed Saint Anthony's parochial school presided over the nursery, and a doctor visited weekly. The nursery took children from age 2 until they entered

[55]*Il Carroccio* XV (1922), 151–836.

[56]The flyers are in CMS, OLP Box 12, Folder 144.

[57]Kathy Peiss, *Cheap Amusements: Working Women and Leisure in Turn-of-the-Century New York* (Philadelphia: Temple University Press, 1986), 150.

school, and had an after-school program for older children. It operated from 7:00 a.m. to 6:00 p.m., and so served breakfast, lunch, and a late-afternoon snack. The menu was an Americanizing experience: oatmeal at 8:00 a.m., soup and tea at noon, and cocoa and bread at 4:00.[58]

As one can see from Saint Anthony's records, the word "settlement" was popular, but Catholics did not use it in the same sense that Protestant and secular philanthropists did.[59] Of the Catholic settlements which served Italians, the Saint Rose Settlement on East 71st Street probably came closest to the original idea. Saint Rose's was incorporated in 1900. Its guiding spirit was Miss Marion Gurney, a convert who lived in the settlement with her parents.[60] Saint Rose's began with a small lending library and English classes for men and boys. Gradually, it expanded into a night school, offering basketweaving, bookkeeping, cooking, crocheting, drawing, dressmaking, rag-carpet weaving, sewing, singing, stenography, and telegraphy.[61] Most Catholic settlements, though, were staffed by sisters who lived in a convent rather than at the settlement. Also, Catholic settlements were not organized to study and meet a variety of community needs. Most provided one special service. Barat was a nursery and catechetical center, Saint John's in East Harlem seems to have been primarily a nursery, and Saint Anthony's "settlement" combined nursery and recreational services.

As mentioned above, Father Joseph Congedo of the Sacred Hearts of Jesus and Mary shared Father Walsh's interest in summer camp. Congedo was an Italian immigrant, the first pastor of his parish, and the founder of its parochial school and its girls' high school. He began his "fresh air" ministry in the summer of 1918 by taking 50 or 60 children to the beach for a day. Having survived that, the next summer he rented a nine-room house in White Plains, New York, and gave summer vacations to 500 youngsters. The White Plains neighbors objected to the noise and activity, and Congedo began looking for a suitable site to buy for a summer camp. He purchased property in Hackettstown, New Jersey. By the early 1920s, Saint Joseph's Summer Institute had a capacity of 175 boys and girls, ages 6 through 13. It was staffed by Congedo and fifteen laity.[62]

[58]*Note di Cronaca . . . di S. Antonio*, 18.

[59]Margaret M. McGuinness, "Response to Reform: An Historical Interpretation of the Catholic Settlement Movement, 1897–1915" (Ph.D. dissertation, Union Theological Seminary [New York], 1985).

[60]Franklin, "Italian in America," 67.

[61]C.W. Thuente, "Charity in New York," *Saint Vincent de Paul Society Quarterly* XV (1910), 164.

[62]*Golden Jubilee, Church of the Sacred Hearts of Jesus and Mary, 1914–1964* (Hackensack, New Jersey: Custombook, 1964), unpaginated.

These were the Italians pastors' actions. What were their thoughts? Some immigrant pastors were not as aware of the long history of Protestant-Catholic antagonism which led native American Catholics to distance themselves from Protestant and secular philanthropy. Father Antonio Demo seems to have been such a person. He never recorded how he thought about the many state and private social welfare agencies represented around his parish of Our Lady of Pompei in Greenwich Village. Rather, he saw opportunities to help his parishioners and he took them. He was on good terms with agencies other American Catholics criticized: the public school system, the Children's Aid Society, the Charity Organization Society, and the nearest settlement to Pompei, Greenwich House. His actions as an intermediary between his parishioners and the institutions that could help them are so well-documented that they could fill chapters unto themselves.[63]

For some pastors and Italian journalists, Progressive charities were, like the Italian churches themselves, a way to preserve the Italians' ethnic identity in New York. While the churches appealed to the adults, the philanthropists' activities extended that sense of community to children. Saint Sebastian's dramatic program emphasized Italian playwrights. Its baseball team allowed boys to defend Italy's honor on the playing field.

For social scientist Caroline Ware, Progressive charities channelled the second generation's assimilation in a way acceptable (if not entirely so) to their parents. The adults who frequented the Greenwich Village Catholic churches which Ware studied preferred to maintain the customs they had known in Italy, but their children wanted to be accepted by their American peers and to that end they rejected everything Italian, including Catholicism. The clergy responded by de-emphasizing some of the uniquely Italian pious customs, and by giving the youngsters an American-style youth program. Both parishes had play space and dramatic clubs. Although Italian parents regarded sports as an American way of wasting time, one pastor coached both boys' and girls' basketball teams. Although in Italy the family screened companions of the opposite sex and arranged marriages, both parishes sponsored dances at which youths met suitable friends under Catholic, not quite parental, auspices. The youth programs helped keep the migration experience from extending the generation gap into a yawing chasm. They also conveyed to the second generation the message that Catholicism was indeed an American institution, and that leaving behind one's italianita' did not necessarily mean abandoning one's faith.

One letter indicates some of the difficulties the younger generation faced. When a young parishioner ran away to join a theatrical troupe, Antonio Demo of Our

[63]Brown, *From Italian Villages to Greenwich Village*, 62–73.

Lady of Pompei wrote to her asking her to reconsider. His letter is full of subtle indications of the various possible attitudes adults could take in such situations. Instead of acting on his authority as an older person and a priest, he made a point of emphasizing he had obtained permission to write. Instead of reminding his parishioner of the biblical obligation to honor one's father and mother, he appealed to her love of family. And instead of assuming she was in the wrong, he indicated his awareness of the possibility of family tensions:

> I have found out your address, and with your friend Ida's permission I am writing you a few lines thinking you might like to hear from me. I am very sorry that you left your house perhaps in too much haste. If you had taken advice [from] someone who could give it to you freely and disinterestedly you would surely be thankful some day if not already now. However it may be not too late to remedy it. I know that you already complain of that vagrant life which leads you from one country to another without much profit. Your place was home and nowhere else. If the past is not pleasant, turn to the future which you may make bright by coming home as soon as possible. If you have any difficult[ies] they can be removed easily, for you may also count upon me for help. Your Parents, your brother and your little sister are dying to see you and embrace you again. I am sure you can picture to yourself the anxiety they are in on your account. Come home. You say you live with a family who takes good care of you, but I fail to understand how they could take you away without the necessary permission.
>
> My dear Providenza I mean to speak to you without reserve. The stage life is not for you or girls like you.
>
> You thought that a stage career would bring you plenty of money to live much more comfortably than you could at home, because you have seen stage girls well dressed and bejewelled living in fancy houses. Now it seems to me, that you understand very well that the stage money is not enough for the support of those expensive girls, and that such girls have other sources of income which you would surely never accept. Therefore take counsel and make up your mind to come home at once. Your friends here preserve good [memories] of you and nobody will wonder at your short absence. As soon as you receive this letter do me the favor to answer me freely and without delay. Inform me of your intentions for I mean to help you where I can.[64]

Although they adopted the tactics, the Italian clergy left no record examining Protestant or secular thought on social welfare. Evidence of this comes from a survey of East Harlem churches (of all denominations) done at the onset of the Great Depression.[65] At that time, East Harlem had several parishes serving either Italian or mixed congregations and offering social services of various types. Saint Ann's on East 110th Street had a boy's recreation program that included boxing, basketball, and football. Saint Lucy's on East 104th Street provided space for a

[64]Demo to Providenza, New York, before 14 January 1919, CMS OLP Box 3, Folder 23.

[65]May Case Marsh, "The Life and Work of the Churches in an Interstitial Area" (Ph.D. dissertation, New York University, 1932), 331–436.

charity that dispensed free milk to families with babies. Our Lady of Mount Carmel on East 115th Street had a day nursery with 100 children, sewing and embroidery classes, and a volunteer social worker who referred people to the appropriate agencies. Saint Cecilia on East 106th Street cooperated with the Harlem Health Center, the Red Cross, the Charities Organization Society, and the Society for the Prevention of Cruelty to Children, had its own day nursery and institute for working girls, and participated in a political campaign to clean up East Harlem by removing the trolley car barns. East Harlem's Italian clergy realized none of these efforts amounted to much in the face of the Depression. However, none was willing to go farther, especially to cooperate with Protestant churches, with most of the secular charities, or with Governor Franklin Roosevelt's Prosser Committee, which funded individuals and organizations that in turn hired the unemployed.

To some extent, the clergy's efforts to help individuals and families were hampered by their needs to meet parish debt payments, but they were even more hampered by their attitudes toward poverty and charity. They took either the traditional Catholic view that poverty was a cross to be borne, or had adopted a version of the theory that poverty resulted from sinful living. In either case, preaching and the sacraments assumed equal importance to any material aid. Charity was a Christian virtue, not mediated by social welfare agencies.

In the period from about 1890 to about World War I, New York's Italian national parishes encountered two trends. Within the parishes, there was a rapidly assimilating second generation. All around the parishes, there were the influences of Progressive philanthropies. The Italian national parishes combined their reaction to these two trends, using the new social services to keep the second generation loyal to the institutional Church which in turn helped preserve the Italian community. This combination of reactions showed most clearly the paradox of the Italian parishes. In order to maintain an Italian identity, the parishes gradually adopted more and more American ways.

In the short run, experiments with Progressive philanthropy reinforced the national parish structure.[66] During the 1900s and 1910s, the Italians added to their churches and schools other social service institutions, such as day care centers, youth recreation programs, summer camps, and settlements, staffed by their own clergy and religious. This may have helped close the gap between Italian parents and Italian-American children, but, had it continued, the self-sufficiency it encouraged may have widened the gap between Italian national parishes and other

[66]For a case study on this phenomenon in another archdiocese, see Stephen Joseph Shaw, *The Catholic Parish as Way-Station of Ethnicity and Americanization: Chicago's Germans and Italians, 1903–1939* (Brooklyn: Carlson (Chicago Studies in the History of American Religion), 1991.

parishes in the archdiocese. Other trends, though, were acting as a counterweight, bringing the Italian parishes into closer conformity with other Catholics in the archdiocese. These trends are the subject of the next chapter.

5

A Progressive Archdiocese

As they Americanized, the Italians assimilated to a moving target. By the 1920s, both Italian and non-Italian Catholics together assimilated to the standards of the twentieth century. These standards may be summed up in historian Robert Wiebe's useful phrase, "a search for order."[1] Wiebe placed this search for order between the years 1877 and 1920, and emphasized the centralization and bureaucratization that took place in nearly every American institution save the family during that time. Historians of American Catholicism have since developed a bibliography of works concerning Catholicism's search for order, its time frame, and how it was accomplished. A pioneering work in this field was Edward Kantowicz's biography of George Cardinal Mundelein, *Corporation Sole*.[2] When Mundelein came to Chicago in 1916, each pastor made his own decisions about building or renovating his parish plant and financing parochial charities, and the various orders of sisters decided how to run their schools. When Mundelein died in 1939, decisions regarding such matters were in the hands of architecture, financial, welfare, and education officials at the chancery. Elsewhere, Kantowicz suggested that other ordinaries must have taken their dioceses through similar developments.[3] Since then, other historians, notably James O'Toole in his work on William Henry Cardinal O'Connell of Boston, have tested Kantowicz's hypothesis for other ordinaries.[4]

[1] Robert Wiebe, *The Search for Order, 1877–1920* (New York: Hill and Wang, 1967).

[2] Edward R. Kantowicz, *Corporation Sole: Cardinal Mundelein and Chicago Catholicism* (Notre Dame: University of Notre Dame Press, 1983).

[3] Edward R. Kantowicz, "Cardinal Mundelein of Chicago and the Shaping of Twentieth Century American Catholicism," *Journal of American History* LXVIII (1981), 52–68.

[4] James M. O'Toole, "The Role of Bishops in American Catholic History: Myth and Reality in the Case of Cardinal William O'Connell, *Catholic Historical Review* LXXVII:4 (October 1991), 595–615.

The Archdiocese of New York's search for order was inspired not only by episcopal initiative but by perceived need. One perceived need concerned the increasing heterogeneity of the parishes. New York had always had different neighborhoods for different socioeconomic classes; modern transportation made it possible to segregate the poor in downtown parishes while the middle class lived within a subway or car ride of where they worked or shopped. The proliferation of ethnic groups, each with its own Catholic history, meant the archdiocese could not rely on a common heritage but had to supervise the parishes to ensure they all adhered to the same standards.

New York's search for order also took a longer time. Archbishop Corrigan took steps to centralize the management of Catholic education.[5] This chapter takes up the administrations of John Cardinal Farley and Patrick Cardinal Hayes, and the role the presence of Italian parishes played in the archbishops' search for order.

Cardinal Farley and the Supervision of Pastoral Care

Cardinal Farley does not have a scholarly biography, so a few words of introduction are in order.[6] John Murphy Farley was himself an immigrant, born in Newton-Hamilton, County Armagh, Ireland, on April 20, 1842.[7] His uncle provided funds for him to come New York, which he did in 1864. That same year, he enrolled at Saint John's College at Fordham. In 1865, he transferred to the archdiocesan seminary, then at Troy, and, in 1866, to the North American College in Rome. After ordination in Rome in 1870 he returned to his first assignment as curate at the rural parish of Saint Peter's, New Brighton, Staten Island. His second was as rector of the poor, teeming urban parish of Saint Gabriel's on East 37th Street.[8] The transfer to Saint Gabriel's resulted from Farley's appointment in 1872 as Cardinal McCloskey's secretary. He held this position when Michael Corrigan became McCloskey's coadjutor, and after McCloskey's death Farley continued to serve in Corrigan's household. Upon the death of vicar-general

[5]Reilly, "The Administration of Parish Schools."

[6]What scholarly secondary literature there is on Farley centers on his role in the Archdiocese of New York's experience with modernism. See Thomas J. Shelley, "John Cardinal Farley and Modernism in New York," *Church History* XLI (June 1992), 350–361.

[7]*The New York Times*, 18 September 1918, 1:1, 13:1–6; and *Dictionary of American Biography*, s.v. "Farley, John Murphy," by James J. Walsh.

[8]Saint Gabriel's closed January 15, 1939, to make way for the Queens-Midtown Tunnel. Its parishioners were transferred to the Italian Catholic Church of the Sacred Hearts of Jesus and Mary. *Golden Jubilee, Church of the Sacred Hearts of Jesus and Mary, 1914–1964.*

Monsignor Thomas S. Preston in 1891, Corrigan promoted Farley to vicar general and president of the Catholic School Board. In 1895, Farley advanced to auxiliary bishop. On September 15, 1902, a few months after Corrigan's death, he was named archbishop. He became Cardinal Farley on November 27, 1911, and died September 17, 1918, after sixteen years as ordinary.

Farley's inheritance from Corrigan was a contradictory one. On the one hand, he was trained in the methods of a bishop with a small diocese, a small chancery, and a few secretaries. On the other hand, he was expected to manage a large and growing archdiocese, each parish and charitable institution of which operated as a self-sufficient unit. McCloskey and Corrigan had assumed each unit shared common values and possessed sufficient economic resources. By Farley's day, that was no longer true. Farley, though, began by using chancery personnel and management capabilities to try to bring about the unity of Catholic practice.

Farley began his efforts among the Italians in December 1902, by delivering a speech to the Association of Catholic Charities in which he deplored Italian leakage from American Catholicism. On December 17, 1902, a group of clergy active in the Italian apostolate met to discuss their work. The discussion followed familiar pathways. None doubted the existence of an Italian problem. Given Protestant organizations' activities, none doubted its seriousness. Everyone agreed the best results with Italians seemed to occur when Italian clergy ministered to their own people. Everyone agreed on the need to work zealously to save the children.[9]

By the time of the second meeting, January 22, 1903, causes for anxiety had increased. Thomas Meehan's lengthy analysis of what was being done and what was needed for Italians had appeared in the Jesuits' *Messenger of the Sacred Heart*; this was the article that called for "the adoption of the tactics of the enemy." This time, all rectors with Italians in their parishes were invited to the meeting. They heard reports from two *ad hoc* committees on what should be done for Italians. Some of the solutions were, again, quite traditional: increased use of chapels, missions, Saint Vincent de Paul societies, and greater efforts toward getting the children into catechism class. On March 5, 1903, the Italian clergy reported some progress in identifying the parts of the city with the greatest concentrations of Italians, and in organizing Sunday schools. They also agreed to split into smaller, geographically-based groups "in order to localize and give earnestness to the work." There are records of only one more meeting, among Lower East Side rectors, on March 31, 1903.

[9]The record of these meetings is in "Minutes of Meetings with Pastors of Italian Congregations held in 1902–1903," photocopy at CMS IAR Box 1, Miscellaneous Correspondence Regarding Italians folder.

The archdiocese made sporadic attempts at supervision, most of them spurred by some immediate concern. For example, in 1907, Farley sent a circular letter to all Italian rectors. Italian bishops had complained to the pope that Italians baptized, confirmed, or married in the United States did not bring certificates of these sacraments with them when they returned to Italy. The migrants claimed that the certificate fees were too high. But there were no certificate fees, so Farley concluded that some Italian rectors were charging for what was supposed to be a free service.[10]

This, though, was merely troubleshooting. The real issue was not a suspected racket in sacramental certificates. The real issue was that even when their spiritual and financial conditions were impeccable, the national parishes followed the interests of their particular ethnic groups rather than those of the archdiocese. In 1912, the chancery laid plans to "supervise accurately and systematically the moral and material conditions of these various elements of the archdiocese," that is, of the national parishes.[11] Even without the reputation of being a problem, the Italian parishes posed a management concern because of their numbers. The person who prepared the study paper on the subject for the archdiocese found 24 Italian parishes, as against 10 Polish, 5 Ruthenian, 4 German, 2 Slovak, and 1 each Bohemian, Bohemian/English, Bohemian/Slavonian, Greek Albanese, Lithuanian, Magyar, Maronite, and Syrian. The plans called for putting all the Italian churches and clergy under the direction of a vicar-general, assisted by a committee. Six people composed the committee: Gherardo Ferrante, an Italian archdiocesan priest who served as dean; Daniel Burke, pastor of the partly Italian Saint Philip Neri in Bedford Park in the North Bronx; and representatives from the Franciscans, Scalabrinians, Salesians and Pallottines, the orders most heavily involved in the Italian ministry. The vicar-general and his committee were to monitor the attendance of the Italian clergy at various clerical meetings, to inspect the financial and spiritual management of Italian parishes, to study the need for new parishes, and "to bring about within [the Italians] a sentiment of solidarity with their fellow Catholics."

The Italian Bureau opened early in 1913, along with bureaux for Slavic, Ruthenian, and Oriental Catholics (those from the Near East and eastern Europe, whose rituals differed from those practiced by western European, Latin-rite Catholics). Archdiocesan officials hoped the Italian Bureau would provide two-

[10]Farley to "Rev. Dear Sir," New York, 2 December 1907, CMS IAR Box 1, Miscellaneous Correspondence Regarding Italians folder.

[11]"Nationalities in the Arch-Diocese of New York," New York, 24 May 1912, CMS IAR Miscellaneous Notes and Letters, 1883–1923.

way communication. During retreats and conferences, the Italian clergy had an opportunity to exchange views and describe to archdiocesan authorities their parishes' special difficulties, and chancery officials had a forum for giving general direction to the national parishes.[12]

The vicar-general entrusted with the Italians was Monsignor Michael Joseph Lavelle. Monsignor Lavelle was born on the Lower East Side in 1856, the son of Irish parents. He was educated at Saint Patrick's parochial school and ordained in the seminary at Troy in 1879. First assigned to the new cathedral as a curate and then in 1887 as rector, among his responsibilities was representing the hierarchy, especially at clerical funerals and occasions of importance to Italians. After the organization of the Italian Bureau, Lavelle acted as retreat master for the Italian clergy.[13]

Monsignor Gherardo Ferrante served as "dean" and secretary for the Italian Bureau, and was another archdiocesan cleric always available for Italian occasions. As secretary, Ferrante corresponded with other dioceses regarding Italian clergy coming from New York and their fitness for exercising their office.[14] He wrote, usually by hand and in Italian, the letters by which the Italian Bureau supervised the Italian clergy in the archdiocese.[15] Ferrante also acted as superior of Italian women religious, handling their property and legal affairs.[16]

The Italian Bureau's five other members represented the archdiocesan clergy and four of the men's religious orders working with this immigrant nationality. The man who represented the secular clergy during the entire time the board operated was Pasquale Maltese. Maltese was born in Italy about 1872 and came to the United States in 1893. He was educated at the archdiocesan seminary, then at Troy, and at the new Saint Joseph's seminary in Yonkers, and ordained June 24, 1898. He served as curate to Daniel Burke at Saint Philip Neri, and at Saint Lucy's on East 104th Street before becoming pastor of Our Lady of the Rosary

---

[12]"Diocesan Bureaux for the Care of Italian, Slav, Ruthenian, and Asian Catholics in America," *Ecclesiastical Review* XLVIII (1913), 221–222.

[13]Michael J. Lavelle to Charles E. McDonnell, New York, 29 July 1913, CMS IAR Archives of the Diocese of Brooklyn folder.

[14]Gherardo Ferrante to McDonnell, New York, 29 October 1916, CMS IAR Archives of the Diocese of Brooklyn folder.

[15]CMS OLP Series I Box 7 Folder 61 contains the correspondence between Ferrante and Italian pastor Antonio Demo, C.S.

[16]Edward Claude Stibili, "The St. Raphael Society For the Protection of Italian Immigrants, 1887–1923" (Ph.D. dissertation, University of Notre Dame, 1977), 250.

at Port Chester in 1904. In 1912, he became the second pastor of Saint Anthony's on Commonwealth Avenue in the North Bronx.[17] Anicetus Silvioni, O.F.M., and Antonio Demo, P.S.S.C, represented the Franciscans and the Scalabrinians, respectively, for the life of the board. Anthony Moeller, P.S.M., represented the Pallottines until about 1925, when Gaspar Dalia, P.S.M., appeared in the Catholic directory's list of board members. Similarly, Ernesto Coppo, S.D.B., represented the Salesians until 1925, when Paul Zolin, S.D.B., replaced him.

It is not clear how effective the Italian Bureau was. When Monsignor Ferrante died in 1921, he was not replaced as secretary nor was another person added to the board to keep up the numbers. The board ceased to appear in *The Catholic Directory* in 1927, when the Archdiocese of New York's directory entry was almost completely revised.

The Italian Apostolate

Farley's other archdiocesan-level organization for Italians was the Italian Apostolate. Its primary function was to preach missions, one of the many popular devotions of the nineteenth and early twentieth century. Jay P. Dolan, the most thorough student of them, termed them "Catholic revivals," and certain elements of Catholic missions were common to Protestant revivals as well. A special preacher came for a set length of time. Through a tight schedule of worship services, featuring dramatic sermons, people were led to an increased commitment to religious practice. In Catholic revivals, the preachers were from religious orders specializing in this ministry, and the signs of increased commitment to religious practice were making a good confession and receiving communion.[18]

The Italian Apostolate followed this model insofar as its leader was the Reverend Roberto Biasotti, a former Scalabrinian. The missions also followed the format Dolan outlined for English-language missions.[19] The missionaries

[17]*New York Catholic News*, 5 December 1936, p. 21.

[18]Jay P. Dolan, *Catholic Revivalism: The American Experience, 1830–1900* (Notre Dame, Indiana: University of Notre Dame Press, 1978).

[19]Robert Biasotti, "Rapporto Morale dell' Apostolato Italiano di New York, 1 Gennaio 1916," manuscript in AANY New York Italian Apostolate folder. Biasotti's interest in preaching missions may have stemmed from his experience as a Scalabrinian. Bishop Scalabrini had envisioned "flying missionaries," who visited Italian communities for a short period of time to preach, administer the sacraments, and foster the formation of a permanent parish. See Graziano Battistella, C.S. *Itinerant Missions: Alternative Experiences in the History of the Scalabrinians in North America* (New York: Center for Migration Studies [Center for Migration Studies Occasional Papers: Pastoral Series #6] February, 1986).

came to a parish for one or two weeks, depending on the size of the parish, its need for spiritual awakening, and the amount it could afford to pay the Italian Apostolate, which charged $50 per week per missionary. If the parish was large and wealthy enough for a two-week mission, the congregation was divided by sex, with the women attending one week and the men the next. The daily schedule remained the same for both weeks. The first devotion each day began at 5:00 a.m., to give laborers a chance to attend services and get to work on time. Usually, these services were "meditations" on the life, passion, or death of Christ. The second service, at 8:00 or 9:00 a.m., was an instruction on the cardinal sins or the sacraments. At 3:30, when the children came, the preacher went over the morning and evening prayers, giving a sort of catechism lesson. The lengthiest service was in the evening. First, the preacher instructed the people on the necessity of meeting religious obligations, the nature of the true Church, how to make a good confession, or the ten commandments or the precepts of the Church—the practical details of Catholicism. Then there was a break during which the congregation sang penitential hymns. The preacher concluded the evening with a meditation on a more abstract theme, such as the purpose of humanity, the salvation of the soul, or mass or communion. Throughout the mission, individuals had opportunities to make their confessions. At the end of the mission there was a liturgy featuring the renewal of baptismal vows and an invitation to receive communion at Sunday mass.

Between its inception on September 10, 1912, and the end of the year, the Italian Apostolate clergy preached nine missions: seven in New York, and two in small towns in Pennsylvania.[20] Between January and June of 1913, which included the busy season of Lent, the Italian Apostolate preached 33 missions, eight in New York City, ten in New York State, and the rest in Pennsylvania, New Jersey, Rhode Island, and Massachusetts, besides which the clergy gave spiritual exercises to four houses of Pallottine sisters, nine panegyrics for saints' feastdays, and one month of special preaching on the topic of the Sacred Heart at Saint Joachim's on the Lower East Side.[21] In 1914, it preached 43 missions; in 1915, 46; and in 1916, 42, besides which there were retreats for Italian sisters, triduums, and panegyrics.

Every year, Biasotti submitted to Farley handwritten, Italian-language annual reports. The reports listed each mission preached, including some comments on the conditions the missionaries found in the various areas and churches. They

[20]Robert Biasotti, "Rapporto Delle Missioni Date Dall' Apostolato Italiano Di New York City Dal 1° Settembre al 31 Dicembre 1912," AANY Italian Apostolate folder.

[21]Robert Biasotti, "Rapporto Delle Missioni Date Dall' Apostolato Italiano di New York Dal 1° Gennaio al 1° Luglio 1913," AANY Italian Apostolate folder.

provide another point of view on the work of the Italian parishes, and preserve
additional detail on parish life.

It may have been because Biasotti wanted to encourage the archdiocese to
support the mission-giving enterprise as fully as possible that he tended to describe
the parishes in bleak terms. The one consolation for the Archdiocese of New York
was that the worst conditions were outside the archdiocese. The mining area in
western Pennsylvania, where small colonies of Italians lived in widely scattered
communities, was particularly disappointing. Jeanette, Pennsylvania, had at least
200 Italians; six or seven attended mass in an "American" Catholic church, and
another ten frequented an Italian Protestant church; there was no Italian Catholic
church. Connellsville had 4,000 Italians, only 100 of whom attended the mission;
they were largely without religious defense against socialist propaganda emanating
from Pittsburgh.[22] Most other places had churches or annex congregations, but
these, too, had problems. Saint Lucy's in Newark, for instance, had 16,000
Italians and a church with a capacity of 500.[23]

New York's Italians had more churches, but some of these churches provided
inadequate service. Epiphany's annex congregation could not have daily mass or
weekday meetings because the regular congregation usually needed the church
basement for its own activities. Mary, Help of Christians, on East 11th Street,
had 20,000 Italians in its neighborhood but room for only 1,000 in its church.[24]
Our Lady of Mount Carmel in East Harlem had only a small priestly staff to deal
with the largest Italian congregation in the city.[25]

Attendance at missions left something to be desired. Sometimes logistical
problems prevented many people from coming. A snowstorm in February and
March of 1914 cut down the size of the congregation at Our Lady of Mount
Carmel in West New Brighton, Staten Island; a heat wave struck during a mission
that May at Immaculate Conception on East 14th Street.[26] The most common
reason for poor attendance, though, was the people's lack of interest. Biasotti used

[22]Biasotti, "Rapporto . . . 1912," visits to Jeanette and Connelsville, Pennsylvania.

[23]Biasotti, "Rapporto . . . 1913," visit to Saint Lucy, Newark.

[24]Robert Biasotti, "Rapporto Delle Missioni Date Dall' Apostolato Italiano Di New York Dal
Primo Gennaio al 31 Dicembre 1914," AANY Italian Apostolate folder, visits to Epiphany and
Mary, Help of Christians.

[25]Robert Biasotti, "Rapporto dell' Apostolato Italiano di New York nell' anno 1916. Gennaio,
1917," AANY Italian Apostolate folder, visit to Our Lady of Mount Carmel on East 115th Street.

[26]Biasotti, "Rapporto . . .1914," visits to Our Lady of Mount Carmel, West New Brighton, and
Immaculate Conception, East 14th Street.

every word in his vocabulary to describe the Italians' inattention to missions: *freddo* (cold), *indifferente, noncurante* (uncaring), and *negligente*. Biasotti's comments on attendance were more than impressionistic. He usually supplied round figures on those who came and those who received the sacraments or on the number of Italians in the neighborhood and the seating capacity of the church. For example, Transfiguration's 1914 mission was a success if measured by the church's size: the old building on Mott Street sat 1,000, and more people than that received the sacraments. The mission's achievements paled beside what was yet to be done: there were 15,000 Italian Catholics in the Chinatown area.[27]

Biasotti's statistics document the continuation of a gender division of labor regarding religious duties. Most missions preached to men and women separately. The difference between the sexes was most striking in Biasotti's report on his 1915 mission at Mary, Help of Christian. The first week, the women attended *en masse*, and 900 went to confession. The second week, a few "spiritually cold" men came, and only 100 confessed. The same gender distinction appeared in other parishes. The 1915 mission at Assumption in New Brighton, Staten Island, attracted 100 women and 70 men The mission at Saint Joachim's on Roosevelt Street that same year was mostly women. Only at Saint Joseph's chapel (precursor of Saint Joseph's church on Catherine Street) were the audiences mostly male.[28]

There were some pleasant experiences, such as visiting Our Lady of Mount Carmel in the Bronx, where the mission succeeded spiritually and financially. More heartening, there were occasions when the mission sparked interest in an annex congregation or chapel. After a mission at Saint Boniface on East 47th Street, the parish, which had German, American, and Italian communicants, set aside a school room for the Italians for Sunday and feastday masses.[29] (Eleven years later, this annex congregation became the nucleus of Holy Family parish on East 47th Street.[30]) After he attended a 1915 Italian Apostolate mission at Saint Matthew's on West 69th Street, one lay man wrote Farley, commenting on the spiritual awakening caused by the mission, and requesting an Italian chapel for the neighborhood.[31] (Biasotti was less enthused. Of the 3,000 Italians in the area

[27]Biasotti, "Rapporto . . . 1914," visit to Transfiguration, Mott Street.

[28]Biasotti, "Rapporto . . . 1916," visits to Mary, Help of Christians, Saint Joachim, Saint Joseph on the Lower East Side, and to Assumption in New Brighton.

[29]Biasotti, "Rapporto . . . 1916," visits to Our Lady of Mount Carmel, Belmont, the Bronx, and Saint Boniface.

[30]*New York Catholic News*, 9 April 1927.

[31]Mario Terenzio to Farley, New York, 30 November 1915, CMS IAR Box 1, Italian Colony, 69th Street folder.

around Saint Matthew's, 500 came to the mission and 425 received communion.[32]) Again, it is difficult to say how effective the Italian Apostolate was. The last report came in 1916, and Biasotti went on to other work.

Beside the Italian Bureau and Italian Apostolate, New York's Italians might have benefitted from another of Farley's projects, United Catholic Works. This was incorporated in 1913 to coordinate fundraising and activities for the many individual charitable institutions in the archdiocese. There was a varied list of organizations to be helped, indicating the scope of the effort: crime prevention (working with juvenile delinquents and paroled prisoners), day nurseries, employment bureaux, fresh air and summer outing works, homes for boys and girls, hospitals, settlements, and welfare agencies. Also included was protection for immigrants and their assimilation into American religion and politics.[33]

World War I's impact on the Italian parishes will be taken up two chapters hence. What is of importance here is that it diverted Farley's attention from the internal workings of his archdiocese. When the United States entered the war, Catholics faced overwhelming demands: Catholic soldiers needed chaplains and recreation centers, and the American war effort required civilians to conserve fuel and food to alleviate civilian needs in Europe. The three American cardinals (James Gibbons of Baltimore, William O'Connell of Boston, and Farley) called for a meeting to take place at Washington, DC, on August 11 and 12, 1917. A number of individuals already involved in war relief combined forces and organized the National Catholic War Council to coordinate varied activities such as chaplain services, soldiers' recreation, and war relief.

Farley himself died just before the end of the war, and so did not live to see the full usefulness of this new institution. The value of a central organization to direct national charitable efforts proved itself to Catholics during World War I. After the war, there were a number of other issues of concern to Catholics which cut across diocesan boundaries; the most pressing of these were post-war economic adjustment and reform. Pope Benedict XV approved the creation of the National Catholic Welfare Council in April 1919, to coordinate Catholic action on matters of importance across the United States. Because the word "Council" has a technical meaning in canon law, implying a legislative body, and because the National Catholic Welfare Council was not a legislative body, the name was changed to National Catholic Welfare Conference in 1922; it is the ancestor of the present National Catholic Conference.

[32]Biasotti, "Rapporto . . . 1916," visit to Saint Matthew's, West 69th Street.

[33]The New York Times, 6 August 1913, 6:7.

Reorganization under Hayes

Like Cardinal Farley, Cardinal Hayes lacks a scholarly biography. Patrick Joseph Hayes's parents emigrated from Killarney.[34] Hayes was born November 20, 1867, near Saint Andrew's Church, just south of Five Points. He received his elementary education at the parochial school of Transfiguration, nearby on Mott Street. At age fifteen, he was sent to live with his deceased mother's sister and her husband, a grocer. Hayes attended the De La Salle Institute next door to Nativity Church on Second Avenue, then Manhattan College, where he received his A.B. in 1888, then the seminary at Troy. In recognition of his good record there, he was ordained on September 8, 1892, ahead of his class. He went on to further studies, and received a theology degree from Catholic University in 1894. Hayes's first assignment was as curate at Saint Gabriel's on East 37th Street, where John Farley served as pastor, establishing a close relationship between the two men's careers. When Farley became Corrigan's auxiliary bishop, Hayes served as Farley's secretary, a position he retained when Farley rose to archbishop. In 1903, Hayes advanced to chancellor, and, in 1914, to auxiliary bishop. He stepped in as archbishop upon Farley's death, being formally installed on March 10, 1919. On March 24, 1924, he followed Farley again when he was appointed New York's third cardinal.

One difference between Farley and Hayes was either Hayes wrote for publication or someone in the chancery drafted articles which were published over his name.[35] None of the articles discussed Italians specifically, but one included the Italians in a more general "immigrant problem." The article presented immigrants as living proof of the compatibility of Catholic faith and American patriotism. Protestants were to be excluded from Catholic immigrant care, lest Catholics be seduced into thinking they needed to convert to a more American religion in order to be fully accepted. Catholics outside the United States had only a minor role in immigrant work. Hayes cooperated with international immigrant aid societies, and invited Italian religious orders into the archdiocese, but these were expedients necessitated by the Italians' unfamiliarity with the English language and American customs. The proper caretaker for the immigrant was the American Catholic:

> . . . . if we are going to save [the immigrants] for our church we ourselves must take care of them. Who can more properly extend this hand of friendship than

---

[34]*Dictionary of American Biography*, supplement II, s.v. "Hayes, Patrick Joseph," by Henry J. Browne, 293–295.

[35]Joseph M. White, *The Diocesan Seminary in the United States: A History from the 1780s to the Present* (Notre Dame: University of NotreDame Press, 1989), 320, 343, indicates Hayes lacked intellectual interests, which may have included writing for publication.

> we, his Catholic brothers in America, loyal to the same holy Mother, yet filled
> with a deep love for America and her glorious ideals?[36]

After his installation as archbishop, Hayes revitalized Farley's plans for a central organization for Catholic eleemosynary activities.[37] He announced his plans at the annual archdiocesan retreat for the clergy in June, 1919. The first step was to distribute questionnaires to over 200 Catholic welfare institutions: all the boys' and girls' clubs, clinics, day nurseries, hospitals, maternity homes, mother's clubs, orphanages, parole-work agencies, rest homes, and settlements. The survey revealed that a number of these agencies, each of which raised its own funds, operated on weak financial bases. Different institutions duplicated efforts in some areas and left other needs untouched.

Armed with this data, Hayes conducted a publicity campaign during 1920 to inform New York Catholics of the many demands made upon Catholic philanthropy and to create a sense among potential donors that these agencies provided important services to the needy. Then he began fundraising in earnest. Hayes calculated he needed $500,000 annually to support Catholic Charities. In the first three years, he raised $2.6 million.[38]

To obtain the money, Hayes relied on the individual parishes' proven fundraising abilities. Previously, each parish maintained a Saint Vincent de Paul committee to raise money and distribute aid to its own poor. Now, each parish had a committee to collect funds for Catholic Charities. During the annual fundraising week (near Easter), the collectors went from door to door. The proceeds went from individual parishes to a district manager and to the main office.[39] Catholic Charities' Finance Division kept careful records of each parish's donation. Each year, the annual report published how much each parish had given in the previous two years, so that parishes competed not only with each other, but with their own previous records.

Five other divisions coordinated activities among and distributed funds to agencies with similar missions. Two guiding principles shaped these divisions' work. The first enjoined keeping families together. The Families Division resembled a welfare department. Trained social workers investigated cases and made referrals, and qualifying families received financial assistance. The second princi-

[36]Patrick J. Hayes, "The Immigrant Problem," 57.

[37]John Joseph Walsh, *Our American Cardinals* (New York: D. Appleton and Co., 1926), 321ff.

[38]Patrick J. Hayes, "The Unification of Catholic Charities," *Catholic World* CXVII (1923), 147–150.

[39]William R. Kelly, "The Cardinal of Charities," *Il Carroccio* XIV (1924), 445–446.

ple was to protect needy Catholics' faith by providing philanthropic aid similar to that given by Protestant and secular agencies. Catholic Charities had four divisions covering institutional care. The Health Division took responsibility for Catholic hospitals, convalescent homes, hospices for incurables, maternity care, and for chaplains at public hospitals. The Children's Division supervised orphanages and foster care. The Protective Care Division was staffed by social workers specializing in criminal work; it provided parole services for men, women, and juvenile delinquents. Social Action brought together a variety of agencies which met recreational needs: summer camps, settlements, girls' and boys' clubs, and Scout troops.

Social Action also oversaw the nine immigrant shelters in the archdiocese. Otherwise, Catholic Charities had no division, or lesser unit, for immigrant or ethnic care. When it was found that immigrant welfare needed some coordination, the archdiocese added "auxiliaries" onto its Catholic Charities structure. Two auxiliaries bear mentioning here.

The Catholic Immigrant Auxiliary, established in February, 1923, represented a joint effort between Catholic Charities and the New York Diocesan Council of the National Council of Catholic Women. The Catholic Women took upon themselves the project of friendly visiting in the homes of newly-arrived immigrants, welcoming them in the name of the Church, and assisting them in finding clergy who spoke their language and in getting their children into parochial school. The director of the New York Diocesan Council's friendly visiting project was Miss Elizabeth Vaughan Dobbins. Its Executive Secretary was Miss Mary Kennedy.[40]

The second important auxiliary, the Italian Immigrant Auxiliary, had its roots in Italy. In 1908, the (Italian) National Society for Assistance to Italian Catholic Missionaries helped to organize Italica Gens, an agency to provide practical help to Italian migrants in transit. By 1910, Italica Gens had a New York branch office. In theory, Italica Gens competed with the Saint Raphael Society for the Protection of Italian Immigrants, the New York branch office of which was established in 1891. However, Saint Raphael had not lived up to its founders' plans.[41] After Bishop Giovanni Battista Scalabrini's death in June 1905, his Scalabrinians ceased contributing to the New York Saint Raphael. Thereafter, the financial burden fell on the Pallottine Sisters of Charity, who managed the immigrant

---

[40]Elizabeth Vaughan Dobbins, "When Catholic Europe Settles in America," paper read at the Annual Conference of Catholic Charities, Philadelphia, 1923. Copy in Center for Migration Studies, National Catholic Welfare Conference, Box 68, New York Catholic Immigrant Auxiliary. Hereafter, CMS NCWC, Box Number, Folder Name.

[41]Stibili, "St. Raphael," 252, 310–311.

shelter. In the same year, Saint Raphael's chaplain, Giacomo Gambera, moved to a pastoral position in Chicago. Saint Raphael's new chaplain, Gaspare Moretto, did not have access to Ellis Island and so could not perform the same functions as his predecessors. Also, Moretto was repeatedly involved in scandals. Early in 1922, he left for Italy and did not return. In 1923, the Scalabrinians ceased their work among immigrants in transit and concentrated on parish work.

Saint Raphael's loss proved Italica Gens's gain. World War I interrupted Italica Gens's work, and, in 1921, its New York Director, Monsignor Giuseppe Grivetti, was appointed secretary to the Apostolic Delegate to Canada.[42] In 1922, Grivetti and a Colonello Guido Romanelli came to New York to reorganize its Italica Gens branch, hoping to make it the main agency ministering to Italians on Ellis Island. Its proposed list of duties indicated Italica Gens was more interested in maintaining Italian loyalties than in fostering American ones.[43] Italica Gens was supposed to:

1) Assist migrants during their voyages,

2) Direct them to places where they would most likely succeed in their work,

3) Assist in developing Italian "colonies,"

4) Teach standard Italian to dialect-speaking adults and children,

5) Give grants to students, doctors, lawyers, and clergy to travel in Italy;

6) Take care of Italian World War I veterans, and,

7) Assist migrants with immigration and military paperwork.

Italica Gens, though, did not have a clear field for immigrant work. An American agency, the National Catholic Welfare Council's Bureau of Immigration, pushed its claims. The Bureau of Immigration's headquarters were in Washington, with the other NCWC offices, but there was a field office in New York, with a director and a number of workers stationed at Ellis Island. The Director of the Bureau of Immigration was a layman, Bruce Mohler, and the head of the New York office was another layman, Thomas Mulholland. By 1923, the stage was set for a three-way competition to care. The Archdiocese of New York, traditional minister to migrants passing through its port, attempted to keep its hand in the field by using the Italian Auxiliary as its proxy. The Italian Auxiliary relied on the archdiocese for legitimacy, but attempted to define immigrant pastoral care in terms of preserving the immigrants' heritage. The NCWC was in agreement with the archdiocese that pastoral care of immigrants should be defined as keeping

[42]Italica Gens and World War I in *Il Carroccio* XV (1922), 548. Grivetti's appointment in *Il Carroccio* XIII (1921), 686.

[43]*Il Carroccio* XV (1922), 710.

the immigrants Catholic while making them American, but represented a new, extra-diocesan method of achieving that traditional goal.

The NCWC and the Italian Auxiliary

On March 16, 1923, representatives of the archdiocese, the Italian Auxiliary, and the NCWC Bureau of Immigration gathered for a meeting on preventing conflict.[44] Present were: the Reverend Ferdinando Baldelli, secretary of the central office of Italica Gens in Rome; the Reverend Robert F. Keegan, Secretary of Catholic Charities of the Archdiocese of New York; the Reverend Gaetano Arcese, chaplain and overseer for the Pallottine Sisters who managed the Saint Raphael house; and the Reverend Giuseppe Silipigni, the New York representative for Italica Gens. The meeting decided to establish a committee to develop guidelines for Italica Gens's work. Monsignor Daniel Burke headed the committee, whose members consisted of Silipigni, Arcese, Keegan, and the Scalabrinians' provincial superior, Antonio Demo, P.S.S.C.[45]

Shortly after the meeting, Burke drafted a set of guidelines which gave almost all power to the NCWC.[46] Since the federal government recognized the NCWC as having a monopoly in Catholic immigrant care, all work with Catholic immigrants was placed under its supervision. This included any cases in which immigrants faced legal difficulties. In addition, they forwarded the names of immigrants to the dioceses in which the immigrants' new homes were located to enable local volunteers to conduct friendly visiting among the newcomers. Although the NCWC conferred with Italica Gens, it had no interest in Italica Gens's mission to preserve cultural heritage. Rather, NCWC's responsibility was for the "preservation of the Catholic feelings of the immigrant and the natural, gradual assimilation of the Italian elements into the American federation."

Italica Gens was anxious to win power for itself and to protect its interests and those of Italy. In May 1923, Italica Gens's New York office heard that the United States and Italy were near agreement to allow exceptions above the quota limits for additional Italian laborers to migrate to the United States. Ferdinando Baldelli wrote to Bruce Mohler, asking "Could you not ask your Government to be

[44]"A Meeting of the Representatives of the Association of Assistance to Italian Immigrants," New York, 16 March 1923, CMS NCWC, Box 36, Italian Auxiliary.

[45]Material on the NCWC and Italian Auxiliary previously appeared as "Competing to Care: Immigrant Aid Societies for Italians in New York Harbor in the 1920s," Mid-America LXXI (October 1988), 137–151.

[46]"Tentative Agreements Proposed by Father Burke," New York, undated typescript, CMS NCWC, Box 36, Italian Auxiliary.

appointed to [select the laborers], so as to enable our Institution to make the work of selection under your supervision in our General Office in Rome?"[47]

By July 1923, the NCWC and Italica Gens had arranged for a division of duties which gave the latter greater power than Daniel Burke's draft agreement had done.[48] Italica Gens agreed to carry out the NCWC's assimilation policies, but there was no mechanism for guaranteeing Italica Gens's adherence on this point. The NCWC agreed to ask Ellis Island officials to refer to Italica Gens Italians seeking assistance, and to assist Italica Gens in appealing cases.

The agreement went for approval to the episcopal committee which oversaw the NCWC Baldelli hoped to receive approval before he sailed for Rome, but just before he left Bruce Mohler informed him that the bishops wanted Vatican credentials for Italica Gens and a clear understanding that the NCWC was upholding its previous agreement with federal authorities not to give responsibility for immigrants to any other agency.[49] Baldelli sailed for Italy in August, and sent the credentials in October.[50]

The bishops supervising the NCWC gave their approval soon thereafter. In early November, Thomas Mulholland informed Bruce Mohler that Italica Gens was re-establishing itself in New York.[51] Besides its agreement with the NCWC, Italica Gens had gained affiliation with Catholic Charities of the Archdiocese of New York, and was listed in the archdiocesan directory as the Italian Immigrant Auxiliary. The director of the agency was an immigrant, Monsignor Giuseppe Silipigni. Silipigni was born in 1877 at Gioia Tauro in Calabria, and educated at Mileto. During his years as a priest in Calabria, he had taught ecclesiastical history at the seminary in Mileto, and edited two journals, one of them entitled *Stella degli Emigranti*.[52] Silipigni migrated to New York in 1912. When the Jesuits

---

[47]Ferdinando Baldelli to Bruce Mohler, New York, 18 May 1823, ibid. See also a memorandum in ibid., dated 30 July 1923, in which Italica Gens asked help in finding out when Italian immigrant men initiated divorce proceedings against wives in Italy, so the wives could be warned.

[48]"Agreement between Italica Gens (Italian Auxiliary, Inc.) and NCWC," typescript, New York, 28 July 1923, ibid.

[49]Conditions in John Burke, C.P.S., to Mohler, Washington, DC, 16 August 1923. Timing for telling Baldelli in Mohler to Baldelli, Washington, DC, 16 August 1923. Both in ibid.

[50]Baldelli's sailing in Baldelli to Mohler, New York, 13 August 1923. Credentials in Cardinal De Lai to Baldelli, Rome, 15 October 1923. Both in ibid.

[51]Thomas Mulholland to Mohler, New York, 10 November 1923, ibid.

[52]*The New York Times*, 27 December 1930, 13:2.

left Our Lady of Loreto in 1919, he took over as pastor. From Elizabeth Street, he travelled daily across Manhattan to the Italian Auxiliary office on West Street.[53]

Ironically, even as the NCWC and the Italian Auxiliary divided up responsibility for immigrant care, the number of immigrants was drastically reduced. In 1921 and 1924, Congress passed legislation designed to preserve, as far as possible, the numerical majority which descendants of British and northern European migrants enjoyed in the United States, and to restrict the inflow of less desirable peoples from southern, central, and eastern Europe. Congress established quotas for the various countries of the world, reducing Italian migration from between 100,000 and 200,000 per years to under 4,000 per year. Most of the Italians who arrived in the 1920s already had relatives in the United States and did not need the services of an immigrant aid society.

The Italian Auxiliary continued to perform traditional services such as meeting immigrants at the ships, but the increasing restrictions on immigration made legal aid more important. Once again, the Italian Auxiliary and the NCWC came into conflict over the division of labor. Representatives of the NCWC, the Italian Auxiliary, and the Catholic Immigrant Auxiliary met in November 1924 to delineate their respective roles when immigrants faced legal difficulties.[54] Immigrants excluded from the United States had the right to appeal the decision. They were then granted hearings at Ellis Island. The testimony was forwarded to the Department of Labor, the Cabinet department responsible for immigrants. The Department of Labor's Board of Review met, in Washington, reviewed the evidence, and made decisions on appeals, while the immigrants waited on Ellis Island. The NCWC was permitted to advise migrants regarding the decision to appeal, and to represent the migrants before the Board of Review.

The Italian Auxiliary was involved because its social workers met the ships and were the first to know when an immigrant was excluded. The Italian Auxiliary also provided free legal advice. It almost always recommended appealing decisions, trying to hold out hope to the excluded. The NCWC refused to accept every appeal case, preferring not to waste time or money on losing cases such as the admission of tubercular patients or persons with criminal records. The NCWC warned the Italian Auxiliary to familiarize itself with immigration law to assure it gave immigrants an accurate idea of the probably success of a particular appeal. If the NCWC decided to accept a case, then the Italian Auxiliary had to prepare it and promptly deliver the documents to Washington. If the NCWC rejected a

[53]*Il Carroccio* XVIII (1923), 146–148.

[54]Mary Jo Kennedy to Joseph Silipigni, New York, 10 November 1924, CMS NCWC, Box 36, Italian Auxiliary.

case, then Catholic Charities would not step on toes by taking it up. If the Italian Auxiliary insisted on appealing a particular case it had to use its own funds, though it could charge the migrant a small fee for legal representation in Washington.

The Italian Auxiliary's prompt delivery of legal material proved most difficult. Mulholland thought the problem lay with the Italian Auxiliary lawyer, who came to the office only in the evenings, from five or six until nine, dragging out the necessary preparations.[55] Sometimes, material came after a case had been decided. The lawyer thought the problem lay with the migrants' relatives. When an immigrant was excluded, relatives usually looked first for help from the Italian Welfare League. Only after they had exhausted this secular agency's resources did they call on the Italian Auxiliary. By then, the case was before the Board of Review.[56]

In August 1924, Monsignor Germano Formica took over the Italian Auxiliary's daily administration, although Silipigni remained the nominal director. Formica was born at Nepi in 1885. He was ordained in Rome in 1909, and returned to Nepi to teach in the seminary. The Vatican sent him to New York specifically to assist Silipigni. In 1926, Silipigni resigned for reasons of health, and concentrated his efforts on Our Lady of Loreto.[57] In August, Hayes appointed Formica Director of the Italian Auxiliary.[58]

That December, the Reverend Edward R. Moore of Catholic Charities' Social Action Division returned to work after a prolonged illness. He called Mulholland to his office to update him on immigrant work. Mulholland informed Mohler that Moore wanted to know whether the Italian Auxiliary really needed to maintain its West Street shelter.[59] Apparently, Moore then checked out the shelter himself, for late in December he notified Mulholland that the Italian home was an extravagance. Few people stayed there. The Italian Auxiliary (and Catholic Charities) could save $5,000 by boarding the women at Saint Raphael and sending the men to a hotel. Formica needed just an office to handle inquiries, attend incoming ships, and edit his monthly magazine. Mulholland was pleased Moore wanted NCWC's advice. In reporting to Mohler Moore's comments on the Italian Auxiliary shelter, he added: "I think it is a more complete recognition

[55]Mulholland to Mohler, New York, 7 February 1925, and Mohler to Germano Formica, Washington, 26 May 1925, ibid.

[56]Gaspare M. Cusomano to Mohler, New York, 2 June 1925, ibid.

[57]*New York Catholic News*, 3 November 1934.

[58]Mulholland to Mohler, New York, 16 August 1926, CMS NCWC, Box 36, Italian Auxiliary.

[59]Mulholland to Mohler, New York, 21 December 1926, ibid.

of the N.C.W.C. Bureau of Immigration than we have had so far from Catholic Charities."[60] Mohler was also pleased. He advised Mulholland to make recommendations, but to "be conservative" and to keep Formica's point of view in mind.[61]

Formica quickly revealed an annoying talent for looking out for his own interests. His major public relations outlet was his monthly magazine, *La Voce dell' Emigrato*. Each issue published a list of services available through the Italian Auxiliary. Chief among these was legal aid, and Formica had a monthly question-and-answer column regarding immigration law. When he wrote his case for the Catholic Charities fundraising campaign of 1927, he used it to explain what Catholic Charities funds enabled the Italian Auxiliary to do.[62] He filled the rest of the magazine with photographs of Italy and articles highlighting prominent Italian Catholics, such as Christopher Columbus.

To his own journal, Formica added press releases which he sent to other periodicals. The Italian Auxiliary appeared in the Italian-American monthly *Il Carroccio* in December 1927; in the *New York Catholic News*, the Brooklyn (Catholic) *Tablet*, and the New York *Sun* in March, 1928; in the New York *Evening Sun* and the Jesuit weekly *America* in 1929; and in the *Sun* again in 1933.[63] Mulholland and Mohler shared these news items, along with the observation that the NCWC should also advertise, "along more dignified lines of course."[64]

Formica also took to the airwaves. He made his radio debut on a New York Italian station in November 1927, with the transcript appearing in *La Voce dell'Emigrato*. Mulholland passed on to Mohler what Formica himself said about his broadcast: "It gives him a good chance of advertising his work."[65] After four broadcasts, Mohler wrote Mulholland: "Monsignor Formica is surely up and

[60]Mulholland to Mohler, New York, 29 December 1926, ibid.

[61]Mohler to Mulholland, Washington, DC, 5 January 1927, ibid.

[62]Germano Formica, "Catholic Charities and the Immigrant," *The Voice of the Immigrant* IV (1927), 1–2.

[63]*Il Carroccio* XXVI 9127, 154. For March 1928 press releases, *see* Mulholland to Mohler, New York, 29 March 1928. For 1929 *Evening Sun* story, *see* Mohler to Mulholland, Washington, DC, 5 February 1929. For *America*, *see* Mohler to Mulholland, Washington, DC, 26 February 1929. For 1933 *Sun* story, *see* Mulholland to Mohler, New York, 8 May 1933. All in CMS NCWC, Box 36, Italian Auxiliary.

[64]Mohler to Mulholland, Washington, DC, 5 February 1929, ibid.

[65]Mulholland to Mohler, New York, 30 November 1927, ibid.

doing and I am afraid he will make inroads in the work of our Bureau unless we are able to do something to expand and meet this competition in the near future."[66]

As a combination promotion and fundraiser, Formica wrote books. His first effort, published in 1929, was on the recent Eucharistic Congress in Chicago. The author himself contacted the NCWC to ask them to review it for their publication.[67] Mulholland dutifully agreed to sell five copies: he sold one to himself and one to Mohler.[68] When Mohler paid him for the book, Mulholland included in his thank-you note the news that Formica had completed a second book, on the Lateran treaties, "which information did not thrill me. I shall not accept any of this issue for disposal."[69] Mohler got a copy anyway. Formica sent one, along with an advertising flyer.[70]

More disturbing than Formica's public relations talents were his coworker's tactics. Formica supervised an office of three: his secretary Elizabeth Salway; a guide who escorted migrants to railroad connections; and another helper who was paid on a per-ship basis to assist when the workload was heavy.[71] Two of these people met ships with normal-length passenger lists; three if the list were long. When a ship docked, Formica installed his two female assistants in an office on board to help those first- and second-class passengers who were cleared for entrance to the United States on board rather than on Ellis Island. The assistants brought disembarking Italians to their relatives on the pier. Migrants who still had a rail journey went to the railroad office. Those who stayed overnight received lodging at the Italian Auxiliary home. Most ships did not discharge migrants to immigrant aid society agents, but Italian ships carried so many passengers that the ship inspectors appreciated the help.[72] Formica's assistants were more adept than the NCWC at obtaining work. One NCWC agent reported watching Salway board the S.S. *Berengaria*. She had come to meet an appointment rather than to act as an agent, but while there she asked if there were any people the Italian Auxiliary could accommodate overnight . Although she was charged with Italian migrants, she offered to take French, Swiss, or German migrants, too, since the

[66]Mohler to Mulholland, Washington, DC, 19 December 1927, ibid.

[67]Formica to Mohler, New York, 1 July 1929, ibid.

[68]Mulholland to Mohler, New York, 14 June 1929, ibid.

[69]Mulholland to Mohler, New York, 21 June 1929, ibid.

[70]Mohler to Formica, Washington, DC, 13 August 1929, ibid.

[71]Mulholland to Mohler, New York, 27 June 1927, ibid.

[72]Mulholland to Mohler, New York, 10 October 1927, ibid.

Italian Auxiliary staff knew the requisite languages.[73] Although the Italian Auxiliary was supposed to meet Italian ships, the staff met French ships as well, since numerous Italians left Europe from Marseille.[74]

Such diligence made the Italian Auxiliary seem more useful. The shelter, which Moore had wanted to close, was now full of guests.[75] At least, so it seemed; the NCWC officers suspected Formica doctored his statistics. In February 1927, Formica reported that in 1926 he had handled 329 appeal cases, 311 successfully. Mohler thought that was an astoundingly high figure, and asked Mulholland to check it.[76] Mulholland reported that Formica told him any inquiry into a case counted as an appeal, not just formal hearings with Labor Department officials.[77]

The Italian Auxiliary received a setback in May, 1932, when its two agents violated prohibition laws by smuggling 15 bottles of wine off a ship.[78] Formica's failing health proved a more serious blow. Formica departed for Italy in June 1934.[79] Shortly thereafter, rumors about his high blood pressure circulated through Catholic Charities agencies.[80] Formica died in Italy in October 1934.[81] Early in 1935, the Italian Auxiliary moved to a smaller office in the Chelsea section of Manhattan, and continued its work without replaced Formica.[82]

New York's Italian Catholics and Catholic Charities

Catholic Charities directed most of its efforts toward New York's permanent Catholic residents. The new agency touched Catholics, Italians included, in three ways: by requiring donations; by supervising benevolent agencies which had been

[73]Mulholland to Mohler, New York, 22 April 1924, ibid.

[74]Mulholland to Mohler, New York, 24 June 1927; Mohler to Mulholland, Washington, DC, 24 June 1927; Mulholland to Mohler, New York, 27 June 1927. All in ibid.

[75]Mulholland to Mohler, New York, 19 December 1927, ibid.

[76]Mulholland to Mohler, New York, 18 April 1927, ibid.

[77]Mohler to Mulholland, Washington, DC, 30 March 1927 ibid.

[78]Mulholland to Mohler, New York, 26 May 1932, ibid.

[79]Mulholland to Mohler, New York, 31 May 1934, ibid.

[80]Mulholland to Mohler, New York, 10 September 1934, ibid.

[81]"Mgr. Formica, Guide to Aliens, Is Dead in Rome," New York *Herald Tribune*, 1 November 1934.

[82]Mulholland to Mohler, New York, 16 January 1935, ibid.

set up a variety of Catholic groups, including ethnic groups; and by providing services, either through institutions or through the Families Division.

The Archdiocese of New York publicized Catholic Charities among Italians. Just before the 1924 fundraising campaign, the Reverend William R. Kelly of Catholic Charities placed an article in *Il Carroccio*. The article emphasized the benefits the Italians derived from Catholic Charities through the nurseries and settlements in Little Italies. The article also described services, such as parole work, which were not just for Italians, but which they might find helpful. Vincent Jannuzzi, P.S.S.C., of Saint Joachim's on Roosevelt Street provided an endorsement. Perhaps to be sure everyone understood something, the article was in English, but Jannuzzi's remarks were in Italian. The article ended by alerting readers to Cardinal Hayes's upcoming radio appeal, and expressing hopes for "a hearty response from all who sympathize with others less fortunate than themselves."[83]

The Italians' response was among the weakest of any. Appendix 3 summarizes the donations from all the Manhattan parishes to Catholic Charities for the years 1923–1925 and 1929–1930. Overall, Italian parishes contributed less than non-Italian parishes. There could be several reasons why. Most Italian parishes were in poor neighborhoods, and drew their offerings from poor people. Most Italian parishes were still young, and money might have been diverted to paying off debts and establishing parochial schools; one can see that the older Saint Anthony of Padua gave more than its younger neighbor, Our Lady of Pompei. Different Italian parishes had different-sized congregations; Our Lady of Mount Carmel on East 115th Street had more parishioners to solicit than Saint Ann's on East 110th Street. Most Italian parishes served only one ethnic group, which limited their appeal. Finally, the 1929 stock market crash effected 1930 donations in all parishes.

None of these, though, is a full explanation. Our Lady of Pompei and Saint Joseph's on Sixth Avenue were within walking distance of each other in Greenwich Village, yet the former gave one-tenth of the latter. Saint Anthony of Padua was founded in 1866; it still gave less than other parishes founded more recently. The size of the ethnic group is more compelling. Our Lady of Vilna was a small Lithuanian parish founded in 1909; it had a modest giving record. However even this is not enough. Saint Stanislaus was a Polish parish larger than Our Lady of Vilna but smaller than some Italian parishes, yet its giving record was better than that of many Italian parishes. The Italian's own history of modest financial support of the Church must also be a factor.

[83]Kelly, "Cardinal of Charities."

Catholic Charities in the 1920s seems to have followed a "from each according to ability, to each according to need" policy. Contributions from Italians was not related to supervision over, or funds given to, Italian agencies. Italian Catholic philanthropies were incorporated into Catholic Charities' programs. For example, Asilo Scalabrini, Our Lady of Pompei's day nursery, was among the day care centers for which the Children's Division sponsored a day-long conference.[84] Catholic Charities enabled the Sisters of Our Lady of Christian Doctrine to operate Madonna House, a settlement in the neighborhood near Saint Joachim on Roosevelt Street and Saint Joseph on Catherine Street.[85]

Not all assistance was provided in the form of services given at institutions. Those requiring financial assistance in order to keep their households together had to apply at the Families Division at 477 Madison Avenue, a few blocks northeast of Saint Patrick's Cathedral. The Reverend Antonio Demo of Our Lady of Pompei preserved his correspondence with that division, providing a glimpse of relations between the Families Division operations.

The Families Division had complex relationships with Protestant and secular agencies providing the same services. It avoided direct competition, and when it turned out that a person who applied for relief at Catholic Charities had previously applied at a competitor agency, Catholic Charities let the other agency handle the case.[86] On the other hand, Catholic Charities clearly preferred to have Catholics cared for under Catholic auspices. Once, when Father Demo succeeded in getting a boy transferred from a non-Catholic to a Catholic foster-care institution, John Philip Bramer, Director of the Families Division, sent a thank-you letter.[87]

Catholic Charities competed with non-Catholic agencies, but it also paralleled them. Like Protestant and secular agencies, it tried to ascertain the worthiness of those asking for help. It did so by asking the supplicants' pastors for reference letters.[88] One measure of worthiness was the degree to which one kept up the practice of one's faith, and occasionally Catholic Charities' efforts to aid a family came to a temporary halt pending reception of the sacraments. Demo once

[84]Bryan McEntegart to Julia Rosetti, New York, 19 November 1926, CMS OLP Box 18, Folder 216.

[85]Kelly, "Cardinal of Charities."

[86]E.g., John Philip Bramer to Demo, New York, 14 December 1925, CMS OLP Box 5, Folder 34.

[87]Bramer to Demo, New York, 18 August 1925, ibid.

[88]Alice B. Claus to Demo, New York, 17 July 1930, CMS OLP Box 6, Folder 40.

administered conditional baptism to two adolescents, issued them baptismal certificates, and returned them to the Catholic Charities worker at New York's Family Court, who was handling the young women's legal problems.[89] On another occasion he baptized an eight-month-old boy to enable the mother to continue to received legal aid from Catholic Charities.[90]

Catholic Charities' records indicate the Protestant work ethic was actually ecumenical. Even before Catholic Charities pastors had done a lively business in job referrals.[91] At Catholic Charities, even families that applied for relief, rather than work, received guidance in employment opportunities. When Demo referred a parish family to Catholic Charities, the district supervisor reported back to him that the male head of the household could not work due to illness, but the family was not receiving relief because, with Catholic Charities' help, the man's mother was taking care of him, his wife and 17-year-old daughter were working, and his 15-year-old daughter was planning to get her working papers and go to work, too, thus sacrificing the daughters' future opportunities to the family's present need.[92] In another case the husband refused to take a job Catholic Charities found for him and Catholic Charities took the family off relief.[93] Demo responded to Catholic Charities' insistence on employment by making it clear when there was no one to employ; in one case, he carefully explained to Catholic Charities that a parishioner needed to place her son in foster care because the husband and father could not support the family because he had deserted his wife and children in 1918.[94]

Like non-Catholic agencies, Catholic Charities tried to operate efficiently. When one woman missed an appointment which Catholic Charities had made between her and a medical specialist, the case worker wrote the woman to express her disappointment, and, indirectly, urge the woman to greater punctuality. Similarly, Catholic Charities tried to operate as economically as possible. When it could, it referred Italians to philanthropies especially for them, thus saving Catholic Charities funds for other people not eligible for Italian care.[95]

[89]Mary Rea to Demo, New York, 13 March 1930, CMS OLP Box 6, Folder 40.

[90]M. H. Lagrille to Demo, New York, 1 June 1926, CMS OLP Box 5, Folder 35.

[91]See CMS OLP Boxes 2–6.

[92]Alice B. Claus to Demo, New York, 22 October 1930, CMS OLP Box 6, Folder 40.

[93]John Philip Bramer to Demo, New York, 28 January 1926, CMS OLP Box 5, Folder 35.

[94]Demo "To Whom it may Concern," New York, 16 September 1930, CMS OLP Box 6, Folder 40.

[95]Catherine Hart to Demo, New York, 18 June 1932, CMS OLP Box 6, Folder 40.

Given the history of anti-Italian sentiment among other New York Catholics, it is no wonder Italian Catholics applying for help at the Families Division sometimes felt themselves as a disadvantage. An Italian social worker at Our Lady of Mount Carmel of East 115th Street who tried to steer her compatriots toward the welfare agencies appropriate to their particular needs concluded that "the weight in Catholic Charities is rather with the Irish and Irish Americans that the Italians."[96] Demo even told Catholic Charities as much. In a second reference letter for a parish family he wrote: "This people are under the impression that you do not care at all to act in their favor therefore this new recommendation."[97]

To be fair, it might have helped Demo's parishioners had he familiarized himself with Catholic Charities' bureaucratic structure. Although he received letters with the names and titles of Catholic Charities' workers typed neatly beneath their signatures, he addressed recommendations "To Catholic Charities." What is interesting about this is that, prior to Catholic Charities' establishment, Demo had taken the time and trouble to establish good relations with non-Catholic agencies in Greenwich Village, and even knew the names of the local public school teachers and charity workers.[98] That Demo knew a surprising amount about Greenwich Village and surprisingly little about Catholic Charities points the way toward one possible conclusion about the Italians' experience in New York in the 1910s and 1920s.

The NCWC took away from the various groups their previous responsibility for their traveling compatriots. This may have improved immigrant care. However, until the NCWC, migrant care was a way of reaffirming ethnic identity. The NCWC made it a way of inculcating American patriotism. Catholic Charities performed the same function for Italian parishes. Catholic Charities may have been a boon to the poor, the sick, babies, toddlers, orphans, adolescents, and mothers. However, before Catholic Charities, providing assistance had been a way of binding the Italian community together, and of allowing Italian leaders to decide what the Italian people needed. Now, charitable serves bound the recipients to the archdiocese, and the pastors and laity that might have provided ethnic leadership was eliminated.

Italica Gens and the Italian Auxiliary did not keep up the old ways. They did not connect New York's Italians with the narrow, insular, provincial world of the

[96]Marsh, "The Life and Work of the Churches in an Interstitial Area," 433.

[97]Demo to Catholic Charities, New York, 23 July 1926, CMS OLP Box 5, Folder 36.

[98]Mary Elizabeth Brown, "Italian Immigrant Clergy and an Exception to the Rule: The Reverend Antonio Demo, Our Lady of Pompei, Greenwich Village, 1899–1933," *Church History* XLII:1 (March, 1993), 41–59.

mezzogiorno, nor with each other in the new environment in New York. Instead, they represented the new nationalist state directed primarily from northern Italy. The emphasis on a national allegiance, whether to Italy or the United States, became even stronger as Mussolini, who came to power the same year Catholic Charities was incorporated, consolidated his hold on Italy and reached out to bring Italians abroad within his orbit.

6

A Second Generation of
Clergy and Laity

In 1944, a small controversy broke out a Nativity, the Jesuits' Italian mission on Second Avenue. One curate reported that the pastor "likes to do away with Italian customs that have produced good fruit for many years," and mentioned particularly the "Italian custom" of getting married late on Saturday afternoon, which the pastor was trying to replace with the American custom of confession.[1] Another curate, however, described the same custom without using the word "Italian," attributing the late afternoon weddings to the neighborhood preference for proceeding directly from the church to the reception hall for dinner.[2] To further complicate getting at the truth of the matter, all three Jesuits were of Italian extraction.

Although the story is from 1944, even by the 1920s Italian immigrants and their offspring had blended elements from their Italian heritage and their American surroundings to create a new culture. Chapter four described the beginning of this process, when parishes founded to provide services for Italian immigrants added American programs to hold on to the second generation. This chapter returns to that story, now in the period from 1920 to 1945, when the youngsters matured and began taking leadership roles in parish life.

There are several ways to document changes in the New York parishes that had been founded for Italian immigrants, and they will be presented in turn in the sections below. The Jesuits' records permit a case study of how Italian-American Jesuits managed one Italian parish. Material on the Italian secular clergy is scattered, but enough exists to answer the question of whether the Archdiocese of New York acted as a melting pot for immigrant clergy. Parish histories describe the laity in the church institution that affected them most directly. There is also scattered evidence that indicate that individual lay persons were changing the heritage of devotions and pious practices which the Italian had brought over from

[1]Anthony Russo-Alesi, S.J., to Father Provincial, New York, 15 March 1944, NYSJ Nativity 1933–1947.

[2]George P. Barbera, S.J., to Father Provincial, New York, 12 May 1944, ibid.

their homeland. Work on the nature and meaning of immigrant adaptation to American life can put this data into historical perspective.

A Case Study of Pastoral Care

Nativity parish's first three pastors have already been introduced: Nicholas Russo, who organized the first chapel at Our Lady of Loreto; William H. Walsh, who expanded the boys' programs; and Daniel J. Quinn, a critic of Walsh's progressive Catholicism. Nativity's fourth pastor was Patrick F. Quinnan. Quinnan was born in 1866 in Hazlingdon, England, of Irish parents. He came to Nativity in 1922. Nothing is known about his preparation for the Italian ministry, but he did possess the necessary sympathy After he left Nativity, remembered his congregation fondly: "The people in general were lovable, kind-hearted, and deeply appreciative of our interest in them."[3] This was not just nostalgia. Dominic Cirigliano, who served as curate to both pastors, wrote that while Quinn attended to the English to the neglect of the Italians, Quinnan attended to the Italians to the neglect of the English.[4]

Quinnan is interesting because where other pastors saw Italians, he saw middle-class families for whom he tried to run a middle-class parish. He did not think the Barat Settlement's type of child care and catechesis was really was the parish needed. As he explained to his provincial superior:

> [The Barat women] took up this work in a missionary spirit and principally among neglected children. The parishioners in general at Nativity took good care of their children and desired and expected more from the church than that which a settlement house could give.[5]

What Nativity needed was a parochial school, and Quinnan sought to provide one. In a letter that might have alerted his provincial superior to the possibility of future financial difficulty, Quinnan wrote:

> At present [Nativity's parishioners] can pay for this building [a structure Quinnan hoped to acquired for his school] and I think it would make them better Catholics, strengthen their faith and get into their hearts a greater devotion to the Church if they felt they were bound in conscience to make this sacrifice for the Christian education of their children. Having a debt of $100,000 or more to pay would give us more reasons to exercise our zeal and at the same time to teach, by preaching the example, the necessity of sacrifice, to our people.[6]

[3] Patrick F. Quinnan, S.J., to Father Provincial, New York 19, December 1947, ibid.

[4] Dominic Cirigliano, S.J., to Father Provincial, New York, 4 January 1924, NYSJ Nativity 1922–1932 folder.

[5] Quinnan to Father Provincial, New York, 19 December 1947, NYSJ Nativity 1932–1947 folder.

[6] Quinnan to Father Provincial, New York, 9 June 1923, ibid.

The building turned out to be unavailable, and Quinnan turned to providing catechesis and after-school recreation through the parish rather than through Barat settlement. He secured use of Public School 63 after hours for parish boys, and put Dominic Cirigliano in charge of the boys' catechetical and social program.[7] Then, he secured use of Public School 91 after hours for parish girls and began looking for a community of sisters to do the girls' work. In order to get the sisters, he had to offer them a place to live. At this point, Quinnan's project began to spin out of his control.

In August 1925, Quinnan found a house for the sisters. He wrote his superiors for permission to buy, stressing what a bargain the parish was getting. The house was on Forsythe Street, right near P.S. 91. It cost $25,000, and repairs and alterations to fit it for a convent added another $10,000, but there was $29,000 in the parochial school fund, thus assuring a small mortgage. Quinnan estimated upkeep at $4,000 per annum, and predicted Nativity's parishioners could meet that expense easily.[8]

His superiors gave him permission to buy, and within a few months Quinnan was in financial difficulty. New estimates raised the costs of alterations and repairs to between $29,155 and $36,136, although part of the reason for the discrepancy was that Quinnan had decided to add a nursery. Quinnan reassured the Jesuits that the debt incurred in making alterations, which he still estimated at $25,000, "is not a very heavy burden for this parish to carry."[9] However, Quinnan's curates were worried. Under the Jesuits' rules, Quinnan and his curates made up a tiny Jesuit community and were obliged to hold consultations regarding major decisions. Quinnan held a consultation about the Forsythe Street house. He reported to his provincial that a decision had been made to sell the house, even at a loss, rather than continue the project.[10]

However, there were no buyers. Even a novena of masses failed to produce one.[11] The house stood vacant, a fire hazard to other buildings on its block, for the next seven months. Then, in December 1926, Quinnan informed his superiors that he wanted to invite the Mission Helpers of the Sacred Heart, a Baltimore-based order, to open the day nursery and catechetical center. He also informed his superiors that he wanted to sell the sisters the Forsythe Street property, at a

[7]Cirigliano to Father Provincial, New York, 24 June 1925, ibid.

[8]Quinnan to Father Provincial, New York, 2 October 1925, ibid.

[9]Quinnan to Father Provincial, New York, 8 March 1926, ibid.

[10]Quinnan to Father Provincial, New York, 18 March 1926, ibid.

[11]Quinnan to Father Provincial, New York, 14 May 1926, ibid.

loss of several thousand dollars, and leave it up to the Mission Helpers to find renovations funds.[12]

His superiors hesitated to authorize Quinnan to proceed. Perhaps they were influenced by the consultors' reports which Quinnan's curates filed. Both the Italian Dominic Cirigliano and the non-Italian J.M. Prendergast objected to certain aspects of Quinnan's project, to the lack of planning, and to the inattention to detail.[13] The curates had other grievances against Quinnan. None resulted from any lack of sympathy for the Italian people. What troubled the curates was Quinnan's attitude toward daily parish life. Most peculiar was his refusal to honor daylights savings time, resulting in confusion between English and Italian masses. The curates also complained that Quinnan baptized babies on the Saturday before Easter, rather than helping to hear confessions, that he scheduled funeral masses for Sunday morning, and that he did not organize sodalities or publicity for fundraisers.[14]

While the superiors hesitated and the curates fretted, Quinnan negotiated with the sisters. In February 1927 he wrote the Mission Helpers' superior with his final offer. The plan called for Nativity to sell the Forsythe Street house to the Mission Helpers, and to help them finance their purchase by giving them an interest-free loan. He also held out the possibility that Catholic Charities might help fund the renovations.[15] The Mission Helpers accepted the terms, and Nativity sold them the property on June 27, 1927.[16] A few months later, possibly as a result of his superiors' investigating his work, Quinnan was transferred.[17]

Quinnan's successor was Dominic Cirigliano. Cirigliano had been born in Potenza in southern Italy in 1883.[18] He was raised in the neighborhood around Nicholas Russo's mission of Our Lady of Loreto. He left for the seminary about the time Willam Walsh became pastor, and he returned to the area as Quinn's

[12]Quinnan to Father Provincial, New York, 14 December 1926, ibid.

[13]Cirigliano to Father Provincial, New York, 2 March 1926, and J. M. Prendergast, S.J., to Father Provincial, New York, 12 March 1926, ibid.

[14]For baptism, see J. Reilly, S.J., to Father Provincial, New York, 26 April 1925. For other comments, see Cirigliano to Father Provincial, New York, 24 June 1925. Both in ibid.

[15]Quinnan to Mother Lambert, New York, 10 February 1927, ibid.

[16]Santo Catalano, S.J., to Father Provincial, New York, July 1927, ibid.

[17]Lawrence Kelly, S.J. to George Gillespie, New York, 24 1927, ibid: "I knew nothing about the transfer [of the property] until a few days before Father Quinnan was removed and Father Cirigliano succeeded him." Kelly was Quinnan's provincial superior, and Gillespie Kelly's lawyer.

[18]Rufo Mendizabal, S.J., *Catalogus Defunctorum in renata Societate Iesu ab a. 1814 ad a. 1970* #24 134.

curate. "Father Ciri" was pastor from 1927 to 1933, and again from 1937 to 1940. From 1937 to 1940, the pastor was Santo Catalano, another Loreto alumnus and a curate during Cirigliano's first term.[19]

Cirigliano's immediate concern was to conclude Quinnan's unfinished business with the new Mission Helpers settlement on Forsythe Street. Cirigliano regarded the Mission Helpers as no end of trouble. The contract Quinnan signed with the Mission Helpers stipulated daily morning mass and evening benediction, but Cirigliano complained that the convent was too far away (five blocks) and he could not spare clergy for the work.[20] Catalano left no record of problems during his short pastorate, but Cirigliano frequently pressed his superiors to send more clergy to Nativity.[21]

Despite his constant fretting about the understaffing at Nativity Cirigliano kept up a full schedule of activities. In most aspects of its life, Nativity seemed more an American than an Italian parish. The one exception was adherence to the parish schedule. If Nativity had set times for confessions and baptisms, no one paid any attention to them, with the result that confessions were heard before all Sunday masses and parents brought children to the rectory to be baptized at any time. Although Italians were reputed to be careful to baptize their offspring, some of Nativity's parents allowed some time to lapse before bringing the baby to the church. One curate complained about the "not so infant-like" infants presented for baptism.[22]

Nativity was not usually involved in *feste* to honor Italian patron saints. Once, in 1933, the local Saint Gondolfo Society asked if it could hold its mass at Nativity, since one of the curates was a *paesano* who had written a life of the saint and who could preach a panegyric.[23] In general, the parish promoted non-Italian devotions, such as the Miraculous Medal, the Jesuit saints, and the patrons of youth.[24]

Far from being aloof from the Church, the Italian parishioners seem to have been all over the place. The women's group met in the rectory parlor.[25] Various

[19]Gabriel A. Zema, S.J., "The Italian Immigrant Problem," *America* LV (16 May 1936), 129–130.

[20]*E.g.*, Cirigliano to Father Provincial, New York, 8 October 1927, NYSJ Nativity 1922–1932 folder.

[21]*E.g.*, Edward C. Philips, S.J., to Cirigliano, New York, ibid.

[22]Anthony De Maria, S.J., to Father Provincial, New York, 16 February 1939, NYSJ Nativity 1933–1947 folder.

[23]Catalano, S.J., to Father Provincial, New York, 17 August 1933, ibid.

[24]De Maria to Father Provincial, New York, 28 March and 1 August 1938, ibid.

[25]De Maria to Father Provincial, New York, 1 August 1938, ibid.

committees and clubs also gathered in the parlor, and friends used it as a convenient place to rendez-vous.[26] The Jesuit superiors voiced concern that the clergy lacked enough peace and quiet for their own spiritual life.[27]

Nativity's clergy continued to emphasize the care of youth, partly "to counteract the work of proselytizing agencies all around us."[28] The clergy still worried that Nativity had no school, but neither Cirigliano nor Catalano pushed for one. They concentrated instead on catechesis. Cirigliano moved the Sunday school to Saturday and provided instruction for public school children during the week.[29] During the 1930s, there were various parochial clubs and sodalities for young men, such as the Nativity Club. There were also branches of diocesan-wide or nation-wide organizations such as the Catholic Youth Organization and the Boy Scouts.[30] Cirigliano kept the Monroe summer camp open, and invited girls as well as boys.[31]

When Cirigliano took over as pastor, he observed that "the parishioners are contributing generously."[32] During the Great Depression, fundraisers augmented regular collections. Nativity sponsored movies, dances, and raffles, distributing tickets for these affairs between Sunday morning masses.[33] Either Nativity continued to rely on the Irish for income, or the Italians Hibernianized, for the parish celebrated Saint Patrick's Day with a fundraiser.[34] Both Catalano and Cirigliano thought Nativity's income sufficient to allow them to make major repairs. In 1936, Catalano took $2,520 from the parish's $6,000 bank account to buy an oil burner.[35] Cirigliano planned major renovations in 1938. When he described them to his superior, he emphasized "I can pretty well assure Your Reverence that *I will not go into debt.*"[36]

[26]De Maria to Father Provincial, New York, 16 February 1939, ibid.

[27]Joseph A. Murphy, S.J., "Memorial of Visitation," 31 March 1939, ibid.

[28]De Maria to Father Provincial, New York, 28 March 1939, ibid.

[29]Cirigliano to Father Provincial, New York, 24 October 1927, NYSJ Nativity 1922–1932 folder.

[30]De Maria to Father Provincial, New York, 1 August 1938, NYSJ Nativity 1933–1947 folder.

[31]Cirigliano to Father Provincial, New York, 16 May 1928, NYSJ Nativity 1922–1932 folder.

[32]Cirigliano to Father Provincial, New York, 16 May 1928, ibid.

[33]De Maria to Father Provincial, New York, 16 February, NYSJ Nativity 1933–1947 folder.

[34]Father Provincial to Cirigliano, New York, 16 September 1929, NYSJ Nativity 1922–1932 folder.

[35]Catalano to Murphy, New York, 14 September 1936, NYSJ Nativity 1933–1947 folder.

[36]Cirigliano to Father Provincial, New York, 16 May 1938, ibid.

Cirigliano, at least, seemed uninterested in emphasizing Nativity's Italian heritage. For example, when he invited a guest to celebrate mass in the newly renovated church in 1938, he did not choose an Italian or even a Jesuit, but someone important to Nativity's own history, a sometime parishioner who had entered the priesthood and become the bishop of Camden, New Jersey.[37]

Secular Clergy in the Archdiocese of New York

Statistics indicate the importance of Italian secular clergy in New York Catholicism.[38] In 1941, the New York City Works Progress Administration compiled an inventory of church archives in the City and Archdiocese of New York.[39] The inventory listed 47 parishes with at least one Italian sermon on their Sunday schedules, 21 of which were founded and maintained by Italian immigrant or Italian-American archdiocesan clergy. Others, such as Our Lady of Loreto on Elizabeth Street, were founded by a religious order and later transferred to archdiocesan clergy, or, such as Holy Rosary on East 119th Street, were founded by non-Italian secular clergy and became Italian parishes.

The Italian clergy resident in the archdiocese came to it in three ways. First, Italian diocesan clergy occasionally migrated from Italy. This is how the archdiocese obtained its first Italian clergy in the nineteenth century. The chancery considered this the most troublesome way.

A second way for the archdiocese to acquire Italian clergy was to recruit Italian seminarians. Some young men went directly to the United States upon ordination. Others completed their seminary training at the archdiocesan seminary, Saint Joseph's, in Dunwoodie, Yonkers. Then, they were ordained for the Archdiocese of New York. Daniel Burke of Saint Philip Neri in Bedford Park went on such recruiting trips for the archdiocese early in the twentieth century. One one of these trips, he brought back a young priests to serve as his curate, Giuseppe Caffuzzi.[40] Caffuzzi became pastor of his own parish, Our Lady of Mount Carmel in Belmont, the Bronx, and went on a recruiting trip of his own in 1927.[41] Another

[37]De Maria to Father Provincial, New York, 27 September 1938, ibid.

[38]Material on New York's Italian archdiocesan clergy previously appeared in "Italian and Italian-American Secular Clergy in the Archdiocese of New York, 1880–1950," U.S. Catholic Historian VI:4 (Fall 1987), 281–300.

[39]New York City Works Progress Administration, "Inventory of the Church Archives in New York City: Roman Catholic Church, Archdiocese of New York," volume 2.

[40][Joseph L.G. Borgatti], Our Lady of Mount Carmel, New York, Celebrates its Golden Jubilee, 1906–1956 (New York: Privately printed, 1956), n.p.

[41]Il Carroccio XXVI (1927), 154.

Italian American priest, Bonaventure Filetti, made a recruiting trip for Cardinal Spellman.[42]

Some seminarians came at their parents' behest. Reuniting the family was a frequently cited reason for migration among seminarians and young clergy. In this matter, Italian and American seminarians differed. In order to build priestly solidarity American seminaries discouraged their seminarians from fraternizing with the families. In Italy, although Joseph M. Pernicone was in the seminary in Sicily when his father decided to move his family to New York, he was still considered part of the family. He, too, left Sicily for New York in 1920. When he learned English, he entered Saint Joseph's Seminary. He was ordained in 1926.[43] Similarly, by the time Francis Cagnina completed his seminary studies and received his ordination in Rome in 1908, his parents had left their native Sicily for New York. Cagnina joined them in 1909.[44] Severino Focacci interrupted his seminary studies in Genoa to join his parents in New York in 1909; he resumed his training at Saint Joseph's and was ordained in 1911.[45] Dominic Fiorentino also left the seminary in Italy to join his parents in New York in 1909; he studied with the Salesians at Hawthorne before entering Saint Joseph's, and was ordained in 1914.[46]

The American clergy complained about inadequately trained Italian clergy, but at least one seminarian who migrated in the middle of his studies found little difference between his training in Sicily and in New York. Joseph Pernicone noted that the seminaries in both places taught the same courses, the only difference being that Saint Joseph's taught them in English.[47]

A third source Italian archdiocesan clergy was vocations among Italian-born boys raised in America or American-born and -raised boys of Italian descent. Irish and Italians agreed that fewer Italian-background boys entered the priesthood than boys from other ethnic groups, and advanced a number of explanations. The first emphasized cultural factors. Italian immigrants considered themselves working class people, not an educated elite, and so found it difficult to conceive that their

[42]Interview with the Most Reverend Joseph M. Pernicone, Bronx, New York, 12 August 1983.

[43]Ibid.

[44][Joseph J. Raimondo], *Saint Clare of Assisi, Bronx, New York, 1929–1979* (Pearl River, New York: Universal Graphics, 1979), 13.

[45]Borgatti, *Our Lady of Mount Carmel . . . 1906–1956.*

[46]*Salute to Saint Dominic's* (New York: Privately printed, 1974), n.p.

[47]Pernicone interview.

offspring might achieve the status of professionals, and become doctors, lawyers, teachers, or clergy. Italian anti-clericism, whether brought about by *mezzogiorno* folk traditions or by radical politics, may have kept boys and their parents from viewing the priesthood seriously.

A second explanation had a more practical base. Italian immigrants were poor people who put their youngsters to work as soon as possible, preventing them from staying in school and testing their vocations.[48] One candidate for the priesthood, Jerome Pasquarelli, delayed his ordination until he was 39 years old in order to work and help educate relatives. Pasquarelli went on to become the first pastor of Most Holy Crucifix on Broome Street.[49] Other young men, whether taken from school by their parents or by their own felt obligation to assist their families, must have given up altogether.

Another practical consideration was that many Italian immigrant boys had limited exposure to institutional Catholicism. Boys who attended public school may have learned of a wide variety of careers, but not necessarily the priesthood.[50] When an Italian boy was exposed to an Italian religious order at his parish and parochial school, he was more likely to consider joining a religious order than he was to consider joining the archdiocesan clergy. For example, the care which Nicholas Russo and William H. Walsh lavished on the boys at Our Lady of Loreto and Nativity paid off handsomely in terms of Jesuit vocations. Between 1927 and 1957, Nativity had four pastors, all of them alumni of the Jesuits' boy ministry there.[51]

When they became priests, the Italians were not integrated into the rest of the archdiocese. They worked mostly in Italian parishes. Perhaps their bilingual skills were too precious to waste. Certainly, the Irish laity did not care to be under Italian clergy.

Early in the twentieth century, the shortage of Italian clergy and the need to open Italian parishes meant that many Italian immigrant clergy advanced quickly from curate to pastor. Giuseppe Caffuzzi was Daniel Burke's curate for under five years before he became rector of Our Lady of Mount Carmel in the Bronx.[52] Philip Leone seems to have spent no time as a curate in New York before becoming

[48]Ibid.

[49]*The New York Times*, 2 September 1953, 25:3.

[50]Pernicone interview.

[51]*Church of the Nativity, New York City* (South Hackensack, New Jersey: Custombook, 1971), n.p.

[52]Borgatti, *Our Lady of Mount Carmel . . . 1906–1956.*

pastor of Our Lady of Peace in 1919, although he may have had experience in his native Palermo.[53] After the number of clergy increased and the number of parishes stabilized, some clergy spent long years as curates before their promotion to pastor. Catello Terrone, for example, had been a curate in Naples for nine years before migrating to New York in 1913. There, he was an assistant for another eight years; finally, in 1921, Cardinal Hayes appointed him pastor of Saint Roch's on Staten Island, a position he held until his death in 1950.[54] Francis Cagnina came to New York as a new priest in 1909. In 1929, Hayes made him the first pastor of Saint Clare of Assisi in the Bronx.[55] Dominic Epifanio might hold some kind of record. He came to New York from Tricarico as a newly ordained priest in 1901. For the next 26 years he was assistant at Saint Patrick's Old Cathedral. Even when pastor John F. Kearney died in 1923, after over 50 years in the parish, Epifanio was passed over in favor of an Irish American. In 1927, Hayes appointed Epifanio first pastor of Holy Rosary on Staten Island, where he remained until his death in 1947.[56]

The need for a link between the Irish-American archdiocesan administration and the Italian national parishes meant that a few Italian clergy found work in the chancery. Gherardo Ferrante, for example, served as Italian secretary for three archbishops during his years in New York. After Ferrante's death in 1921, Hayes seems to have had confidence in Gaetano Arcese at Holy Rosary on East 119th Street. However, when he needed an official representative with the Italian community, he used two Irish-Americans, Michael J. Lavelle and Daniel Burke. Not until 1954 was another Italian raised to a prominent position, when Joseph M. Pernicone became the archdiocese's first auxiliary bishop of Italian descent.

Changes at the Parish Level

The Italians have a reputation for lagging behind other immigrants in socioeconomic mobility. The Jews, whose migration peaked about the same time as the Italians' were supposed to move rapidly on to better jobs, higher pay, nicer neighborhoods, and more education, while the Italians were supposed to have remained in unskilled jobs, lower income brackets, and poorer housing, and to

---

[53]*Il Carroccio* XXVI (1927), 332, gives Leone's birthplace. *The New York Times*, 30 May 1945, 9:2, gives his New York career.

[54]*The New York Times*, 30 March 1950, 29:2.

[55]Raimondo, *Saint Clare of Assisi*, 13.

[56]*The New York Times*, 5 June 1947, 25:5.

have received less education. However, it is difficult to tell how many Italians fit this stereotype. Thomas Kessner, who compared both groups in New York City, concluded that as early as 1915 the Italians showed signs of upward mobility, measured by occupation, income, and residence.[57] Father Quinnan's assessment of his Italian parish's ability to pay off debts has already been noted. For other parishes, there is more than the pastors' word: there are records of increased expenditures.

During the 1920s, a number of Italian parishes replaced older church buildings with new ones. Sometimes, the new building was a step from pioneer poverty to middle-class luxury. For example, on Christmas Day 1930, the congregation of Saint Vito's in Mamaroneck moved out of its unheated wooden church with the uncushioned kneelers into a more comfortable building.[58] Sometimes, the move reflected the rise of a new generation. Saint Joachim's on Roosevelt Street was a small chapel. In 1925, the congregation completed a huge second structure on Catherine Street, containing a church, a parochial school, and a parish hall.[59]

Sometimes, the new church stated that the Italians had arrived. Our Lady of Pompei, for example, had to rebuild in the 1920s, when the city extended Sixth Avenue across Bleecker right through the lot on which the congregation's church stood. The new church more than replaced the old. The parish bought a lot a few blocks from the old one, at the corner of Bleecker and Carmine Street. In 1928, it dedicated its new church, which was contained in a building which also housed a parochial school, several meeting rooms, and space for a convent (completed in 1952); the rectory, built at the same, time, was separate but connected to the building. The lot and building cost abut $1,170,000, and the congregation had not yet completed the decorations.

Pompei's building showed the continuation of a pattern noticed earlier: adopting American fundraising techniques while preserving the outward appearance of Italian culture. The parish hired a consultant to assist in the preparation of its fundraising. The consultant designed a campaign which began with a fancy fundraising banquet in the midtown Pennsylvania Hotel and which collected pledges from many of the business leaders of the Italian community, then continued by organizing a committee to go door to door to solicit pledges among the Greenwich Village parishioners and neighbors. The finished building, though, resembled a church in southern Italy; it even had a *campanile* at one corner. The

[57]Thomas Kessner, *The Golden Door: Italian and Jewish Immigrant Mobility in New York City, 1880–1915* (New York: Oxford, 1977), 165–177.

[58]*Church of Saint Vito, Golden Jubilee, 1911–1961* (New York: Privately printed, 1961), 6.

[59]*Fiftieth Anniversary, Saint Joseph Church* (New York: Park Publishing Company, 1977), 9–10.

interior decoration, completed in 1939, was what a southern Italian church might have looked like if the southern Italians had as much money as the American Italians. The entire ceiling was covered with frescoes. The focal point was over the altar: there sat Our Lady of the Rosary (to which a shrine at Pompei was dedicated; hence the parish name); Christ Child on her lap, giving her rosary to Saints Dominic and Catherine, while angels and saints gathered around. Even the parishioners were included in the fresco, through a picture of the church's bell tower. On the ceiling over the center aisle was a series of pictures drawn from the Joyful, Sorrowful, and Glorious Mysteries of the Rosary. Near the organ were singing angels, Saint Cecelia, the patroness of church music, and King David, traditional author of the Psalms. The stained glass windows included pictures of saints and scenes of the seven sacraments. Around the altar and in niches in the back of the church was a collection of saints' statues that grew larger over the years.[60]

Other parishes had similar stories. Our Lady of Mount Carmel had met in various locations in White Plains since its foundation in 1902. In 1927, the congregation celebrated its silver jubilee with a campaign to raise funds for a church. The campaign received $270,000 in pledges. The finished structure was a copy of a southern Italian church, including a *campanile* visible to travelers arriving from New York aboard the commuter railroad.[61]

The Italians also used their newly earned wealth to build, or rebuild, parochial schools. Our Lady of Mount Carmel on Belmont Avenue in the Bronx purchased Saint Elizabeth's Industrial School in 1923, and opened a parochial school there in 1925.[62] That same year, Joseph Congedo opened a school at Sacred Hearts of Jesus and Mary, on East 33rd Street in Manhattan. Congedo also opened a high school for girls.[63] Saint Joseph's on Catherine Street and Saint Ann's on East 110th Street both opened their schools in 1926.[64] Our Lady of Pompei in Greenwich Village opened its school in 1930. Saint Anthony's in the Van Nest section of the Bronx opened its school in 1931.[65]

[60]Brown, *From Italian Villages to Greenwich Village*, chapters 7 and 8.

[61]*Diamond Jubilee of Our Lady of Mount Carmel Parish* (New York: Privately printed, 1977), n.p.

[62]Borgatti, *Our Lady of Mount Carmel, New York . . . 1906–1956.*

[63]*Golden Jubilee, Church of the Sacred Hearts of Jesus and Mary, 1914–1964.*

[64]*Fiftieth Anniversary, Saint Joseph Church*, 10; and *Golden Jubilee Dinner Dance of Saint Ann's Parish, 1905–1955* (New York: Privately printed, 1955), n.p.

[65]*Saint Anthony's, Commonwealth Avenue, the Bronx, New York City* (New York: Privately printed, 1931), n.p.

Studies of German and Polish Catholic immigrants indicate these groups advocated parochial schools as a way of passing on the parents' culture to the younger generation.[66] Some of the clergy involved in Italian immigrant pastoral care echoed the same theme. Bishop Giovanni Battista Scalabrini preached it to the clergy of his missionary community, and the laity who attended his missionaries' churches.[67] Saint Joseph's on Catherine Street appealed to racial pride in soliciting contributions to its parochial school.[68] Joseph Congedo of Sacred Hearts left the most succinct example of such thought. Congedo used the popular analogy in which Italy was the male immigrant's mother, and American his bride. A good relationship with one's mother was considered a necessary foundation for a good relationship with one's wife. Similarly, Italians' children needed to acquire a proper understanding of and appreciation for their parents' homeland to gain the self-respect necessary to become good citizens of their parents' adopted land. Self-respect started with the study of Italian, so that parents and children could communicate. Italian history and literature demonstrated Italy's contribution to western civilization and allowed the children to be ambassadors of the "real Italy" to non-Italians. Congedo thought of a good American education only in terms of its practical application; it allowed children to achieve material success. Even religion was subordinate to culture. Parochial school curricula included religion because "To deny [Italian pupils] religious education is to deny them a part of their glorious heritage."[69]

Plans for an Italian curriculum missed an important element of Italian immigration. Most Italian immigrants hailed from southern Italy, whose rich culture had been transmitted mostly via the family, the local church, and the community, not via the school. Teaching southern Italians' children standard Italian did not allow parents and offspring to communicate, because the parents spoke a southern dialect. Some schools did have some bilingual education. Mother Cabrini thought bilingual education was a useful approach for the young children and the girls in her care.[70] The *Maestre Pie Filipini*, or Religious Teachers Filipini, also offered

[66]For the Germans, see Barry, *The Catholic Church and German Americans*. For Poles, see John J. Bukowcyzyk, *And My Children Did Not Know Me: A History of Polish Americans* (Bloomington: Indiana University Press, 1987).

[67]Andrew Brizzolara, C.S., "100 Days: The Visit of Bishop Scalabrini to the United States and Its Effects on the Image of Italian Immigrants as Reflected in the American Press of 1901" (M.A. Thesis, Hunter College, City University of New York, 1986).

[68]"Pages describing the inception of St. Joahim, St. Rocco and St. Joseph," CMS Saint Joachim, Box 5, Folder 158.

[69]Joseph M. Congedo, "Bearers of Rich Gifts," *Il Carroccio* XX (1924), 471–473.

[70]Sullivan, *Mother Cabrini*, 156–159.

bilingual education in their schools.[71] Usually, schools reflected the American attitude toward languages. As one pastor, himself a Sicilian immigrant, explained, American children did not usually study "foreign languages," so the children in his parochial school waited until high school to study Italian.[72]

Several factors entered into the choice of a community of sisters to staff the parochial school. Parishes staffed by men religious sometimes chose a related community of women religious, as the Franciscans at Saint Anthony of Padua on Sullivan Street chose a community of Franciscan Sisters. Bishop Giovanni Battista Scalabrini had played a role in the founding of the Missionary Zelatrices (after 1967, the Apostles) of the Sacred Heart, and the Scalabrinian pastor at Saint Joseph secured these sisters for his school, and the Scalabrinian pastor at Pompei later followed suit. Joseph Congedo, a secular priest and author of the article cited above, recruited a non-Italian order, the Sisters of the Immaculate Heart of Mary, for his school. Some parishes invited an order such as the Religious Teachers Filipini specifically for their bilingual skills. Other parishes tried to get a steady supply of Americans of Italian descent. The Missionary Zelatrices who staffed the Scalabrinian parochial schools came not from the mother house in Italy, but from an American provincial house in Connecticut.

One well-documented discussion of the relative merits of Italian and American sisters took place at Nativity. Patrick Quinnan's first thought was to recruit an American order for his children's program. When the first American order he asked turned him down, his provincial superior raised the possibility of getting Italian sisters. Quinnan referred the suggestion to his Italian curates, and reported to his superior that "They are anxious to have American women who know the language and the ways of the country."[73] In response, the provincial superior explained that he was interested in introducing Italian sisters partly for the sisters' sake: "They have a large number of Americanized Italian girls now . . . and would get many more if working in Nativity Parish."[74]

Changes in Individual Devotional Life

The newly built churches may have looked Italian, but what went on inside them indicated that the Italians had adopted elements from their American surround-

[71]Myles Muredach, "An Experiment in City Home Missions," *Extension* XVII (1923), 35–36, 62.

[72]Pernicone interview.

[73]Quinnan to Father Provincial, New York, 17 January 1927, NYSJ Nativity 1922–1932.

[74]Kelly to Quinnan, New York, 27 March 1927, ibid.

ings. One example was language. As early as 1896, the Franciscans at Most Precious Blood had to use English to hear the second generation's confessions.[75] References to the changing of the generational guard appeared in notices of events at Italian churches in the 1910s and 1920s.[76] Sometimes, Italian and English speaker separated by language: in 1927, one parish held a two-week mission, the first week in English and the second in Italian.[77] On other occasions, both groups were recognized. When Saint Roch, in the North Bronx, laid its new building's cornerstone, the ceremonies featured two sermons, one in Italian and one in English.[78] Regular mass schedules, though, usually offered separate masses with English and Italian sermons.

Italian pious practices changed over the years, too, in response to changes in society and to the rise of a new generation. The best documented changes in devotional customs are those practiced by Italians as a community, that is, the annual *feste* honoring the Madonna and the patron saints.

Chapter two cited Jacob Riis's account of a feast day celebration in 1899. His article was touched with the comic humor inherent in the absurd situation of transplanting an outdoor festivity from a rural Italian village to the American Gotham. Newspapers in the 1910s and 1920s still carried stories emphasizing the *feste* as the Italians' effort to preserve their Old World customs and express their Catholic faith, but they added another image of the outdoor affairs, a picture which stressed crowding, traffic blockage, and a potential for violence. In May 1922, *The New York Times* reported panic at a Saint Rocco *festa* in the East 30s, when a man fired an automatic pistol at a crowd for no apparent reason. Police shot and wounded the gunman, and took him into custody.[79] In July of that same year, police staked out the Saint Gerlando *festa* along Mott Street, arrested a suspect and four associates, and disarmed all five.[80]

The city passed ordinances forbidding the carrying of statues in parades without prior permission. Some devotees took the new ordinance calmly: there was no serious incident when police halted a procession heading north on Second Avenue with a statue of Saint Guiliano in the lead, and told the marchers they could continue but Saint Guiliano had to return to his niche at Saint Sebastian's

[75]J.H. Senner, "Immigration from Italy."

[76]E.g., *New York Catholic News*, 9 December 1916.

[77]*New York Catholic News*, 16 April 1927.

[78]*Golden Jubilee of Saint Roch's Parish . . . 1949* (New York: Privately printed, 1949), n.p.

[79]*The New York Times*, 8 May 1922, 19:7.

[80]*The New York Times*, 31 July 1922, 15:5.

church.[81] Other groups protested, and the newspapers emphasized the threat to public order:

> The mob of Italians in Hicks Street, Brooklyn, yesterday stormed the rectory of their parish church, broke down the doors and partly wrecked the building because the church had refused to let them carry a statue of their patron saint in a parade. In wreaking vengeance on the helpless parish priest the mob dealt roughly with a patrolman, overcame a whole fire company that rushed to his aid, and finally fought a pitched battle with 300 policeman. Not until heavy reserves from Manhattan had been rushed across the Brooklyn Bridge to reinforce their hard-battling brothers in the other borough did the police succeed in scattering the angry celebrants.[82]

The articles finished with the note that a similar incident occurred at Mary, Help of Christians, on East 12th Street.

One way for the Italian community to preserve the image of the festa as an occasion for devotion was to follow the American custom of practicing devotions at churches. Our Lady of Mount Carmel on East 115th Street had long been the main sponsor of the festa honoring its patroness. Mount Carmel's festa changed only slowly. In its early days, one could see elderly women proceeding toward the Madonna's statue on hands and knees, tongues dragging on the floor as they crept. That extravagant display of humility died out by the 1930s. However, vendors still sold and people still bought wax images of afflicted body parts to offer to the Madonna to request a cure. Outside the church, hungry participants bought sausages, Italian cakes and candy, and American frankfurters and watermelon. They amused themselves listening to the band play Italian opera music and riding on American amusement park rides, such as the Ferris wheel and the merry-go-round.[83]

Saint Anthony of Padua on Sullivan Street tied its patron's cult even more firmly to the church. The parish had no outdoor festa until after World War II. Instead, it sponsored a traditional, novena-like service of thirteen consecutive Tuesdays of devotions to Saint Anthony. At Saint Anthony's the thirteen Tuesdays were held during the weeks before Christmas.[84] Other churches scheduled thirteen Tuesday devotions so that they culminated on Saint Anthony's feast day, June 13. On the feast day itself, there was a Solemn High Mass (with music), and the distribution to the faithful of bread and lilies, Saint Anthony's symbols.[85]

[81]New York Herald, 24 May 1925.

[82]The New York Times, 4 September 1923, 19:1.

[83]The New York Times, 15 July 1935, 17:1; 17 July 1935, 14:6; 15 July 1936, 17:3, and 16 July 1936, 19:4.

[84]New York Catholic News, 25 September 1937.

[85]New York Catholic News, 25 June 1927.

Feste had to be planned annually, so there was a yearly opportunity to examine the celebration and decide what Italian elements to keep and what American ones to incorporate. Other Italian customs persisted without such conscious effort. Sometimes, this was because certain individuals had begun practicing particular devotions when they were young, and then the individuals lived into old age, keeping the customs of their youth no matter how much the world around them changed. One example of this comes from Our Lady of Pompei on Bleecker Street. Women immigrants from San Stefano, a town south of Genoa, established at Pompei their home town devotion to Our Lady of Guadeloupe. Parishioner Catherine Zerbarini's mother was among this first generation, and she inherited her mother's piety. Every year in mid-August, she sent the parish money in honor of Our Lady of Guadeloupe, even though she herself lived in Stamford, Connecticut. Every year she noted how long she had been contributing to the feast day, and eventually achieved a 33-year record of faithfulness.[86]

Some Italian customs held such rich associations with home and family that they were psychologically comforting and thus were preserved. Christmas customs are an example. In Greenwich Village, the Italian parishes displayed creches. The Christmas masses included a ceremony somewhat like the modern veneration of the cross on Good Friday, in which members of the congregation formed a line along the center aisle to take turns stooping, bowing, or kneeling at the creche to kiss the face of the Christ Child statue.[87]

The American and Italian devotional tradition were different in that the American Catholics did not have such a long history of local saints, nor any pious customs integrated into the local culture. Italians did not adopt American devotions. Rather, Italians and non-Italians acquired new devotions as the twentieth century progressed. During the 1930s, both Italian and non-Italian churches experimented with a new pious practice, the "perpetual novena." The name was something of an oxymoron. Novenas were nine days of special services to honor God, the Madonna, or a saint; they usually led to, and were in preparation for, an important feast day. Perpetual novenas were held weekly, with no limits on how many consecutive weeks it could be held. The actual service consisted of several short prayers; reciting them in common took under a half an hour. Perpetual novenas were defended as a necessary concession to the modern age. Working people could not afford to take off a week for a novena, but they could schedule a short weekly prayer service.[88] In October 1937, in response to parishioners' and devotees'

[86]Catherine Zerbarini to Demo, Stamford, Connecticut, 17 August 1923, CMS OLP Box 4, Folder 30.

[87]Ware, *Greenwich Village*, 313.

[88]*New York Catholic News*, 29 January 1938.

demands, Our Lady of Mount Carmel on East 115th Street instituted a perpetual novena to honor its patroness. The perpetual novena was held one morning a week: the Italian-speaking devotees met at 7:00 a.m., a priest said daily mass at 7:30, and the English-speaking devotees had their service after mass. Both Italian- and English-speakers heard a short sermon, recited prayers in unison, sang hymns, and formally enrolled new members in the Society of Our Lady of Mount Carmel.

Italians joined non-Italians in worshipping new saints. Robert Orsi has demonstrated how the cult of Saint Jude spread from Chicago throughout American Catholicism after 1929.[89] In 149, the Jesuits introduced the Italians at Nativity to Mary, Mediatrix of All Graces.[90] In 1946, Frances Cabrini was proclaimed saint and in 1950 proclaimed patroness of immigrants; her cult was practiced in both Italian and non-Italian American Catholic churches.

American Catholicism lacked a long tradition, but there was the American civil religion of patriotic and secular holidays. Some of these also appeared in Italian American religious practice. For example, when the Scalabrinians' Father Superior visited Our Lady of Pompei in 1939, the parish treated him to its parochial school's Mother's Day recital, explaining to the foreign dignitary that la festa della madre had a special significance to Americans. The visitor responded by making motherhood the subject of his speech, and by imparting his blessing on all mothers present.[91]

Italian Clergy and National Leadership

The Italians never imitated the Germans in taking people from many parts of the homeland, now scattered across many parts of the United States, and trying to maintain a sense of common peoplehood. However, by the 1920s, some Italian clergy had assimilated to other nations' customs, and were trying to provide some form of national leadership for their people in the United States.

One such priest was the Reverend Aurelio Palmieri, O.S.A., an immigrant and a member of the Augustinian order. In 1920, Palmieri was assigned as a curate at the Italian church of Our Lady of Good Counsel in Philadelpia. He was fluent in both Italian and English, and a versatile writer. He wrote a survey on the progress of Protestantism among Italian immigrants that appeared in the American

[89]Robert A. Orsi, "What Did Women Really Think When They Prayed To St. Jude?"*U.S. Catholic Historian* VIII:1–2 (Winter/Spring 1989), 67–79.

[90]Francis Doino, S.J., to Father McMahon, New York, 25 November 1949, NYSJ Nativity 1948–1959.

[91]Sassi, *Madonna di Pompei*, 80–81.

monthly *Catholic World*, and he contributed an article on Italian immigrant clergy to a symposium on American Catholic history. He also wrote articles for Italian journals and published pamphlets in Italy criticizing American Catholic handling of Italian immigrants.

Palmieri tailored his writing to his various audiences' interests. In an article intended for Americans, he predicted:

> I am convinced that after another half century there will no longer be "Italian" churches in the United States. The children of immigrants will not longer talk Italian nor preserve remembrance of Italian life or traditions. They will be completely "Americanized."[92]

But for the coming half-century, clergy, sisters, churches, and school were to have the task of protecting the Italians from the Irish. In his English-language publications, Palmieri assumed the American clergy lacked understanding of the Italian situation.[93] In his Italian-language publications, he accused the American clergy of considering the Italian laity a burden. imposed by the Italian clergy's deficiencies, and he quoted numerous anti-Italian articles published by Irish Americans in the previous 20 years to prove his point.[94]

Italian clergy and churches not only protected the laity from anti-Italianism, they played an important role in the transition from Italian to American Catholicism. Palmieri held to the belief that culture and Catholicism were so interwoven that to pull out the strands of one led to the unraveling of the other. Immigrants fresh from Italy were more responsive to a clergy who understood their dialects and "the peculiar psychology of Italian Catholicism." If they attached themselves to Catholicism in the United States through these clergy and parishes. the Italian would raise their families in the faith, and the clergy would then somehow be "imbuing them with the spirit of the American organization of the Catholic Church."[95]

John Zarrilli, a diocesan priest in Duluth, Minnesota, questioned the demise of Little Italy in American even in the next half-century. He went much farther than had Palmieri in advocating the preservation of Italian culture and in doing so involved himself in much greater controversy with other American Catholics.

[92]Aurelio Palmieri. O.S.A., "The Contribution of the Italian Catholic Clergy in the United States," 144–145.

[93]Ibid., 143.

[94]Aurelio Palmieri, *Il Grave Problema Religioso Italiano negli Stati Unity* (Florence: Librería Editrice Fiorentina, 1921), 28–29.

[95]Palmieri, "Contribution of the Italian Catholic Clergy," 144. *See also* his "Il Clero Italiano negli Stati Uniti," *Vita Italiana* XV (1920), 113–127.

Zarrilli published his "Suggestion for the Solution of the Italian Problem" in the January 1924 issue of the clerical monthly *Ecclesiastical Review*. Zarrilli proposed establishing an "Italo-American Centre" in a major city, preferably Chicago. His Centre was to house a variety of activities: a mission band (similar to New York's Italian Apostolate), a national Italian Catholic newspaper, and national Catholic lay organizations for men and women. Most importantly, the Center was to provide a port of entry for the Italian immigrant clergy, supplementing the work of the new pontifical college, and allowing new arrivals to study the American language, customs, and finances before their parish assignments. Zarrilli wanted to crown this separate-but-equal system of Italian Catholicism with a few Italian bishops, one of whom should head the Italo-American Centre to "add credit to the institution."[96]

Appointing bishops in a kind of affirmative-action plan had aroused the hierarchy's ire when Peter Paul Cahensley and Giovanni Battista Volpe-Landi suggested it in 1891, and it still provoked anger among American clergy. Two of them published critiques of Zarrilli's proposals, both of them anonymously. One critic conceded that, in the past, the pressures of migration had led American bishops to invite foreign-born clergy to the United States to minister to the migrants. Such recruitment had its drawbacks "when seen from the important viewpoint of unifying the Catholic body under a common discipline in which religious and civic aims combine for the improvement of the national spirit." Foreign clergy and national parishes perpetuated Old World loyalties while diluting the New World ones, and they isolated immigrants from the rest of the diocese, which sometimes kept the local bishop unaware of mismanagement and scandal. The critic agreed with Zarrilli that incoming clergy needed a port of entry, but he thought such a place should do more than familiarize them with American ways: it should Americanize them completely.[97]

Zarrilli responded by publishing a pamphlet on the subject. The pamphlet's first section reprinted his *Ecclesiastical Review* article and the third reprinted an article on bilingual education in Trenton, New Jersey. In the second section, Zarrilli answered his critics. He defended bilingual education as a legitimate tool which Protestants used to proselytize and which Catholics needed to use to save the children for the faith. He also defended Italian bishops as a way of recognizing the Italians and showing them their value to the Church. He reminded his critics

---

[96]J. Zarrilli, "A Suggestion for the Solution of the Italian Problem," *Ecclesiastical Review* LXX (1924), 70–77.

[97]"Pastoral Care of Foreign Catholics in America," *Ecclesiastical Review* LXX (1924), 176–181. See also, Fidelis, "Nationalism and the Catholicity of the Clergy in the United States," *Ecclesiastical Review* LXX (1924), 295–299.

that forced Americanization produced hypocritical Americans as surely as forced conversion produced hypocritical Christians.[98]

Zarrilli mentioned in his pamphlet that he had sent a rebuttal to the *Ecclesiastical Review*, but the editors rejected it for publication. He finally had his rebuttal published in 1928. In it, he gave consideration to his opponents' suggestions and incorporated some them, such as moving the site of his proposed Italo-American Centre from Chicago to Catholic University in Washington, D.C. He held to his opinion that Italian clergy ought to preserve their own and their parishioners' *italianità* through separate parishes. He agreed that Italian national parishes ought to be turned into regular territorial parishes, but one of his reasons for agreeing with this was that the territorial parishes, with their definite borders, were easier for the clergy to manage. Zarrilli continued to press for bilingual education. If he could not get Italian bishops, he wanted Italian vicars-general to assist the bishops in supervising Italian parishes, and he still suggested "a small representation of ecclesiastical leaders of Italian nationality in responsible places," to foster Italian Catholic pride.[99]

Zarrilli's grand plans were never implemented. There were sporadic attempts to shape New York's Italian clergy into ethnic leaders on an archdiocesan level. There was a short-lived *Unione del Clero Italiano nell'America del Nord*, with an equally short-lived bulletin, and also records of meetings of *L'Associazione del Clero Italiano della diocesi di New York* in 1919 and 1920.[100] The Italian clergy, though, were really leaders of numerous Italian parishes. They did come together for each other's cornerstone-layings, school dedications, and, as the community aged, parish and priestly anniversaries. This was socializing rather than collective action.

The last chapter pointed out the irony of "preserving Italian culture." The Italian culture of most immigrants was transmitted through family and community, not through education or institutions. This chapter brings out another two other ironies. First, there is some irony in the phrase "adapting American ways." American Catholicism was itself so new that it was developing while the Italians were settling in the United States: all ethnic groups together adopted new devotions and pious practices.

[98]J. Zarrilli, *A Prayerful Appeal to the American Hierarchy* (Two Harbors, Minnesota: Privately printed, 1924).

[99]J. Zarrilli, "Some More Light on the Italian Problem," *Ecclesiastical Review* LXXIX (1928), 256–268.

[100]CMS IAR, Box 3, Archives of the Diocese of Brooklyn, Miscellaneous folder.

Second, the Italy being held up as the immigrants' homeland had developed only since the immigrants left. Italian nationalism was a new sentiment. The next chapter turns to the development of the new Italian identity, its relationship with the older Catholic identity of most Italian people, and the effect of this relationship on the Italian American Catholics of the Archdiocese of New York.

7

Italian, American, and Catholic

At that the same that they Americanized the Italian immigrants also "Italian-ized," becoming more aware of a common Italian identity. Some aspects of this process were straightforward: succeeding American-born generations loos-ened their ties to particular provinces or villages and adopted the name "Italian" that Americans bestowed on them. There were, however, three complicating aspects of this process. Examining these complexities as they affected the develop-ment of the Italian parishes in the Archdiocese of New York is the subject of this chapter.

The best-known complication was Benito Mussolini, who was not just an important national figure but also the earliest exponent of the fascist theories American came to oppose in World War II. A second complication was the presence of Catholicism in the mix. Italy was usually regarded as a Catholic country, but Church and state were at odds throughout the nineteenth and early twentieth centuries. American Catholics had a particularly difficult time accepting modern Italian nationalism until a way was found to reconcile it with the traditional privileged position Catholicism held on the Italian peninsula. Third, the Italians under study here did not develop their Italian national sentiments in Italy, but in New York, and their *italianità* had to complement, not supersede, their Ameri-canization.

Harmonizing the conflicts between Italian, American, and Catholic identities took place in a series of steps over a period of time. Italian identity was heightened during World War I but the possibilities for conflict with other identities was muted by the alliance system. Italian and Catholic identities were reconciled in 1929. Ironically, this reconciliation was made possible partly by Mussolini, against whom Americans went to war in 1941. Not until the Cold War did a common enemy create a situation in which Italian, American, and Catholic identities reinforced, rather than conflicted, with each other.

The Early "Italian Community"

Late nineteenth- and early twentieth-century Italian immigrants were not *nationalists*, loyal to a particular people, but *patriots*, loyal to a home land. Americans and uninitiated Danes such as Jacob Riis might call an area a "Little Italy," but insiders knew any "Little Italy" could be divided into well-defined areas reserved for particular provinces and villages. This was as true of the densely populated Manhattan neighborhoods as it was in the small towns on Staten Island.[1]

Italian immigrants planned their social lives along provincial lines. Women had few formal social contacts, and those they did have – work, church, relatives, and shopkeepers – were, because they were confined to kin and neighborhood, confined to a particular province or village. Men had more formal social contacts, particularly through mutual benefit societies. One purpose of these societies was to provide sick and death insurance. Another purpose was to preserve ties between former residents of a particular place. The mutual benefit societies sponsored "members only" clubs and *bocce* courts where those who belonged met for conversation and recreation. Annual *feste* honoring home town patron saints served as formal celebrations of loyalty to one's roots. Gino Carlo Speranza, an Italian American who worked with Progressives to assist Italian migrants, outlined in a letter to the editor of *The New York Times* the disadvantages of multiple regionally based mutual benefit societies. Although New York City had numerous Italians, their political strength was dissipated by mutual benefit societies' intramural quarrelling. Although the societies did some good, providing reasonably priced sick and death benefits and wholesome family recreation at annual balls, the men who ran the societies were too concerned with personal and provincial honor to advance the concerns of the Italian population as a whole.[2]

The greatest expressions of Italian unity came at times of natural disaster. For example, on December 28, 1908, a severe earthquake levelled the town of Messina and shook Calabria. The earthquake was followed by flood, fire, fear of famine and epidemic, and over 150,000 deaths.[3] King Victor Emmanuel II came personally to direct rescue and relief efforts, a gesture emphasizing the national scope of southern Italy's misfortune.[4] Italians abroad almost immediately began

[1]John Horace Mariano, *The Italian Contribution to American Democracy* (Boston: Christopher Publishing House, 1921), 19–21.

[2]*The New York Times*, 8 March 1903, 34:4–5.

[3]*The New York Times*, 29 December 1908, 1:7, 2:2–3.

[4]*The New York Times*, 31 December 1908, 3:1, 4–6.

raising funds for earthquake relief. Most New York Italians gave money through the Italian Chamber of Commerce, the American branch of the Italian Red Cross, or one of the Italian newspapers. Local leaders went from door to door in the various Little Italies soliciting contributions. Apparently, the tragedy united the fragmented Italian community of New York, which the *Times* described as "dwelling in little settlements independent of each other."[5] New York's Italian Catholic churches did not take a leading role in earthquake relief fundraising, but perhaps this was because they did not have to. Pope Pius X contributed 200,000 lire to the earthquake victims, and rumor had it that he planned to ask for a general collection through Catholicism. Whatever the Holy Father's role, Cardinal Farley appealed to all parishes, not just Italian, to make collections.[6]

War also turned Italians' thoughts toward their homeland. In 1911 and 1912, Italy and Turkey fought for possession of Tripoli and Libya. In January of 1912, Our Lady of Mount Carmel in Mount Vernon hosted a procession and Solemn High Mass for the repose of souls of Italian soldiers fallen in battle.[7]

Donations to Italian causes and attendance at public observances commemorating events in Italy provide a window into what ordinary immigrants might have thought about their relationship to their homeland. The socioeconomic layer just above them left a much fuller record. In February 1915, a group of Italian American entrepreneurs led by Agostino De Biasi launched a monthly magazine, *Il Carroccio*. *Carroccio* aspired to speak for the Italian "colony" in America, and to reach an audience across the United States. Eventually, it drew news from Little Italians across the country, but there is no indication it influenced opinion greatly. It did not rate mentioning in the bibliography of index of John Diggins's survey of *Mussolini and Fascism: The View from America*. However, *Carroccio* may be taken as an indicator of the sentiments of one group that is of importance here: New York's Italian Catholic clergy. Among the members of its founding editorial committee were Robert Biasotti, director of the Archdiocese of New York's Italian Apostolate; Giuseppe Grivetti, director of New York branch of the international traveler's aid agency *Italica Gens*; and Vincenzo Jannuzzi, P.S.S.C., pastor of Saint Joachim's on Roosevelt Street and then Saint Joseph's on Catherine Street.[8]

From its beginning one of *Carroccio's* distinguishing characteristics was its equation of nationalism and religion. Church and state were still in conflict in Italy,

---

[5] *The New York Times*, 30 December 1908, 3:3–4.

[6] *The New York Times*, 31 December 1908, 3:4.

[7] *The New York Times*, 8 January 1912, 24:3.

[8] "Il Manifesto dell *Carroccio*," *Il Carroccio* I (1915), 3.

but in the United States, the flags of *la religione* and *la patria* flew from the same staff, that of *la patria* above that of *la religione*. The nationalist fervor was in the title: a *carroccio* is a special type of ox-drawn cart which carried an army's insignia into battle. It was also present in some of the pseudonyms under which authors submitted articles: "La Martinella," one author's pseudonym, was the name of the bell that called Renaissance Florence's army into action. These sentiments' sources are not clear. Vincenco Jannuzzi and other Scalabrinians may have brought to *Carroccio* some of their founder's sense of the necessity of preserving culture in order to preserve faith. When Bishop Scalabrini sent forth his first missionaries, he reminded them: "And beside the standard of religion, let the flag of our country, of this Italy, fly glorious and revered, for here is the heart of the Church; it is here God willed to establish the center of religious life, the See of his Vicar. . . ."[9] When Scalabrini visited his missionaries in 1901, he spoke to reporters of the importance of establishing parochial schools that taught both American and Italian language and culture.[10] *Carroccio* praised Scalabrini for "wanting to give to the immigrants the combined comforts of Religion and Fatherland."[11]

To what extent did the parish leadership which read and supported *Carroccio* shape community opinion? A look at World War I will be helpful in answering this question. The war generated numerous documents, and perhaps the war's seriousness impressed upon the clergy the necessity of keeping these documents. It also provided an emergency in which the leaders could exercise their leadership powers.

World War I

Carroccio began publishing in February 1915. Italy's entry into World War I, which took place in May of that year, could have put its clerical supporters in a delicate position, for while the nation armed for battle, Pope Benedict XV tried to persuade Allies and Central Powers to negotiate a settlement. Instead, *Carroccio* devoted its July issue to celebrating Italy's declaration of war. Among its articles that month was one on "La Religione e la Patria," which is a good example of the magazine's concept of the relation between the two social institutions.[12] The article started with the premise that Catholicism was an attribute of the Italian

[9]Caliaro and Francesconi, *John Baptist Scalabrini*, 190.

[10]Brizzolara, "100 Days," 82–85.

[11]*Il Carroccio* I (1915), 61.

[12]La Martinella, "La Religione e la Patria," *Il Carroccio* II (1915), 40–42.

character, and not an attribute of the characters of the other countries fighting. Germany was supposed to have petulantly refused the pope's peaceful mediation partly because to do so was to sacrifice its plans for a Protestant hegemony. France, too, refused Benedict's peace overtures, partly because its government was riddled with Freemasons, and Masons and Catholics had been enemies since the eighteenth century. A more important motive for refusing to negotiate was that both France and Germany thought they could win on the battlefield, and thus demand concessions later. The article closed with a reminder that the strength of Italian arms in the continuing war depended on Italy's unity, meaning not so much geographic unity as unity in loyalty to the two great Italian institutions: the national government and the papacy.

Carroccio's clerical supporters expressed their support in other ways. In October 1915, a group of New York Italian priests formed a *Comitato Del Clero Italiano de New York Pro Famiglie Dei Soldati Italiani* to coordinate efforts to dispense charity among families whose male breadwinners had returned to Italy to fight.[13] Unlike other Italian organizations, the committee was not based on provincial or village loyalties. Rather, it tried to unite the city's Little Italies by including among its officers clergy from all neighborhoods. Gerhardo Ferrante, secretary of Cardinal Farley's Italian Bureau, acted as president. There were three vice-presidents: Ferdinando Parri, an official of the Franciscan Custos of the Immaculate Conception, the headquarters of which was at Saint Anthony of Padua on Sullivan Street; Ernesto Coppo, whose Salesians had two parishes on the Lower East Side; and Giacinto Cardi, whose Pallottines had two parishes in East Harlem. The treasurer was Antonio Demo, whose Scalabrinians also had two parishes. The secretary was Giuseppe Grivetti of *Italica Gens.*

The committee first met on October 26, 1915, at Saint Anthony of Padua, and appointed a subcommittee to make suggestions for raising funds to distribute among needy families of soldiers. The committee reported back at a second meeting on November 9. Some of its ideas involved tapping established sources: pastors, curates, and *L'Unione del Clero Italiano*, the clergy's professional association. The subcommittee also advocated soliciting among the laity by taking up collections at requiem masses for fallen soldiers and by holding a concert featuring Father Parri's music. Those who had no money could donate goods: pastors were urged to organize women to knit stockings. Finally, the subcommittee recommended placing all money in one fund, and disbursing it to parishes according to the number of needy families reported.

[13]"Circular Letter of Comitato Del Clero Italiano di New York Pro Famiglie Dei Soldati Italiani," minutes of meetings in CMS IAR Box 3, Archives of the Diocese of Brooklyn, Miscellaneous folder.

Vincenzo Jannuzzi implemented the suggestion to hold requiems for fallen soldiers, offering such a mass on November 14, 1915.[14] In December, Giuseppe Grivetti sent out a circular to solicit from the Italian clergy and, more importantly, to explain the significance of their participation. Translated into English, he wrote:

> This war will undoubtedly leave profound traces on the European nations as well as on the individuals who participate therein. The appearance of the nations of Europe as well as the map will be changed, and undoubtedly the attitude which the world will take toward the Church after the rendering of accounts of this monstrous cataclysm will depend on the activity of the clergy in this present hour.
>
> Lay committees have already done much and will do much for our families with *feste*, collections, and periodic contributions from the various members.
>
> The clergy should endeavor to do at least as much, and as much more as possible. The Italian colony will watch and will judge them; our Italy likewise expects us to work. We should like, therefore, reverend and dear Father, for you to give all your sympathy and all your support. Christian charity urges us and no other motive.[15]

Carroccio took notice of the clergy's efforts in January 1916, when it printed Grivetti's letter, down to "our Italy likewise expects us to work," omitting the direct appeal and the reference to Christian charity. Instead, the magazine expressed its gratitude at finding a minister of God taking the part of the sacred rights of nations and the honor of civilized people.[16]

The Italian clergy's committee held its first benefit for needy families of soldiers on January 12, 1916. The affair took place at Tammany Hall, and consisted of a concert directed by Francesco Magliocco and a speech by Ferdinando Parri, which *Il Carroccio* described as being about "our war." Besides the public, the affair attracted other clerical patrons: Michael J. Lavelle, Cardinal Farley's special assistant for ethnic concerns, and Giuseppe Caffuzzi, pastor of Our Lady of Mount Carmel on Belmont Avenue, appeared in the audience.[17] The committee held a second benefit in May 1916. This time, the featured speaker was Giuseppe Silipigni of Our Lady of Loreto on Elizabeth Street. What Silipigni said was not quoted, but *Il Carroccio* reported that he said it with "patriotic fervor."[18]

[14]*Il Carroccio* II (1915), 106.

[15]Giuseppe Grivetti to "Reverendo e caro Padre," New York, December 1915, CMS IAR, Box 3, Archives of the Diocese of Brooklyn, Miscellaneous folder.

[16]"Discussioni del *Carroccio*," *Il Carroccio* III (1916), 35.

[17]*Il Carroccio* III (1916), 55–56.

[18]*Il Carroccio* III (1916), 377.

The money thus raised went to the pastors and from there to the parishioners. Vincent Jannuzzi of Saint Joachim's left a record of how this worked. He compiled a list of 68 parish families of Italian soldiers, listing the families by the woman who headed the household and including the ages of minor children.[19] He then kept monthly accounts of receipts by the committee and disbursements to the families.[20]

Father Jannuzzi's records indicate that American entry into World War I changed his work even more than Italian entry into the war. Even though their home country was fighting in the same coalition as the United States, Americans did not think Italy was fighting for the same reasons, such as making the world safe for democracy, and the press urged the foreign-born to abandon their former loyalties and profess "heart's allegiance" the United States.[21] However, Italians could not be expected to read the periodicals in which Americans of a different birth and a different class background discussed "Does America Americanize?"[22] They had to be reached through their established leaders. Taking Jannuzzi for a community leader, numerous private and public agencies put him on their mailing lists, soliciting his help in instructing the Italians as to how to support the war effort.

One agency which tried to recruit Jannuzzi and his colleagues for the war effort was the Food Administration. Joan Hoff Wilson's biography of Herbert Hoover described how the Food Administration's director used the mass media of the time—meaning print media—to urge voluntary food conservation efforts.[23] Another type of mass media was the mass, and other church services. In a letter regarding an upcoming "Food Conservation Sunday," Hoover requested a sermon on this topic, and even gave suggestions for a specific appeal to women:

> The women of America have never failed to answer such a call as comes to them now. The saving of food is within their sphere. Without food conservation we cannot win the war. The woman who conserved the food supply of America and her Allies renders a high service to her country and to all humanity as well. In very truth, the outcome of the world war is in the hands of the women no less than in the hands of the men."[24]

The Food Administration sent Jannuzzi numerous circulars on the economical use of particular foodstuffs. The handouts were in English. Judging from the activities of the settlement house near another Italian parish, the brochures

---

[19]"Famiglie dei Richiamati dall'Italia, 1916-1917," CMS Saint Joachim, Box 5, Folder 161.

[20]"Comitato Pro Famiglie dei Richiamati Resconto Riassuntivo Anno 1917," ibid.

[21]Gino Carlo Speranza, "Hearth's Allegiance," Outlook CXIX (1918), 105–107.

[22]Gino Carlo Speranza, "Does America Americanize? Atlantic Monthly CXXV (1920), 263–269.

[23]Joan Hoff Wilson, Herbert Hoover: Forgotten Progressive (Boston: Little, Brown, 1975), 59–61.

[24]Herbert Hoover, circular letters, 18 June 1917, CMS OLP Box 4, Folder 20.

educated volunteers who in turn ran demonstrations for those who could not read the instructions.[25] At some point, the Food Administration began distributing multilingual public relations material, and sent Jannuzzi a four-color poster with a portrait of Garibaldi (who had been dead for years, but who was widely recognized as an Italian patriot even among Catholics who resented his opposition to their Church's position in Italy) and an Italian-language injunction to conserve food.[26] When shortages grew critical, the Food Administration kept track of the use of basic foodstuffs, including the wheat used to bake communion wafers.[27]

The war increased the need for money, on the part of both voluntary agencies and the government. Voluntary agencies had to raise money through solicitation. The Catholic Church used its parishes as part of its fund raising mechanism. In 1917, the American bishops created a National Catholic War Council to coordinate war-related charitable activities and the fundraising for them. The Knights of Columbus did much of the work of taking up collections and also of using the money to provide spiritual and recreational opportunities for armed forces personnel. Although before the war, the Italian parishes had rarely contributed to eleemosynary activities outside their ethnoreligious community, they contributed to the fund. In 1918, Saint Joachim raised $2,789.27 during the fundraising campaign, and even sent in a late donation of $55.[28]

It was even more unusual for non-Catholics to solicit in Italian Catholic parishes. Antonio Demo, who saved practically everything that crossed his desk in his during his 33 years at Our Lady of Pompei, received very few such letters until World War I. During the war, the American Red Cross sent Father Jannuzzi solicitations with an ecumenical note: "We appeal to you to bring before your people, in a Special Service, or as part of your regular service, the needs and achievements of that Red Cross which is the organized effort of piety and gratitude of all American people irrespective of race or creed."[29] Even after the war, the Red Cross continued to solicit funds, now on behalf of veterans and refugees: "The American Red Cross has prepared the enclosed pamphlet for the use of clergymen, and we

[25]CMS OLP Box 4, Folder 20 contains many letters from Greenwich House regarding presentations given to area housewives and food merchants.

[26]CMS Saint Joachim, Box 5, Folder 175.

[27]B. Hoffmann to Dear Sir, New York, 16 May 1918, CMS Saint Joachim, Box 5, Folder 174.

[28]G.P. Cooke to Vincent Jannuzzi, New York, 30 March 1918, CMS Saint Joachim, Box 5, Folder 174.

[29]William C. Breed to Jannuzzi, New York, 10 May 1918, CMS Saint Joachim, Box 5, Folder 163.

believe that you will find in it the suggestions needed to make your church a strong factor in the appeal to be made for the Red Cross."[30]

The Greater New York United War Work Campaign also canvassed the Italian parishes. Its Director of Publicity sent Jannuzzi public relations material. "I trust you will have this poster hung in a conspicuous place before your next service, and that you will see that it remains there until the end of the campaign."[31] It was a quick end: this particular campaign was scheduled for the week of November 11, 1918.

The federal Treasury Department raised cash not through donations but through bond sales. It used Sunday services to sell bonds. "There is no question of the service you may in this way render the government," an official assured Jannuzzi in a letter requesting a war savings sermon.[32] As the war went on, federal officials became more insistent:

> The campaign for the Fourth Liberty Loan furnishes the clergy an opportunity to use their powerful influence for the country's welfare. As the campaign draws near, it is well to emphasize once more the principle that a Liberty Loan is not primarily an *investment* of our money; it is a *consecration* of our money to the most sacred cause for which men have ever fought
>
> The better to accomplish this result [marketing bonds], a program of activities to be carried on in the churches is being drawn up and will be placed before you a little later.[33]

Besides food and funds, the war needed military personnel. Historian David M. Kennedy reported that as much as 18 percent of the armed forces was made up of foreign-born individuals. Many service personnel wrote home in languages other than English.[34] The military leadership worried not only about the soldiers' and sailors' ability to understand commands, but also that they "have not been fully advised as to the causes of the war" and "do not fully understand the democracy of the United State for of government and its traditions and ideals."[35]

---

[30]C. S. Clark to Reverend Sir, New York, 6 December1918, ibid.

[31]Leo L. Redding to Rev. B. Januzzi [sic], New York, 30 October 1918.

[32]Frederic W. Allen to Reverend and Dear Sir, 17 January 1918, CMS Saint Joachim, Box 5, Folder 162.

[33]Guy Emerson to the clergy in the Second Federal Reserve District, New York, 16 September 1918, CMS Saint Joachim, Box 5, Folder 164.

[34]David M. Kennedy, *Over Here: The First World War and American Society* (New York: Oxford University Press, 1980, 157.

[35]P. P. Claxton to "Gentlemen," New York, undated, CMS Saint Joachim Box 5, Folder 165.

A Commission on War Work Extension thus recruited ethnic community leadership, including the ministry, to assist in making the inductees "fit to fight." A form letter arrived at Jannuzzi's mail box informing him that the War Department intended to appoint civilians to provide preliminary training to individuals drafted into the armed forces, and to expect them to do their patriotic duty without monetary compensation. The letter further directed Jannuzzi to contact the New York City draft board and offer assistance.[36] Apparently Jannuzzi followed the instructions, for he later received letters from the Local [Draft] Board for Division 91. One invited him to a meeting of those nominated to provide preliminary education for those entering the armed forces.[37] Another requested his presence on the day a group of inductees were to leave for boot camp.[38] A third sent instructions for assisting on a day when those eligible for the draft registered with the Selective Service.[39]

As can be seen by the concern that soldiers and sailors understand the causes of the war, what the American government wanted more than food conservation, money, or military personnel was signs of support for the American effort. The clergy were among the intermediaries who explained the war to their congregations and called for demonstrations of support. Father Jannuzzi heard from a private group, the North American Civic League for Immigrants, which asked for his assessment of whether his congregation understood U.S. war aims and whether they needed "protection" (in the form of counter-propaganda) from radical or disloyal forces. The League also requested that Jannuzzi pass on to his parishioners those government and other official communications which "*meet with your full endorsement.*"[40] Jannuzzi saved a folder of correspondence with the Committee on Public Information regarding its "Four Minute Man" program (they explained the U.S. position on the war in that amount of time.)[41]

Acting as a link to the government came on top of traditional pastoral duties. Jannuzzi was asked to assist when the armed forces wanted to contact a soldier's

[36]Ibid.

[37]Ilegible to Father Vincent Januzzio [sic], New York, 9 August 1918, ibid.

[38]Jeanette Bongiorni to Jannuzzi, New York, 23 August 1918, ibid.

[39]Chairman, Legal Advisory Board to Dear Sir, 9 September 1918, ibid.

[40]D. Chauncey Brewer to Dear Father, Boston, 13 March 1918, CMS Saint Joachim Box 5, Folder 172.

[41]CMS Saint Joachim Box 5, Folder 170.

family but did not have a usable address.[42] He also assisted families in need, and once wrote to a commanding officer requesting that an enlisted man, be released from the army so that he could come home and support his elderly parents and ailing brother.[43]

The mail from private and public agencies concerned with the war effort poured in. How did the clergy respond? The answer depended on who was asking and what they wanted. It is not clear that the clergy ever comprehended the reasons for fighting the war. In 1918, an Italian-American organization drafted a telegram, in Italian, quoting approvingly Wilson's statement about making the world safe for democracy, and asked various Italian-American groups across the country to sign the telegram and send it to the White House on Independence Day of that year. The idea was to create the impression of solid Italian-American support. Jannuzzi tried to translate the telegram into English before sending it, and ended up thanking the president for his "new declaration of freedom and of safe democracy for mankind."[44] His colleague Antonio Demo thanked the president for "making Democracy safe for Mankind."[45] Both Jannuzzi and Demo proved better at selling Liberty bonds, probably because these fit into the Italians' need to accumulate money for later use.[46] Jannuzzi supported the Committee on Public Information to the point of reporting to its local representatives "pro-German" activity in his neighborhood.[47] Demo hesitated to recommend too much food conservation to his poor parishioners; asked to read an announcement urging his congregation to conserve food, he merely reminded them, in Italian, that "the mayor of New York and the cardinal recommend that everyone cooperate in every possible way . . . in these times of great communal sacrifice."[48] On the other hand,

[42]Form letter dated 19 October 1918, CMS Saint Joachim Box 5 Folder 172.

[43]Jannuzzi to Robert B. Jackson, New York, 24 June 1919, CMS Saint Joseph, Box 1, General Correspondence and Miscellaneous Documents 1919 Folder.

[44]Jannuzzi to Woodrow Wilson, New York, before 4 July 1919, CMS Saint Joachim Box 5, Folder 166.

[45]Undated draft, Box 3, Folder 22.

[46]For Jannuzzi, see Ernest Iselin to Jannuzzi, New York, 15 May 1918, CMS Saint Joachim Box 5, Folder 164. For Demo, see Iselin to Demo, 10 and 18 October 1918, CMS OLP Box 3, Folder 22.

[47]Antonio Stella to Jannuzzi, New York, 4 September 1918, CMS Saint Joachim Box 5, Folder 168.

[48]Sunday announcements, 16 June 1918, CMS OLP Box 29, Folder 316.

the Italian clergy supported the war effort that began in Italy before the American war effort, and they continued their efforts on behalf of post-war Italy.

Il Carroccio, for example, carried its wartime nationalism unchanged into the post-war era. The best example of its attitude came in 1919, in response to a series of articles in the Jesuit weekly *America*. *America* had sent a correspondent to the Versailles conference. Among the stories which he reported were two which reflected badly upon Italy. One claimed the Italians wanted the Adriatic port of Fiume not so much to use it themselves as to prevent would-be threats to Italian security from using it.[49] A second claimed the Italians took underhanded advantage of Ireland's plight, backing Ireland's request for self-determination in order to embarrass England into support Italian claims at the negotiations.[50] Coincidentally, *America* published two other articles, charging that the Waldensian Aid Society, ostensibly a church for the only Protestant denomination native to Italy, was actually a joint effort of Italian and American Protestants to win Italian away from Catholicism.[51] The latter two articles touched off a flurry of letters to the editor, reiterating the traditional description of the "Italian problem."[52] *Carroccio* then ran an article on the Jesuits entitled "Why Do They Hate Us?" charging that the Jesuits created the church-state conflict in Italy, calculating that if Catholicism were alienated from its natural supporters, it would be more vulnerable to jesuitical manipulation. In the course of the article, the author disposed of the argument that the Italian government could not claim the papacy's traditional lands in central Italy. Even Benedict XV, the article claimed, agreed with Wilson's doctrine of self-determination. Why should self-determination be applied everywhere but Italy?[53]

In the years after World War I, memorial services for battlefield casualties continued to link Catholicism and *italianità*. The most important such memorial was that honoring Italy's unknown soldier, who was entombed on November 4, 1921, beneath the allegorical figure of Rome in the Victor Emmanuel monument. At the same time as the Roman obsequies, Italians in New York gathered at Saint

[49]J.C. Walsh, "Cross Currents at Versailles," *America* XXI (17 May 1919), 141–143.

[50]J.C. Walsh, "Ireland and Article X," *America* XXI (31 May 1919), 193–196.

[51]Francis Beattie, "The Waldensian Aid Society," *America* XXI (14 June 1919), 245–247; and "The Waldensian and Protestant Episcopal Entente," *America* XXI:273–275.

[52]*America* XXI (16 August, and 6 and 27 September 1919), 475, 545, and 617.

[53]Nicholas Fusco, "Why do They Hate Us? Jesuitism and Italian Immigrants," *Il Carroccio* XI (1920), 170–179.

Patrick's Cathedral on Fifth Avenue for a requiem mass. Archbishop Hayes presided, Monsignor Lavelle preached, and many clerical *prominenti* attended: Daniel Burke of Saint Philip Neri; Ernesto Coppo, S.D.B.; Antonio Demo, P.S.S.C., Vincenzo Jannuzzi, P.S.S.C.; and Giuseppi Silipigni of Our Lady of Loreto and the Italian Auxiliary. Also present were General Armando Diaz, an Italian war hero, and Italian envoys on their way to a disarmament conference. After the mass, the dignitaries went by motorcade down Fifth Avenue to Washington Square Park, where General Diaz laid wreaths honoring George Washington and (of all people to be recognized in a Catholic event) Giuseppe Garibaldi. The only objection to the ceremonies came from New York's Italian Protestant Minister's Association, which condemned "the selfish sectarian spirit which is manifest in the commemoration of the glorious unknown soldier in the Roman Catholic cathedral," and asked that civil and military observances be held in another place.[54]

The unknown soldier's requiem provided a graphic example of the problem of this sort of piety. According to *The New York Times*, Lavelle "made a solemn prayer for disarmament, and that the work of the coming conference might be 'wise and just.'"[55] According to *Il Carroccio*, he eulogized the unknown soldier in Italian and English.[56] Lavelle may have done both, and reporters and editors gave the story particular spins for their audiences. Remembering the dead is a traditional act of Christian charity, and it could also be construed as an act of support nationalism. Such confusion became more common when Mussolini came to power.

Mussolini and the Archdiocese of New York

From the moment he became Italy's premier on October 28, 1922, Benito Mussolini was no ordinary usurper. He justified his actions with a new political theory, fascism. Mussolini expounded on fascist doctrine in speeches to his own people and in interviews with foreign journalists. Journalists, political scientists, philosophers, and theologians treated fascism as a subject for careful analysis. However, as John P. Diggins has shown, most American "thought" on Italian fascism was laced with "reactions" or "sentiments." For example, Americans generally approved of fascism for Italy because they perceived the country as

[54]*The New York Times*, 31 October 1921, 4:6.

[55]*The New York Times*, 5 November 1921, 6:1–2.

[56]*Il Carroccio* XIII (1921), 655–656.

charming but desperately behind time, and in need of someone like Mussolini to bring it up to date.[57]

American Catholics shared their conationalists' views of Italy, and their own reasons for favoring Mussolini. Mussolini opposed the liberal politicians who had for so long opposed Catholicism. Some years earlier, Mussolini had been violently anti-clerical; now he announced he was a Catholic who looked to the Church for guidance. Surely, Catholicism could fare better under Mussolini's regime. Diggins has the most complete analysis of the non-Italian American Catholic popular press response to Mussolini. According to him, *Catholic World*, the Paulists' monthly, opposed fascism from the start. *Commonweal*, a weekly journal published by lay Catholics, waffled. *America* was usually favorable.[58]

Understandably, Diggins omitted the *New York Catholic News* from his survey, but the archdiocesan weekly newspaper is of importance here. One *Catholic News* column was always anti-fascist. That was *Sursum Corda [Lift Up Your Hearts]: What's Right with the World.* This was a weekly commentary written by James M. Gillis, C.S.P., who also edited *Catholic World.* Other columnists and editors were neither pro- nor anti-fascist. They had other things on their minds.

The first example of *Catholic News* priorities came in 1929, when Mussolini and Pope Pius XI signed the Lateran Treaties, which established relations between Italy and the independent state of Vatican City to the present day. *Catholic News* coverage of this event began with an defense of the necessity of the treaties. From 1870 to 1929, the paper explained, Italy had claimed the Holy Father was really an Italian citizens. If that were true, the Italian government, which did not have a Bill of Rights, might censor papal speeches and hinder church work. Popes who were Italian citizens might be accused of favoring Italy when they spoke on international affairs. Sovereignty over an independent territory theoretically carried with it the political freedom necessary for spiritual leadership.[59] This explained the situation to Catholics and justified it to non-Catholics

Non-Catholics' education continued with Cardinal Hayes's pastoral letter announcing the concordats. *The New York Times* quoted an oblique passage about how "the spiritual sovereignty of the Holy See cannot impinge on nor impair nor belittle the civil supremacy of the state by the latter's appreciation of a realm above and beyond its domain," which seems to have been intended to allay fears that the Lateran Treaties represented a reunion of church and state in Italy and that

[57]John P. Diggins, *Mussolini and Fascism: The View from America* (Princeton: Princeton University Press, 1972), 21.

[58]Ibid., 182–197.

[59]*New York Catholic News*, 16 February 1929.

Catholics wanted to do the same in America.[60] This impression was strengthened by the cathedral's celebration of the treaties. Saint Patrick's had engaged the Reverend John McClorey, S.J., a professor at the University of Detroit, to preach during Lent, when, coincidentally, the treaties were signed. McClorey hurriedly changed his topic for March 10, 1929, from "The Futility of Birth Control" to "The Church and the Republic." His sermon emphasized that the pope was temporal sovereign only in tiny Vatican City. In the unlikely event that the Holy Father declared war against the United States, American Catholics would fight for the United States. McClorey quoted from Cardinal Gibbons on the impossibility of a church-state union in the United States, cited Al Smith as an example of a politician who combined Catholicism and patriotism, and drew comforting parallels between American democracy and the spiritual democracy that supposedly existed in Catholicism, which drew its popes from all social classes. He closed by reassuring his hearers that if the pontiff favored any nation it was the United States, which had entered World War I only to secure the peace Benedict XV had so ardently desired.[61]

Almost immediately after signing the Lateran Treaties Pius XI and Mussolini quarrelled over education. Later in 1929, Pius issued an encyclical, *Divinus Illus Magistre*, outlining the Catholic position on education.[62] Pius avoided mentioning Mussolini by name, and Mussolini ignored the broad hint of Pius's action in publishing the encyclical. Both Fascists and Catholics sponsored clubs for adolescent boys and young men. The Fascists had various groups, and the Catholic had Catholic Action, an umbrella organization that included youth clubs. Both Fascists and Catholic Action provided opportunities for recreation, socializing, and the inculcation of their respective doctrines. Relations between them were strained. Catholic Action insisted it was not a political party, and that men could belong to both Catholic Action and a Fascist organization. The Fascists argued that Catholic Action was a rival.[63]

The tension worsened in May 1931. To mark the fortieth anniversary of *Rerum Novarum*, Leo XIII's influential encyclical on economic ethnics, Pius XI issued *Quadragessimo Anno* (the title translates as "Forty Years After"). Pilgrims visiting

[60]*The New York Times*, 24 February 1929, 25:1–4.

[61]*The New York Times*, 11 March 1929, 4:1.

[62]*Christian Education of Youth: Official and Complete English Text of the encyclical Letter of His Holiness Pope Pius XI* (Washington, DC: National Catholic Welfare Conference, 1936).

[63]Albert C. O'Brien, "Italian Youth in Conflict: Catholic Action and Fascist Italy, 1929–1931," *Catholic Historical Review* LXVIII (1982), 625–635.

Rome that year heard Pius speak on "distributive justice." The Fascists claimed Pius's preaching on economics constituted political interference. Then, on June 2, a Roman newspaper, *Il Lavoro Fascista*, carried a news item claiming the archbishop who was the ecclesiastical assistant to Catholic Action's Central Council had urged Catholic Action to go into politics. *Catholic News* reported that upon hearing this, Fascist youths rioted against Catholic Action youths, shouted threats against Pius, burnt copies of the Vatican newspaper *Osservatore Romano*, sacked the offices of the Roman Jesuit paper *Civiltà Cattolica*, vandalized the parochial school office of Saint Laurent in Damisco (though the office and school were in a building supposedly protected by the Lateran Treaties), and harassed the drivers of a Vatican postal truck who had halted their vehicle as a Fascist parade passed by.[64]

Mussolini responded by ordering not only Catholic Action, but also women's and children's religious societies disbanded, lest they prove subversive. Pius XI responded with another encyclical, *Non abbiamo bisogno*. This time, Pius wrote specifically about the situation in Italy, blaming the Italian government (he did not use the word "fascist") for what had happened. He further charged that Mussolini's order to disband Catholic Action was a "pretext" for a renewed attack on Catholicism's role in education. He cited Fascist harassment of women's and children's societies as evidence that the government wanted to go beyond stamping out Catholic Action and take over the entire educational process beginning with the smallest children. Pius reiterated his position he had outlined in *Divinus Illus Magistre*, and argued that to accept the proposition that the government should dominate education was to bow to "a regime based on ideology which clearly resolves itself into a true and real pagan worship of the state."[65] The method of publishing *Non abbiamo bisogno* furnished additional proof of fascism's dangers. Fearing censorship, Pius had his encyclical translated secretly (by Francis Joseph Spellman), hustled off to Paris, and published there.[66]

Catholic News explained the fascists' chief error:

> The present Italian government is what is called an integral state, that is to say, a state which is to rule practically all of life and dictate the consciences of its subjects in all those many parts of life that is wishes to rule.[67]

[64]*New York Catholic News*, 6 June 1931.

[65]*Catholic Action: Encyclical Letter of His Holiness, Pope Pius XI* (Washington, DC: National Catholic Welfare Conference, 1931), 22.

[66]Robert I. Gannon, S.J., *The Cardinal Spellman Story* (New York: Doubleday and Company, 1962), 75; and John Cooney, *The American Pope: The Life and Times of Francis Cardinal Spellman* (New York: Times Books, 1984), 42–48.

[67]*New York Catholic News*, 20 June 1931.

Catholicism, though, subjected conscience to a higher power than the state. When put this way, one could see that church-state conflict spread far beyond Italy. In Soviet Russia, in anti-clerical Mexico, and in the United States, individuals urged granting the state the sole right to educate youth. *Catholic News* became so interested in running down examples to illustrate this abstract theological point that it never returned to fascism.

The one *Catholic News* columnist who used the controversy to write specifically about fascism was the anti-fascist James M. Gillis. At one point during his quarrel with Mussolini, Pius XI received a visit from the Boston politician James Michael Curley. Apparently thinking two politicians might understand each other, Pius sent Curley to reason with Mussolini. Curley came away from the encounter converted, and returned to the United States announcing that President Herbert Hoover ought to be more like Mussolini. Gillis used this as this as the premise for a satirical column illustrating the fascist threat to individual liberty.[68]

Late in 1931, Mussolini and Pius agreed upon legislation permitting Catholic Action to continue, but limiting its work. The Archdiocese of New York maintained its practice of commenting on Italian affairs only insofar as they affected the United States. For example, in 1935, when the Italo-Ethiopian War began, *Catholic News* repeated other papers' warnings: American citizens should learn to discriminate between news and propaganda, and the United States itself should remain neutral, even if the Ethiopian crisis led to another general European war.[69]

During the late 1930s, the threat of European war loomed large, except in the pages of *Catholic News*. There, the headlines highlighted the atrocities against Catholicism in Mexico. The only other subjects to attract much notice were Patrick Cardinal Hayes's death on September 4, 1938, and Francis Spellman's installation on April 15, 1939. The Archdiocese of New York ceased giving much press space to Mussolini, leaving him to the Little Italies.

Mussolini in Italian Parishes

Mussolini had support among Italian Americans. Sociologist William Foote Whyte recorded one reason why: "He has done more to get respect for the Italian people than anybody else."[70] An Italian American raised on the Lower East Side thought that "The Italian American population was not at all split regarding

[68]*New York Catholic News*, 27 June 1931.

[69]*New York Catholic News*, 12 October 1935.

[70]William Foote Whyte, *Street Corner Society*, second edition (Chicago: University of Chicago, 1955), 274.

Mussolini. They upheld the Italian government . . . ." During World War II, two of this man's uncles volunteered for the Italian army.[71] A Brooklyn Italian, though, explained that "In the fascist period, Italian Americans for the most part favored fascism, not actively but spiritually."[72]

The most detailed study of the relationship between New York's Italian American clergy and Italy's Fascist movement was done by Gaetano Salvemini. Salvemini was a scholar, political activist, and anti-Fascist before the party came to power. He organized a resistance movement at the University Florence in 1924. In June 1925, the Fascists jailed him for six weeks. Upon his release in August, he left for France. He first toured the United States in January 1928. His admiration for American political values led him in 1933 to settle in the States and become a citizen, but he was dismayed by the groundswell of pro-Fascist sentiment among Italian Americans, and tried to trace it to its sources. By 1941 he had a manuscript on the subject. The book went unpublished while Salvemini involved himself in post-war reconstruction in Italy.[73]

A list of New York Italian Catholic clergy whom Salvemini considered Fascist supporters appears in Appendix 4. Some of the problems with using the list are immediately noticeable. Salvemini listed several people as Fascists without providing any evidence for his charges. In other cases, he considered individuals guilty by association. In still others, he used evidence open to several interpretations. Omitting the individuals for whom the evidence is shaky leaves a smaller group for whom Salvemini's evidence is more convincing. Chief among these are the clerical shareholders of *Il Carroccio*, because one can go through the magazine to see its policy on fascism. News of the March on Rome reached New York in time for *Carroccio's* November 1922 issue. Almost every article discussed the Fascist triumph. The editorial demonstrated that the periodical's support for fascism had been long standing. The editorial was illustrated with a reproduction of the April 1921 cover: a drawing of the *fasci*, the bundle of sticks around an axe from which fascism took its name.[74]

When Pius XI and Mussolini clashed, *Carroccio* published an article by Il Duce's brother Arnaldo, which responded to Pius's charges point by point. Pius

[71]Salvatore J. LaGumina, *The Immigrants Speak: Italian Americans Tell Their Story* (New York: Center for Migration Studies, 1979), 133–134.

[72]Ibid., 187.

[73]Gaetano Salvemini, *Italian Fascist Activities in the Untied States*, ed. Philip V. Cannistraro (New York: Center for Migration Studies, 1977), introduction.

[74]*Il Carroccio* XVI (1922), 542–544.

gave the dominant role in education to the Church, because, he claimed, in everything, including education, the most important thing is to work for salvation. True, Arnaldo conceded, and irrelevant: fascism taught the same virtues Catholicism did, only with an eye to earthly service to the nation rather than heavenly reward. Similarly, Pius placed the family after the Church as the institution with the most authority over children's education. According to Arnaldo, the family educated children in order to secure its own advancement, while, again, fascism gave them the same education but for the good of the whole nation. If Pius and Mussolini agreed on the type of virtues to be taught, why then did they argue? Arnaldo Mussolini offered two possible answers, neither of them flattering to Pius. Either he did not understand what was really going on in the Catholic Action organizations he sponsored, or his special interest in youth blinded him to objective realities.[75]

This was what the clerical shareholders supported. Did they read it and act upon it? Evidence apart from Salvemini's collection indicates that New York's Italian Catholic clergy reacted favorably to the Fascist regime. Antonio Demo, P.S.S.C., who had served in the army under the liberal Italian government, answered a letter soliciting a donation to a fascist cause by writing, in Italian: "This old grenadier of long ago cannot answer the call for money [but he will] honor in his thoughts the heroes of the homeland."[76] Demo also manifested his approval more publicly. He visited Italy in 1931 and reported to his congregation, again in Italian: "I observe in Italy that by the work of the man sent by Divine Providence, Benito Mussolini, there has been made and continues to be made grand progress, that no longer are there divisions into turbulent factions, that there is discipline and duty leading to the enjoyment of perfect order and respect for all, and there is a government which can truly be called a government."[77] Joseph Rosa, C.S.S., of Our Lady of Mount Carmel, White Plains, visited Italy several times during the Fascist years, and reported that under Mussolini order was restored, the Black Hand stamped out, strikes suppressed, and, echoing the classic praise of Mussolini, "trains were made to run on time."[78]

The available documents, though, do not indicate that New York's Italian clergy played a role similar to that which Philip V. Cannistraro has documented for

[75]Arnaldo Mussolini, "Vaticano e Italia; Il Pensiero di Mussolini," *Il Carroccio* XXXIII (1931), 307–313.

[76]Demo to Luigi Barzini, 19 November 1926, CMS Box 5, Folder 35.

[77]*Il Progresso Italo-Americano*, 6 November 1931.

[78]White Plains, New York, *Dispatch*, 10 June 1939.

building contractor, publisher, and would-be politician Generoso Pope.[79] Had the clergy wanted to exert political influence, several forces limited their ambitions. By the 1930s, New York had several politicians of Italian extraction, such Salvatore Cotillo, Edward Corsi, Vito Marcantonio, and Fiorello La Guardia, who were identified as non-fascist or positively anti-fascist.[80] Also, some of the most prominent clergy were near the end of their New York careers. Giuseppe Silipigni, associated with the Italian Auxiliary, died in 1930.[81] Giuseppe Caffuzzi, who had for a generation been the most prominent Italian cleric in the Bronx, died in 1931.[82] *Il Carroccio* went out of business in 1935. The next year, Antonio Demo, the senior Italian priest in Greenwich Village, died; he had already been forcibly retired from his position as pastor for three years.[83] In 1938, Vincenzo Jannuzzi, P.S.S.C., long time pastor of Saint Joachim's and Saint Joseph's on the Lower East Side, returned to Italy.[84]

World War II

Francis Spellman (named a cardinal in 1946), New York's archbishop during World War II, has had two biographers, Robert I. Gannon, S.J., and John Cooney, both of whom stressed his role in national and international affairs. Spellman's work in New York complemented his extra-diocesan activities. He organized his clergy, who in turn organized their parishioners, to provide war time service. During World War II, rationing replaced voluntary food conservation, and film and radio replaced posters and pulpits as propaganda outlets. Demonstrations of

[79]Philip V. Cannistraro, "Generoso Pope and The Rise of Italian American Politics, 1925–1936," Lydio F. Tomasi, ed., *Italian Americans: New Perspectives in Italian Immigration and Ethnicity* (New York: Center for Migration Studies, 1985), 264–288.

[80]Ronald H. Bayor, *Fiorello La Guardia: Ethnicity and Reform* (Arlington Heights, Illinois: Harlan Davidson, 1993), 135, 141, and 159; Ronald H. Bayor, *Neighbors in Conflict: The Irish, Germans, Jews, and Italians of New York City, 1929–1941* (Baltimore: Johns Hopkins University Press, 1978), chapters 3 and 7; Edward Corsi, *In the Shadow of Liberty: The Chronicle of Ellis Island* (New York: MacMillan, 1935); Diggins, *Mussolini and Fascism*, 302–312; and Thomas M. Henderson, "Immigrant Politician: Salvatore Cotillo, Progressive Ethnic," *International Migration Review* XIII (1979), 81–102.

[81]*The New York Times*, 27 December 1930, 13:2.

[82]*The New York Times*, 30 September 1931, 25:2.

[83]*The New York Times*, 4 January 1936, 15:2.

[84]*Fiftieth Anniversary, Saint Joseph Church* (New York: Park Publishing Company, 1977), 10.

support for the American war effort continued to be important, especially for the Italians, and there were some forms of charitable activity in which the government could not replace the parish.

Italian parishes, for example, organized to pray for those in the U.S. armed forces. The Holy Name Society of Saint Clare of Assisi in the Bronx set aside the second Sunday of each month to pray for military personnel, and used the traditional all-night vigil on Holy Thursday (the celebration of the Last Supper just before Easter) to pray for peace.[85] Saint Joachim on Roosevelt Street held a novena to Blessed Mother Frances Cabrini, asking that their soldiers be spared unnecessary hardship, and for a speedy end to the war.[86] Our Lady of Mount Carmel on East 115th Street maintained a special chapel for those who wanted to pray for military personnel.[87]

Parishes collected funds to meet the spiritual and social needs of those in the armed forces. Saint Philip Neri in Bedford Park used the proceeds of its1943 Thanksgiving Dinner to buy Christmas presents for soldiers.[88] Saint Philip's Altar and Rosary (women's) Society used its annual events to fund chaplains.[89] Our Lady of Mount Carmel in Belmont admitted service people free to its social events, and had a Parish Military Committee to distribute donations to charities benefitting the armed forces.[90] Other parishioners donated time. Saint Clare of Assisi's Holy Name Society published a newsletter to keep members in the service abreast of affairs at home.[91] When Staten Island's Fox Hills Country Club and Gold Course was turned into a temporary hospital, Saint Joseph's parishioners volunteered there.[92]

All New York Catholics could engage in the above activities; other activities reflected the special nature of the Italian-American position during the war. The

[85]*Year Book Commemorating the Silver Jubilee of the Parish of Saint Clare of Assisi . . . 1930–1955* (New York: Privately published, 1955), unpaginated.

[86]*New York Catholic News*, 6 November 1943.

[87]Robert Anthony Orsi, "The Madonna of 115th Street: Faith and Community in Italian Harlem, 1880–1950" (Ph.D. dissertation, Yale University, 1982), 122.

[88]*New York Catholic News*, 20 November 1943.

[89]*New York Catholic News*, 4 December 1943.

[90]*New York Catholic News*, 10 June 1944.

[91]*Saint Clare of Assisi.*

[92]*Church of Saint Joseph, Staten Island . . . 1902–1977* (New York: Privately published, 1977), unpaginated.

Archdiocese of New York facilitated ministry to Italian prisoners of war held in the United States. In 1943, *Catholic News* announced it was going to run the names and descriptions of Italian prisoners, and that people who recognized the names could contact the newspaper, which would put them in touch with the prisoners.[93] Our Lady of Mount Carmel on East 115th Street involved the whole congregation in the prisoners' apostolate. In 1943, after a preparatory sermon on loving one's enemy, the pastor invited 500 Italian prisoners of war to Sunday dinner in various parish family homes. The parishioners originally hesitated, but later recalled the event as a precious afternoon of reconciliation.[94]

In 1943, the situation in Italy changed. On 24 July, the Fascist Grand Council voted to restore King Victor Emmanuel III to his position as constitutional monarch, effectively putting Mussolini out of office. Thereafter, two governments competed for Italy: one supported by German and Italian Fascists, and another which the Allies recognized as a co-belligerent. Italy continued to be military battlefield during the war and a political battlefield immediately thereafter, but the Allies held the peninsula securely enough to permit relief activities to begin. When the National Catholic Welfare Conference organized a Clothing Campaign for Italy, Gaetano Arcese and Joseph Pernicone headed up New York's efforts.[95] Pasquale Lombardo of Saint Lucy's in the Bronx sent food to his home town of Marsela, and money with which to rebuild its church.[96]

After the war, Italian American Catholic performed one more act of charity, remembering their veterans and war dead. Saint Clare of Assisi and Our Lady of Mount Carmel in Poughkeepsie opened chapels within their churches in honor of parishioners killed in action.[97] Saint Joseph's, Staten Island, displayed an honor role naming all those who had served in the war.[98] Saint Philip Neri placed a memorial tablet on the church lawn. Assumption in White Plains erected a statue of the Sacred Heart.[99] Italian churches, which had in the 1920s been characterized by distinctive architectural styles and decoration joined other archdiocesan churches in modifying their appearance to indicate their participation in this significant event in American history.

[93] *New York Catholic News*, 21 August 1943.

[94] Orsi, "Madonna of 115th Street," 121–123.

[95] *New York Catholic News*, 13 May and 10 June 1944.

[96] *Saint Lucy's Church, Bronx, New York* (New York: Privately published, 1977), 13.

[97] *Saint Clare of Assisi*, and Lumia, *Golden Jubilee: Our Lady of Mount Carmel, Poughkeepsie, New York*.

[98] *Church of Saint Joseph, Staten Island*.

[99] White Plains, New York, *Dispatch*, 1 and 5 May 1947.

The Cold War

World War I and II gave Italian Americans the occasion to prove their loyalty to the United States through active military service.[100] The Cold War provided a similar opportunity without the dangers of actual combat. It extended the chance to prove one's loyalty to those who were not eligible for the armed forces, and by adding a religious component it completed the development of an Italian American Catholic identity.

Cardinal Spellman encouraged his pastors to establish Catholic War Veterans' posts in their parishes. Saint Clare of Assisi on Rhinelander Avenue preserved the most extensive description of its post, which was a study-and-action group dealing mostly with issues related to Communism. As Saint Clare's parish history explained: "The true philosophy [the Catholic War Veterans] demonstrates places patriotism on a strong base of religion. Thus, the love of country is not a house built upon the shifting sands of revolutionary changes, but a house built upon a rock, which is God."[101]

In the late 1940s, it seemed that the most important theatre in the Cold War was Italy. The Italian Communist Party was well-organized and well-financed, and looked especially powerful in the light of recent victories by Communist parties in eastern Europe. Conventional wisdom emphasized the Italian peninsula's strategic importance in the Mediterranean and also emphasized that all Communist parties ultimately served Moscow; thus, a Communist victory in Italy threatened the west.

In 1948, Cardinal Spellman organized a campaign that joined the forces of Catholicism, Americanism, and *italianità* in an effort to aid Christian Democrat Alcide De Gasperi in the Italian general elections. He encouraged the Italian Americans in his archdiocese to write their relatives in Italy, warning them away from Communism and urging them to vote Christian Democrat. De Gasperi profited from an unusually large voter turnout and won handily.[102]

Even if there was no cause-and-effect linking Spellman's work and De Gasperi's victory, the incident reinforced the notion that the offspring of Italian immigrants had a new image.[103] No longer were they accused of anti-clericalism or lack of

[100]Gabriel A. Zema, S.J., "Jottings in Italy," *Ecclesiastical Review* CXXXIX (1953), 95–99.

[101]*Saint Clare of Assisi.*

[102]James E. Miller, *"Taking Off the Gloves: The United States and the Italian Elections of 1948,"* *Diplomatic History* VII (1983), 33–55.

[103]For an example of this new image, *see* Richard J. Cushing, "Italian Immigrants," *Catholic Mind* LII (1954), 604–609.

support for Catholicism. No longer was Catholicism accused of fostering loyalty to a foreign temporal power. The three identities together created a new identity for a third generation of Italian American Catholics.

8

A Third Generation

The next major event in the New York Italian community after World War II was probably Vatican II, which took place from 1962 to 1965. The time periods between World War II and Vatican II and between Vatican II and the present contain two sorts of problems for historians.

The years 1945–1965 have recently become of interest to American Catholic historians. Church bulletins and other documents that might be considered ephemeral still need to be collected, and interviews need to be done with those who lived through the times. Historiographical work also needs to be done. Much of the work on American Catholicism and Vatican II presents both in a monolithic way. However, Vatican II can be divided into units (e.g., the liturgy, the laity, the Oriental-rite churches), each unit with its own influence. American Catholicism can also be broken down into communities differentiated by factors such as class, age, and ethnicity. The issues confronting a history from Vatican II to the present include a problem in structuring the narrative. The present is not an absolute watershed; it is just the end of the story for now.

This narrative, then, cannot finish conclusively. What it can do is sketch out the trends in studying the period since World War II, and suggest ways to identify what might be of continuing importance.

Demographic Shifts

Fluctuations in income caused many of the other changes in New York's Italian parishes. People with money supported their churches better than people without. However, people with more money moved away from one parish to another parish where they liked the housing. Parishes in neighborhoods where the housing was perceived as unsuitable, and parishes which had to offer social services that did not generate income easily (it could be difficult to get parents to donate for a school; however, there might be no one even to ask to give money for a senior citizens' program) had to develop new fundraisers.

Some priests discussed the changes in income in their parishes explicitly. The parishes along the Bowery, for example, experienced financial instability. As early as 1940, the Jesuits noticed an increase in the number of "panhandlers" knocking on the rectory door at Nativity, a block east of the Bowery.[1] In 1947, one curate described Nativity as "financially stable" and "poor."[2] By this time, Nativity's neighbor, Our Lady of Loreto, a block west from the Bowery, had ceased being an Italian parish and had become a center for missionary activity among homeless men. For Our Lady of Pompei on Bleecker Street, which did not experience the removal of old buildings and their replacement by government housing stigmatized as being for those with low incomes, the decline in parish income became serious a generation later, in the 1960s.[3]

Other priests commented not that their parishes were getting poorer but that they were getting smaller. As early as the 1920s, parishes such as Our Lady of Sorrows on Stanton Street, with little decent affordable housing within their boundaries, noticed that as the Italians acquired the money for better housing, they moved to other neighborhoods where that housing was available.[4] In the 1930s, government housing projects reinforced certain neighborhoods' identities as financially disadvantaged and led people with economic resources to go elsewhere for housing. In January 1943, George P. Barbera, S.J., curate at Nativity on Second Avenue, reported to his provincial superior declining attendance at mass, confession, and Miraculous Medal devotions. Barbera at first attributed the smaller congregations to tension among the Jesuits spilling over to the parishioners. "On second reflection," he also mentioned that "because of the building of many housing projects, many of our parishioners have moved [and] now live in Astoria, Corona, and Coney Island."[5] Nativity's baptism register confirmed Barbera's observation. Someone at Nativity in the 1930s carefully updated the baptismal register to include information on the subsequent marriages of the persons listed therein. In 1918, Nativity baptized 208 souls, most of them Italian. Of those entries, 57 were updated to include information about marriages which took place a generation later, in the 1930s and 1940s. Twelve married at Nativity, five at other Lower East Side parishes, two in other Manhattan parishes, but 22 in Brooklyn and eighteen on Staten Island, in the Bronx, in New Jersey, and elsewhere in New York State.[6]

[1] Di Maria to Father Provincial, New York, 20 February 1940, NYSJ Nativity 1933–1947 Folder.

[2] Barbera to Father Provincial, New York, 25 August 1947, ibid.

[3] Brown, *Italian Villages to Greenwich Village*, chapter 10.

[4] *Our Lady of Sorrows* (South Hackensack, New Jersey: Custombook, 1967), unpaginated.

[5] Barbera to Father Provincial, New York, 27 January 1943, NYSJ Nativity 1933–1947 Folder.

[6] Baptismal Register, Church of the Nativity, New York City, entries for 1918. Access courtesy of the Reverend Nicholas Connolly, S.J.

Losses in the older Little Italies of the Lower East Side, Greenwich Village, and East Harlem meant gains in the newer Italian communities in the suburbs. The clergy at Our Lady of Mount Carmel in White Plains were careful to note exactly where candidates for marriage in their church had been baptized. All of the persons who married in 1903 had been baptized in Europe: seventeen in southern Italy and one in Poland. By 1913, the marriage register indicated marriage candidates migrated shorter distances: three of the 64 persons married that year were baptized at Our Lady of Mount Carmel on East 115th Street. Of the 64 persons married in 1923, two were from the East 115th Street Mount Carmel, and one from that Mount Carmel's East Harlem neighbor, Saint Ann on East 110th Street. The rivulet of migrants from East Harlem was still apparent in the 1943 marriage register.[7]

The East Harlem Italians could have chosen White Plains because they had relatives there. They could also have chosen White Plains because they had easy transportation there. The commuter railroad from Grand Central Station to the northern New York City suburbs stopped at East 125th Street. One reason why so many Nativity parishioners married in Brooklyn was that the two places were linked by a short subway ride. Saint Joseph's on Staten Island noticed that its post-World War II boom began in 1964 after the Verrazano Narrows Bridge joined Staten Island with Brooklyn.[8]

Other priests noticed their parishes' shifting age profiles. North Bronx parishes were overwhelmed not so much by migrants from Manhattan Little Italies as they were by children. Parishes hastened to build schools before the post-World War II babies reached kindergarten age. Saint Clare of Assisi on Rhinelander Avenue opened its school in 1951. Saint Lucy on Mace Avenue and Saint Theresa of the Infant Jesus on Saint Theresa Avenue opened theirs in 1955. Our Lady of Mount Carmel on Belmont Avenue opened a new school in 1946 and had to expand it in 1956.[9] Even Nativity on Second Avenue revived its dreams of a parochial school.[10]

The new generation caused special concern in parishes in low-income districts. Parents and pastors worried that adolescent boys might take to crime to supplement their incomes and acquire a glamorous status among their peers. Inner-city parishes devoted funds and personnel to preventing juvenile delinquency. Both Greenwich

[7]Marriage Register, Our Lady of Mount Carmel, White Plains, New York, 1903–1943.

[8]*Church of Saint Joseph . . . 1902–1977.*

[9]Borgatti, *Our Lady of Mount Carmel Parish . . . 1906–1956.*

[10]"Statement of Financial Condition," and attached papers, typescript, 31 December 1946, NYSJ Nativity 1933–1947 Folder.

Village parishes had programs for young men. Our Lady of Pompei had a Maria Goretti Club, which, despite its female name, was for adolescent boys.[11] The Franciscans at Saint Anthony of Padua sponsored a football team to encourage youngsters to work out their frustrations through socially acceptable contact sports. An article on the team included a photograph, unfortunately irreproduceable, of the pastor, in his Franciscan habit, sandals, and rosary beads, standing tall among a group of short, helmeted youths, demonstrating a long pass.[12]

The Manhattan Little Italies participated in the baby boom, but when families increased past the point where they could be easily housed in the small apartments available in those neighborhoods, and when family income increased, the young families moved out and the average age increased. During most of the history of Italian American Catholicism, the particular needs of older people were met in the course of regular parish activities. As the number of Italian speakers dwindled and interest in Italian saints waned, the elderly emerged as a special group, clustered at the Italian-languages masses and the older devotional services. In the 1970s, parishes took up the senior citizens' apostolate. In 1971, Our Lady of Pompei on Bleecker Street inaugurated a lunch program for its older parishioners.[13] Saint Anthony of Padua on Sullivan Street had similar programs for its elderly.[14] In 1975, Saint Lucy's on Mace Avenue assigned an Italian priest to say mass and otherwise serve the parish's Italian-speaking senior citizens.[15]

A third group of priests noticed the change in their Italian parishes' ethnic profiles. The changes at Transfiguration were earliest and most dramatic. In the 1880s, Jacob Riis caught Transfiguration's façade in the frame of photograph of Chinatown.[16] Although in the 1890s pastor Thomas P. McLoughlin spent much of his time fretting about his Italian parishioners his biographer eschewed McLoughlin's Italian ministry in favor of a chapter on his adventures in Chinatown.[17] In 1902, the archdiocese gave Transfiguration to the Salesians because

[11]Brown, *Italian Villages to Greenwich Village*, chapter 9.

[12]"A Priest's Campaign Against Delinquency," *Jubilee* (November 1959).

[13]Brown, *Italian Villages to Greenwich Village*, chapter 11.

[14]Donald Tricarico, "The Italians of Greenwich Village: The Social Structure and Transformation of an Ethnic Community" (Ph.D. dissertation, New School for Social Research [NY], 1980), 309–310.

[15]*Saint Lucy's Church, Bronx, New York*, 27.

[16]Riis, *How the Other Half Lives*, 79.

[17]Peter McLoughlin, *Father Tom: Life and Lectures of Rev. Thomas P. McLoughlin* (New York: G.P. Putnam's Sons, 1919), 77–103.

that religious order was prepared to minister to Italians. By 1923, the Salesians were expanding their apostolate to include the Chinese.[18] The Chinese increased in number after World War II, and in 1950, the Salesians relinquished Transfiguration to the Maryknoll Missionaries, an American community with experience in China. According to the parish historian, the Italians were as apprehensive about the Salesians' departure as the Irish had been about the archdiocesan priests' departure almost a half-century earlier, taking it as a sign Transfiguration was soon to be completely Chinese.[19]

In the 1950s, as the area east of the Bowery evolved into the Loisida, the Jesuits' Italian mission evolved into a Puerto Rican mission. Pastor Francis Doino's first comments on his new parishioners revealed a combination of new tolerance for racial diversity and an old fear of Protestant proselytizing:

> In our endeavor to get interracial justice we cannot afford to neglect or by-pass this very large portion of our own Catholic vineyard. If we lose these already baptized Catholics to the Church our enemies will surely welcome their immense numbers in our midst by hook or crook . . . .[20]

The Jesuits searched among the members of their order for a priest well-versed in Puerto Rican culture.[21] They then created a lay committee of 25 men, carefully chosen to provide leadership for the Hispanic community, to begin the process of integrating the Puerto Ricans into this Italian parish.[22]

Both Chinese and Hispanics came to Saint Joseph's on Catherine Street. The same Scalabrinians who had ministered to the Italians remained to serve all three groups. The parish historian, at least, was determined to avoid having the Italians do unto others as had been done unto them. He or she looked forward to the day when the Chinese had one mass each week, instead of the monthly mass they had in the 1970s. "Unlike the Italian immigrants who were turned away from other ethnic churches, these groups will not be turned away by Saint Joseph's."[23]

Post-World War II Portuguese immigrants settled in Greenwich Village and affiliated with Saint Anthony of Padua. Saint Anthony himself had been born in

[18]John Voghera, S.D.B., to "Dear Sir," New York, 14 June 1923, CMS IAR, Box 6, Miscellaneous Letters Folder.

[19]*Transfiguration Church: A Church of Immigrants, 1827-1977* (New York: Privately printed, 1977), unpaginated.

[20]Francis D. Doino, S.J., to John J. McMahon, S.J., New York, 2 February 1952, NYSJ Nativity 1948–1959 Folder.

[21]McMahon to John J. Quinn, S.J., New York, 31 August 1953, ibid.

[22]McMahon to Walter Janer, S.J., New York, 21 and 23 September 1953, ibid.

[23]*Fiftieth Anniversary, Saint Joseph's Church*, 13.

Lisbon and had a following among Portuguese. More importantly, the Franciscans provided a Portuguese-speaking friar. The Portuguese experience at Saint Anthony resembled the Italian experience at the same parish in the nineteenth century. The Italians kept the Portuguese at arm's length, and criticized them for insufficient interest in their parish. By the 1970s, the Portuguese gathered themselves into a parish-within-a-parish, much like the Italian annex congregations before World War I.

The newcomers of Harlem were African American and Hispanic. Black Harlem began a little later than Italian Harlem; Spanish Harlem dated from World War I. The presences of African Americans may have done as much as rising income to stimulate Italian movement out of Harlem; however, the Italian Catholic parishes' records did not reflect the African American or Hispanic presence until after World War II. By the 1960s, some Italian Harlem parishes offered one Spanish mass on Sundays.[24] Spanish-speaking Augustinian clergy took Holy Rosary on East 119th Street.

Hispanic *barrios* also appeared in the South Bronx, where the Italians' hold was weakest. Here, the lack of Spanish-speaking secular clergy and the surplus of parishes with dwindling Italian congregations led the chancery to invite Spanish orders to the Bronx mission. Spanish-speaking Augustinians took over the work at Saint Rita of Cascia.

The North Bronx Hibernianized. Saint Philip Neri in Bedford Park had always had Irish-American Italian-speaking pastors to satisfy both ethnic groups in its congregation. After 1944, the pastor was selected without reference to his fluency in Italian.[25] Saint Anthony's on Commonwealth Avenue had Italian-surnamed pastors until 1946.[26]

Our Lady of Pompei on Bleecker Street may have pioneered a new trend, ministering to ethnic groups that did not settle in the immediate area. In September 1988, a Filipino priest took up residence in Pompei's rectory and began ministering to the Filipino Catholics who actually lived elsewhere but traveled to Greenwich Village via public transportation and private car.[27] By the early 1890s, Pompei also attracted Catholics of Vietnamese and Cambodian background willing to travel to the parish to worship with their ethnic community.

[24]Patricia Caye Sexton, *Spanish Harlem* (New York: Harper and Row, 1965), 73–76.

[25]Hanley, *Golden Jubilee of Saint Philip Neri Church, 1898–1948.*

[26]*Dedication of Convent of Church of Saint Anthony . . . 1964* (New York: Privately printed, 1964), unpaginated.

[27]New York *Philippine News*, 17-13 September 1988 and 12–18 October 1988.

Saint Anthony on Sullivan Street reported, in addition to the changes in parishioners' numbers, age, and ethnicity, a change in their class status. Artists came to Greenwich Village in the 1950s and 1960s, attracted by the cheap rents and the SoHo loft space. Then came the *nouveau riche*, drawn by the Village's bohemian reputation, landmark buildings, convenient location, and cultural opportunities. Saint Anthony's people and clergy studied the artists and their associates carefully. On the one hand, an influx of wealthy people heralded a neighborhood revival. On the other hand, the new people's customs were reported to be stranger than those practiced by any ethnic group.[28] As it turned out, the most important factor was that few of the newcomers were practicing Catholics, and those that were preferred the atmosphere at New York University's campus ministry or at Saint Joseph's on Sixth Avenue, the Village's oldest parish and one with a long history of interest in social justice issues outside the immediate parish community.

An area awaiting suitable methodologies for study is the possibility of modernization of the Italians' traditional gender division of labor. Observations at New York's historically Italian churches are only so helpful. One can see a variety of men exhibiting a variety of religious behaviors (attending church by sitting up front and saying prayers, attending church by sitting in the back and appearing withdrawn, or assisting with the service by ushering, reading from the Scriptures, leading the music or administering communion), but one cannot tell if these men are typical of all Italian men, or even if these men consider themselves Italian. Nicholas J. Russo's dissertation on generational change in Italian American religious practice, done in the mid-1960s before the outburst in gender studies, did not include much on this issue.[29] Salvatore La Gumina's collection of interviews includes some references, but it was not a well-developed topic.[30]

Devotional Shifts

The devotion which is most fully identified with the Italians and which has left the largest body of accessible historical records is the *festa*. In one sense, the historical record shows how the *festa* came to be identified with Italians, rather than being from the start an Italian devotion, and came to be a sort of Italian American Catholic public relations and fundraising device.

[28]Tricarico, "Italians of Greenwich Village," 305–307.

[29]Nicholas John Russo, "The Religious Acculturation of the Italians in New York City" (Ph.D. dissertation, Saint John's University [New York], 1968), 219–287.

[30]La Gumina, *The Immigrants Speak*, 131, 184. Peter Occhiogrosso, *Once a Catholic* (New York: Houghton-Mifflin, 1987), 96–111 includes an interview with an New York Italian Catholic male, but hardly a typical one – Martin Scorsese.

Until the 1950s, Saint Anthony on Sullivan Street celebrated only the indoor devotions of the thirteen Tuesdays and novenas to their patron. In 1956, under financial pressure, pastor Arthur Lattanzi, O.F.M., added an outdoor *festa*, scheduled for the days before the June 13 feast day. During the day, the parish sponsored devotions: the novena, the blessing of the sick, the distribution of blessed lilies and bread. In the evening, it sponsored a street fair and bazaar. The parish added a procession at the close of the affair, but it featured benediction rather than a display of the saint's statue.[31]

Our Lady of Pompei's *festa* evolved quickly. There are no records of outdoor feast day celebrations at Pompei in the early twentieth century. In 1973, pastor James Abbarno, C.S., proposed adding one. Pompei had recently suffered rapid depopulation, and those who remained needed senior citizens' and youth services, so the *festa* was a way of attracting money to fund the community social services the parish provided. A *festa* sponsored by a parish and managed by parishioners might circumvent a problem which had come up in other New York area Italian celebrations. The 1971 Italian American Unity Day observance had been marred by the shooting of its organizer, Joseph Columbo. Columbo was reputedly involved in organized crime. Police speculated that his interest in Italian-American ethnic celebrations stemmed from a desire to tar law-enforcement officials' investigations of him as just another example of the stereotype of Italian male criminality, and that he had been shot at his own celebration by a rival for control of criminal activities.[32] Pompei scheduled its first *festa* to coincide with the feast of the parish patron, Our Lady of the Rosary. This was in early October, and presented the problem of holding an outdoor event during unpredictable weather. In 1977, the parish moved its *festa* to mid-July, to take advantage of the more predictable summer weather and the presence of summer tourists. Although the church remained open during the *festa* and volunteers were on hand to answer questions and to sell religious items the main events were out on the street and among the games of chance conducted in the parish auditorium.[33]

Other parishes furnish examples of the same process by which the *festa* became an increasingly secularized event. Our Lady of Mount Carmel in White Plains ceased holding its traditional *festa* about 1952. It revived the custom in 1977 as part of its diamond jubilee and the golden anniversary of its chapel, Assumption. The new *festa* was linked to the past, not the supernatural. The attractions

[31]New York *Villager*, 7 June 1956.

[32]*The New York Times*, 29 June 1971, 1:1, 20:5 and 6.

[33]Denise Mangieri DiCarlo, "The History of the Italian *Festa* in New York City: 1880's to the Present" (Ph.D. New York University, 1990), 216–221.

advertised in newspapers were not religious, but homemade sausages, peppers, meatballs, pizza, fried dough, calzone, and Italian nuts and ice cream. The reformed *festa* became a way to share the Italian heritage with non-Italians.[34]

In other parishes, the *festa* remained a religious event, but still underwent transformations. In the 1950s, Saint Clare of Assisi on Rhinelander Avenue commemorated the completion of its parochial school with a "huge parade" involving "practically every member of the parish." Italians recognized the outdoor religious procession, and non-Italians recognized the "huge parade" aspect.[35] In the 1980s, Our Lady of Mount Carmel on East 115th Street attracted a new generation of immigrants from the Caribbean to its century-old *festa*.

The more private devotions left fewer records, but the records that are there are suggestive. On December 3, 1963, the Second Vatican Council published its Constitution on the Sacred Liturgy. Section 13 discussed paraliturgical devotions in these words:

> Popular devotions of the Christian people are warmly commended, provided they accord with the laws and norms of the Church. Such is especially the case with devotions called for by the Apostolic See.
>
> Devotions proper to individual churches also have a special dignity if they are conducted by mandate of the bishops in accord with customs or books lawfully approved.
>
> Nevertheless these devotions should be so drawn up that they harmonize with the liturgical seasons, accord with the sacred liturgy, are in some fashion derived from it, and lead the people to it, since the liturgy by its very nature far surpasses any of them.[36]

The American Catholic press began to predict a sea change in religious practice, as focus changed from private prayer to the public liturgy. Some people looked forward to it, thinking of the traditional pious practices as being associated with an uneducated view of Catholicism. Some people feared the passing of everything that had helped maintain the faith in the past. The prospect of changing devotional habits had particular implications for Italians, who had long been thought of as focusing on the paraliturgical rather than the liturgical.

Our Lady of Pompei on Bleecker Street preserved a collection of parish bulletins from the 1960s and 1970s. The bulletins from the period of the Vatican Council itself, which were monthly magazines compiled by a commercial company, did not discuss the council in any detail. The schedule from that time period reflected minimal change. When Catholics began celebrating the mass in the

---

[34]White Plains, New York, *Reporter Dispatch*, 8 July 1977, D:13:1.

[35]*Year Book Commemorating the Silver Jubilee of the Parish of Saint Clare of Assisi . . . 1930–1955.*

[36]Walter M. Abbott, S.J., editor, *The Documents of Vatican II* (New York: American Press, 1966), 13.

vernacular rather than in Latin, Pompei was ready. The church had long had a schedule which indicated which masses had English and which had Italian sermons; now the whole mass, rather than the sermon, was in the appropriate language. The schedule of perpetual novenas remained the same: Monday was for the Miraculous Medal and Mother Cabrini, Tuesday for Saint Anthony of Padua, Wednesday for Saint Rita, Thursday for an Italian-language devotion to Mother Cabrini, Friday for the Blessed Sacrament, and Saturday for Our Lady of Pompei. Vatican II had its greatest impact on the parish in 1974, when in the course of making necessary repairs the pastor introduced alterations in the church's decoration and explained these alterations in decoration as being in accord with Vatican II. However, the only change in the schedule was to shift the perpetual novenas from the early evening to the lunch hour (to attract area workers and senior citizens who went out only during the daylight hours), and to add a devotion to Saint Jude. In 1985, the parish had to repair its ceiling again, and restored the decorations that had been there from 1937 to 1974. Only mass in the vernacular remained.

After World War II, two Italian women were canonized as saints. The first was Mother Frances Xavier Cabrini, who had been born in 1850, died in Chicago in 1917, and was recognized as a saint in 1946 and as patroness of immigrants in 1950. New York's Little Italies were full of places sacred to Mother Cabrini's memory. She began her missionary career at Saint Joachim's on Roosevelt Street in 1889. Her sisters taught at Transfiguration on Mott Street, catechized at Our Lady of Pompei on Bleecker Street, staffed Columbus Hospital, and ran an orphanage. Most of her mortal remains are in a chapel in Washington Heights, near a girls' high school run by her order. Appropriately, many Italian parishes erected shrines to her. However, her cult was not limited to Italians, as she was the patroness of all immigrants, and especially honored in the United States as the first citizen to be named a Roman Catholic saint. The Archdiocese of New York erected a parish under her patronage, on Roosevelt Island rather than in a traditionally Italian district.

The second woman was actually a twelve-year-old adolescent, Maria Goretti, who died in 1902 of stab wounds inflicted during an attempted rape. In 1950, she was recognized as a saint. Saint Clare of Assisi on Rhinelander Avenue named a chapel for her. Our Lady of Pompei dedicated its adolescent boys' club to her.[37] She was also used as a model of sexual purity for non-Italian adolescents.

The most complete study of New York Italian devotional practices is Nicholas J. Russo's unpublished sociology dissertation. However, with the benefit of

[37]*Year Book Commemorating the Silver Jubilee of the Parish of Saint Clare of Assisi . . . 1930–1955.*

hindsight, it is easy to see a place where current researchers might find a difficulty with Russo. Russo concluded in his study that the longer the Italians remained in American, the more closely they came to resemble the Irish whose practices he took as an American Catholic norm. However, he collected his survey data in the wake of Vatican II, and did not factor the council into his statistical analysis. Hence it is difficult to tell if the Italians assimilated to the Irish, or if Irish and Italians together assimilated to Vatican II. Given the findings that Vatican II had little effect on devotional life at Pompei, it is also difficult to say if Vatican II affected Irish and Italian piety, or if some other factor (age, class, gender) shaped religious life.

Italian National Parishes Become History

As the comments on Russo's study indicate, assimilation theory has a history of its own. The pioneer thesis of what happened when immigrants arrived in the United States first appeared in Oscar Handlin's 1951 book, The Uprooted. Handlin's study pictures the immigrants as being plucked from peasant villages by the bewildering forces of overpopulation, agricultural decline, and industrialization. Nothing in their rural, communal experience prepared them for life as autonomous, anonymous members of the urban, industrial working class. The institutions they erected to maintain their culture—ghetto neighborhoods, ethnic theatres, foreign-language presses, ward politics—actually furthered their Americanization. Immersed in American culture, the immigrants had no choice but to assimilate.[38]

The "uprooted" thesis has undergone such tremendous alterations that in 1985 John Bodnar titled his survey of nineteenth- and twentieth-century immigration not The Uprooted but The Transplanted.[39] Numerous specialists in Italian migration have produced monographs that support Bodnar's contentions. Rudolph J. Vecoli held up The Uprooted to the light of his own research among Chicago's Italians, and has found the theses do not apply.[40] John Briggs has demonstrated cultural continuity among Italians in Rochester and Utica, New York, and Kansas City, Missouri.[41] Virginia Yans-McLaughlin has show how Italians adapted their

[38]Oscar Handlin, The Uprooted: The Epic Story of the Great Migrations that Made the American People (New York: Grosset and Dunlap, 1951).

[39]John Bodnar, The Transplanted: A History of Immigrants in Urban America (Bloomington: Indiana University Press, 1985).

[40]Rudolph J. Vecoli, "Contadini in Chicago: A Critique of The Uprooted," Journal of American History LI (1964), 404-417.

[41]John W. Briggs, An Italian Passage: Immigrants in Three American Cities (New Haven: Yale University Press, 1978).

traditional family and work patterns to new conditions, in Buffalo, New York.[42] Judith Smith did the same for Italian migrants to Providence, Rhode Island. Miriam Cohen made "family strategies" a main theme in her work on two generations of Italian women in New York City.

More recent work by historians such as Kathleen Cozens and George Pozzetta and sociologists such as Richard Alba and Mary Waters have confirmed two elements of the "transplanted" thesis. First, their research reinforces Bodnar's finding that ethnic traits persist through several generations; contrary to "melting pot" or "uprooted" imagery, ethnic groups indeed transplanted some aspects of their culture. Second, immigrants deliberately picked and chose among cultural elements, selecting what to keep from the Old World and what to accept of the New World, and taking steps to act on their choices.[43] New research adds a new question though: how significant to overall ethnic identity are the elements which are preserved? The Italians, for example, have lost the history of radical politics represented by Carlo Tresca and kept their cuisine.[44] This recent research is reminiscent of a passage in John Higham's classic *Strangers in the Land*. In the early twentieth century, according to Higham, some reformers encouraged immigrants to preserve their culture and to find ways to present their heritage to people outside their ethnic group. Underneath this activity lay the thesis that all immigrant groups had some gift to bring to America. Perhaps the "immigrant gift" thesis sounded more welcoming than a "melting pot" or an "uprooted" thesis. On the other hand, as Higham noted: "When examples of specific gifts came to mind, they turned out invariably to be things to which Americans attached slight importance: folk dances, music, exotic dishes, handicrafts, perhaps certain literary fragments."[45]

Assessing the Italians' degree of assimilation or cultural preservation is more complex because whether they assimilated or preserved their culture, they did it in a Catholic setting, so one must know something about American Catholic historiography as well as migration historiography. Just as migration histiography divides into two broad schools, "uprooted" and "transplanted," American Catholicism also divides into two broad schools.

[42]Virginia Yans-McLaughlin, *Family and Community: Italian Immigrants in Buffalo, 1880–1930* (Ithaca: Cornell University Press, 1977).

[43]Kathleen Neils Conzen, *et al.*, "The Invention of Ethnicity: A Perspective from the USA," *Altreitali* III (April 1990), 37–62.

[44]Mary C. Waters, *Ethnic Options: Choosing Identities in America* (Berkeley: University of California Press, 1990).

[45]Higham, *Strangers in the Land: Patterns of American Nativism, 1860–1925*, 122.

The older school might be called that of "American Catholicism," after John Tracy Ellis's survey of the sujbect. The "American Catholicism" narrative makes it clear Spanish and French Catholics had developed colonies in America before the English Protestants even started, but its real narrative begins with English Catholics in Maryland. Wealthy, educated, and influential Maryland Catholics made Catholicism an American religion right from the start. However, the tradition they initiated was overshadowed by three other developments. First, Catholics were numerically small and belonged to a religion other English people suspected; they were targets for prejudice and discrimination. Second, the immigrant Catholics who came in the nineteenth and twentieth centuries overwhelmed the American Catholics with their own version of the faith. Third, Rome did not appreciate the American contribution to the universal Church until the mid-twentieth century. In the "American Catholic" narrative, Vatican II functions as a dramatic turning point. By Vatican II, the immigrants had successfully assimilated, and American theologians such as John Courtney Murray, drawing on the American Catholic traditions begun in Maryland and continued by a minority through the difficult nineteenth and twentieth centuries, led the ecumenical council toward a new understanding of religious liberty.[46] Ellis took the long view. A more recent historical school has also taken Vatican II as the dramatic turning point, but rather than starting with the colonies and working their way forward, it starts with Vatican II and work their way backward, studying changes American Catholicism as precursors to the council.[47]

The second and more recent school of thought might be called "the immigrant church," after Jay P. Dolan's pathbreaking monograph. In the "immigrant church narrative," immigration did not bury the American Catholic tradition for over a century; it became the tradition. American Catholicism incorporated not just the immigrants, but their devotional patterns and their approach to issues such as social justice or education. Dolan formulated his model in his work with Irish and German immigrants. As can be seen in the chapter on the "Italian problem," there has been discussion of whether the Italians fit the model. Silvano Tomasi might say they did because, although their coreligionists discriminated against them, the Italians did ask for and get national parishes and clergy who spoke their language and knew their customs; they then used their parishes to preserve their heritage. Historians such as Henry Browne and Stephen Michael Di Giovanni might say

[46]John Tracy Ellis, *American Catholicism*, second edition (Chicago: University of Chicago Press, 1969).

[47]There is no survey text which takes this point of view. However, one can often see it in articles in journals such as *U.S. Catholic Historian*.

the Italians did not fit Dolan's model; the American hierarchy supplied the national parishes, invited the religious orders, and provided the conditions for sustaining the immigrants' faith. Rudolph Vecoli might also say they did not, because southern Italian Catholicism was more a matter of folk culture than of parish structure. One scholarly exchange illuminates well the different schools of thought. When sociologist Francis X. Femminella suggested that the Italians, with their emphasis on lay community responsibility for religious life, contributed to an American Catholicism that was ready to implement the teaching of Vatican II, sociologist Andrew M. Greeley responded that the Italians had nothing to do with it: if Americans were ready for Vatican II, it was because Irish and German immigrants had entered the middle class and gone to college, where they were educated in issues such as liturgical reform and social justice.[48]

The research presented here argues for precise stages of assimilation. Some specific vocabulary is needed to understand the first stage. Although contemporary American Catholics use "parish" and "community" interchangeably, it might help to distinguish between them in the Italians' case. Membership in a community was based on residence in a town or village, and the Italians continued that sense of campanilismo in New York. Although national parishes had permission to minister to all who needed their linguistic skills, membership in a parish was generally based on residency in a particular section of New York. Communities had distinct duties for men and women; parishes had distinct duties for clergy and laity. Communities spent their money and effort on feste. Parishes spent theirs on maintaining the parish plant, conducting the liturgy, sponsoring an educational institution for youngsters, and distributing charity. The Italians did not automatically cease being members of a community and start being members of a parish, but upon immigration, the die was cast. If the Italians were going to be considered Catholics, it was within the framework of the parish system, financed by lay contributions, under clerical leadership. When Italians turned to parishes, they found the space to preserve their devotions and customs, but it was no longer the old communal arrangement.

The second stage began as soon as there were sufficient numbers of Italian children to initiate it. While the children were young, the parents attempted to bind them to their faith and their ethnic group. This meant becoming more immersed in American Catholic structure, erecting parochial schools and inaugurating youth programs. It also meant becoming more immersed in American Catholic culture, so that the parish sponsored American devotions and American

---

[48]Francis X. Femminella, "The Impact of Italian Migration and American Catholicism," American Catholic Sociological Review XXII (1961), 233–241; and Andrew M. Greeley, "The Impact of Italian Migration and American Catholicism," American Catholic Sociological Review XXII (1961), 333.

social events. Again, the transition was not made overnight, but the die was cast. The Italian parishes had "their" youth programs, but the programs copied those of other parishes. In this stage, American Catholic reorganization furthered the Americanization process. When in the name of efficient financing, the Archdiocese of New York established Catholic Charities, they reduced the importance of parish charity and took over a function performed by national parishes and ethnic benevolent groups. Thus they tied Catholics not to their parishes, with the particular ethnic histories, but to the archdiocese.

The third stage began as the youngsters grew up. The third generation then furthered the process of selecting which Italian customs to continue and which to discard, and they did so in the American structure of the parish and according to their Americanized tastes. They reduced the use of Italian in parish activities, ceased celebrating some saints' days, and transformed others into fundraisers. This particular stage can keep going as long as successive generations come to maturity, take their heritage from generation immediately before them, and go through the same process of selection.

If migration and pastoral care were indeed history—dead and gone—this book could stop here. However, migration seems to be a constant in human history: Italian migration may have slowed, but other groups have begun to migrate. Pastoral care is an ongoing issue. What does this research have to say about the desireability and practicality of various methods of pastoral care?

The historical actors who were the chief exponents of a distinctly American Catholicism tended to argue that the best form of pastoral care was to encourage uniform American Catholic practice. This turned out to be impractical: immigrants did not assimilate fast enough. Critics from Michael Augustine Corrigan to Joseph Varacalli have questioned whether it was desireable: could American Catholicism be Roman Catholicism, sufficiently united to the universal church, obedient to the hierarchy, and attentive to Church teaching?

The "immigrant church" approach seems to have been practical in the past. It was an efficient way to handle linguistic and cultural differences. Andrew Greeley has questioned whether it remains practical today, when there is a shortage of clergy and sisters, let alone those that speak various languages, and when costs make building new churches and maintaining old ones difficult.[49]

Insofar as the desireability of immigrant churches are concerned, so far, no one seems to have publicly resurrected one old arguement against the desireability of the "immigrant church" approach. Critics of Italian parishes argued they retarded the Italians' assimilation into American Catholicism. Perhaps somewhere someone

[49]Andrew M. Greeley, *The Church, the National Parish and Immigration: Same Old Mistakes* (New York: Center for Migration Studies, 1972).

has published something to the effect that establishing parishes especially for contemporary Hispanic, Caribbean, or Asian Catholics will retard their assimilation, but it did not surface during this research – and hopefully it never will. Also, perhaps someone somewhere has published something echoing Archbishop Corrigan's sentiments that Catholicism ought to be neither American nor Irish nor German but Roman and meant it to enforce a certain uniformity of devotion, but the writing did not surface during this research.

One possible argument against the "immigrant church" approach to pastoral care is that in theory it privileges the group above the individual. The "immigrant church" is committed to maintaining faith in a particular cultural context, regardless of whether the indiviudals attending the parish are comfortable with that context. The research presented here shows that argument is a specious one. Individual choice acted as a force in parish life. After countless parents decided against teaching Italian to their offspring, after countless Catholics decided against continuning Italian pious practices, the Italian parishes removed Italian masses and devotions from their schedules. The "immigrant church" provided for individual identity in the midst of group identity. This would seem to make it a desireable strategy for pastoral care.

A more difficult problem with the "immigrant church" approach to pastoral care reflects the comments John Higham made about "immigrant gifts." The Italians could keep their particular devotions because they did not interfere with other groups' devotions. However other elements of Italian Catholicism—the gender division of labor, the importance of lay men in managing the financial aspects of community religious affairs – did interfere. It may be argued that the gender division of labor and the lay committees organizing *feste*, while they were more important structurally than the Madonnas and the saints, were not part of "real" Catholicism, and thus were good things to lose. But the fact remains that the society around the Italians, not just the Italians themselves, had a role in deciding what parts of their heritage the Italians kept and what they jettisoned.

Perhaps the best argument for the "immigrant church" is that it keeps American Catholics honest. If one is raised entirely within one culture, it is hard to separate out what is essential to the culture. On the other hand, the constant supply of immigrants, and especially the ones who have, like the Italians, such a different and complex Catholic practice, forces American Catholics to think again and again about what is intrinsic to Catholicism and what is not, or, in terms Archbishop Corrigan would have used, what is substantial and what is merely accidental. It is a constant lesson in the difference between uniformity of practice and real unity of spirit.

Appendix 1

1889 Balance Sheet for Saint Brigid's, Tompkins Square

Receipts

On hand, January 1, 1889	3,715.89
Quarterly Pew Rent	1,824.90
Weekly Pew Rent	6,703.61
Ordinary Plate Collection	4,723.70
Special Donations for Windows	1,315.00
Special Collection for Renovation	1,331.50
Collection on Consecration Day	486.00
Mission Collection	422.37
Book Sales	234.75
Net Proceeds of School Exhibit	434.50
Special Collection for Schools	845.02
Net Rents	4,780.19
Debt Paying and Catholic School Society	1,237.00
Rosary Society	153.50
Altar Society	15.20
Library	16.00
Church's Poor Boxes	335.37
Sale of Mutilated Foreign Coin	21.14
Special Collection for Seminary	191.61
Total	**$28,787.25**

(The total excludes the following special collections)

Easter and Christmas Collections	911.24
Indian and Negro Missions	94.79
Church of Saint Thomas Apostle	231.09
For the Supreme Pontiff [Peter's pence]	200.55
African Missions	52.36
Church of Father Matthew [temperance organization]	45.26
Total	**$1,535.29**

Disbursements

Interest	1,440.00
Rectory Rent	97.50
Water	60.00
Principal on Account	1,000.00
Gas for School, Church,and Rectory	330.32
Coal	445.54
Windows	2,041.40
New Pews	2,210.97
Altar (Balance [on account])	375.00
Decoration (Balance)	1,614.00
Skylights	161.23
Wire guards	184.56
Gas Fixtures	719.75
Painting Church and School	994.24
Carpenter	960.60
Church Furniture and Repairs	171.85
Rectory Furniture and Repairs	72.04
Altar Furniture, Candles, Vestments	346.46
Altar Wash	70.83
Printing	97.75
Plumbing	76.56
Sundries	169.79
Church Cleaning	313.00
Consecration Day Expenses	262.35
Discount on Mutilated Coin	6.77
Seminary Assessment	500.00
Archbishop's Dues [Cathedraticum]	200.00
Clergy Salaries	2,000.00
Outside Clergy	180.00
Maintenance	1,249.30
Tenor [to sing at mass]	144.00
Blowers [part of organ]	236.00
Other	44.85
Organist	750.92
Sexton	490.00
Assistants to Sexton	482.86
Janitor	490.00
Mission Fathers	700.00
Mission Expenses	231.10
Teachers' Salaries	4,786.11
Books	507.99
Other School Expenses	403.49
New Piano	300.00
Cash on Hand, December 31, 1889	618.02
Total	**$28,787.25**

Source: *Souvenir of the Consecration Year of Saint Brigid's Church* (New York: Privately published, 1889).

Appendix 2

Italian Parishes in the City and Archdiocese of New York Mentioned in this Text

(This list is taken from the New York City Works Progress Administration, "Inventory of the Church Archives in New York City: Roman Catholic Church, Archdiocese of New York," volume two [typescript, 1941], Catholic directories, and parish histories The parishes are listed in chronological order by borough. For each parish, the following information is provided: name, date of founding, rectory address, source of priests, existence of parochial school, source of sisters, and whether the parish has since closed.)

MANHATTAN

Saint Patrick's Old Cathedral
1809; some Italians beginning in 1870s; Italians in this parish became nucleus of Our Lady of Loreto
263 Mulberry Street
Staffed by secular clergy; pastor of Italian extraction appointed in 1940s
Parochial school founded 1817
Staffed by Sisters of Charity of Saint Vincent de Paul of New York

Transfiguration
1837; some Italians beginning in 1870s; Italians in this parish became nucleus of Most Precious Blood
29 Mott Street(At the time the Italians came to it. It had several previous addresses.)
Staffed by secular clergy from 1837 to 1902, by Salesians from 1902 to 1950, then by Maryknoll Missionaries, then by secular clergy
Parochial school founded 1858
Staffed by various orders of sisters over time

Saint Vincent de Paul
1840; some Italians by 1850s; Italians in this parish became nucleus of Saint Anthony of Padua
116 West 24th Street (at the time the Italians attended, it was on Canal Street)
Staffed by the Fathers of Mercy

Nativity
1842; some Italians by 1910s
44 Second Avenue; at the time the Italians attended, it was housed in a Greek Revival church, which had to be taken down in the 1960s.
Staffed by secular clergy from 1842 to 1917, since then staffed by the Society of Jesus

Saint Brigid
1848; some Italians by 1900s; Italians in this parish became nucleus of
Mary, Help of Christians
119 Avenue B
Staffed by secular clergy
Parochial school founded 1879
Staffed by Sisters of Charity of Mount Saint Vincent

Saint Boniface
1858; some Italians by 1910s, among whom Holy Family was formed
Church now closed, was at Second Avenue and 47th Street
Staffed by secular clergy

Saint Anthony of Padua
1859, 1866; Italian and Irish from the beginning
154 Sullivan Street; services originally at 105 Sullivan Street; present
building dedicated 1888
Staffed by the Order of Friars Minor; first friars came from Italy by way
of Saint Bonaventure College
Parochial school founded 1874
Staffed by Franciscan Sisters of Allegheny, a community founded by the
community of Franciscans that later founded the parish

Our Lady of Sorrows
1867; parish ministered to English, Italian, and German speakers in
1941
213 Stanton Street
Staffed by the Order of Friars Minor Capuchin
School founded 1874
At one time staffed by Dominican Sisters

Holy Rosary
1884; some Italians by 1910s
444 East 119th Street
Staffed by secular clergy beginning in 1884; by 1914 had a separate
rectory for Italian clergy staffing the parish; in 1925 an Italian named
pastor; in 1990s staffed by Augustinians
School founded 1949

Our Lady of Mount Carmel
1884; founded as an Italian parish
448 East 116th Street (this is the rectory; the church faces East 115th
Street)
Staffed by the Pious Society of Missionaries (now Society of the Catholic Apostolate); who came to attend to Italian immigrants
Parochial education as early as 1884
Originally staffed by Pallottine Sisters of Charity who came from Italy
for the purpose; then by the Sisters of Charity

Saint Joachim
1888; founded as an Italian parish
Church closed 1958; was at 22 Roosevelt Street
Staffed by the Society of Saint Charles

Resurrection
1889
Now closed; was on 174 Centre Street
Staffed by the Society of Saint Charles

Most Precious Blood
1891; founded as an Italian parish out of a congregation meeting at
Transfiguration
113 Baxter Street
Staffed by Society of Saint Charles from 1891 to 1894; then by the Order of Friars Minor, which had taken care of the congregation when it
met in the basement of Transfiguration

Our Lady of Loreto
1891; founded for the Sicilians in the area
Now closed; was in a converted tenement house at 303 Elizabeth Street
until late 1980s
Staffed by the Society of Jesus until 1919, then by secular clergy
Parochial school from 1895 to 1919
Staffed by Sisters of Jesus and Mary

Our Lady of Pompei
1892; founded as the chapel for the Saint Raphael Society for the Protection of Italian Immigrants
Parish met at 113 Waverly Place from 1892 to 1895; at 214 Sullivan
from 1895 to 1898; at 210 Bleecker Street from 1898 to 1927; and
since then at 25 Carmine Street
Staffed by the Pious Society of Missionaries
Parochial school founded 1930
Staffed by the Missionary Zelatrices (since 1967 Apostles) of the Sacred Heart

Saint Lucy
1900; Italian congregation by 1930s
344 East 104th Street
Staffed by secular clergy; an Italian-background priest appointed in
1932

Saint Clare
1903
Now closed, was at 436 West 36th Street
Staffed by the Order of Friars Minor
Parochial school operated from 1922 to 1936
Staffed by Franciscan sisters

Our Lady of Grace
1906
Now closed; was at 18 Stanton Street
Staffed by secular clergy of Italian-Albanian extraction; clergy and congregation spoke Italian, acknowledged the papacy, and practiced eastern-
rite liturgies

Mary, Help of Christians

1908; created out of an Italian congregation meeting at Saint Brigid's
440 East 12th Street
Staffed by Salesians of Don Bosco, who came from Italy for this purpose
Parochial school founded 1925
Staffed by Salesian sisters

Saint Ann

1911
308 East 100th Street
Staffed by Pious Society of Missions (now Society of the Catholic
Apostolate)
Parochial school founded 1928
Staffed by Maestre Pie Filippine, or Religious Teachers Filippine, who
came from Italy for that purpose

Sacred Hearts of Jesus and Mary

1914
309 East 33rd Street
Staffed by secular clergy; first pastor (Joseph Congedo) was an Italian
immigrant
Parochial school founded 1925
Staffed by Sisters of the Immaculate Heart of Mary

Saint Sebastian

1915; founded from an annex congregation which met at Epiphany par-
ish on East 22nd Street and Second Avenue
Now closed; address was 312 Second Avenue
Staffed by Salesians of Don Bosco from 1899 to 1902 (while at Epiph-
any), by secular clergy from 1902 to 1917, then by the Order of Friars
Minor

Our Lady of Peace

1918
236 East 62nd Street
Staffed by secular clergy; first pastor was from Sicily

Holy Family

1925; created out of an Italian congregation meeting at Saint Boniface
321 East 47th Street
Staffed by secular clergy; first pastor (Daniel De Nonno) was of Italian
extraction

Most Holy Crucifix

1925
378 Broome Street
Staffed by secular clergy; first pastor (Jerome Pasquarelli) was of Italian
extraction

Saint Joseph
1925; grew out of congregation at Saint Joachim
64 Catherine Street
Staffed by the Society of Saint Charles
Parochial school founded 1925
Staffed by Missionary Zelatrices (after 1967 Apostles) of the Sacred
Heart

BRONX

Saint Philip Neri
1898; founded for Italians working at the Jerome Park Reservoir
3025 Grand Concourse
Staffed by secular clergy
School founded 1913
Staffed by Ursuline Sisters of the Roman Union

Saint Roch
1899
Wales Avenue at 147th Street since 1932; prior to that at 150th Street
and Jackson Avenue
Staffed by secular clergy; first pastor (John Milo) of Italian extraction

Saint Rita of Cascia
1900
East 145th Street at College Avenue since 1904; at 152nd and Court-
landt from 1900 to 1901; at 148th and Courtlandt from 1901 to 1904
Staffed by secular clergy; first pastor (Carlo Farina) an Italian immi-
grant; now staffed by Augustinians
Parochial school founded 1914 (prior to that, catechesis provided by
Missionaries of the Sacred Heart)
Staffed by Dominican Sisters

Immaculate Conception
1903
739 Gun Hill Road at Williamsbridge; originally at 214th Street and
White Plains Avenue; then at a site opposite the present one until
1921; then, when the church burned, in temporary quarters until 1924
Staffed by secular clergy; first pastor (Giuseppe Cirriginione) from Italy; now staffed by Orders of Friar Minor Capuchin
Parochial school staffed by Pallottine Sisters of Charity

Our Lady of Mount Carmel
1906
187th Street at Belmont Avenue
Staffed by secular clergy; first pastor (Giuseppe Caffuzzi) an Italian immigrant
Parochial school founded 1925
Staffed by Pallottine Sisters of Charity

Saint Anthony
1908
Commonwealth Avenue and Mansion Street
Staffed by secular clergy; first pastor (Henry De Vivo) an Italian immigrant
Parochial school founded 1931
Staffed by Sisters of Charity of Saint Vincent de Paul of New York

Our Lady of Pity
1908
276 East 151st Street; from 1908 to 1909 at 149th Street between Morris and Courtlandt Avenues
Staffed by the Order of Friars Minor
Parochial school founded 1909
Staffed by Franciscan Sisters of the Immaculate Conception, Newton, Massachusetts

Saint Anthony
1919
4505 Richardson Avenue
Staffed by secular clergy; first pastor (Gaetano Spina) of Italian extraction
Parochial school founded 1953

Our Lady of Grace
1924
3985 Bronxwood Avenue
Staffed by secular clergy; first pastor (Victor Bassi) of Italian extraction, educated at the archdiocesan seminary
Parochial school information lacking

Saint Dominic
1924
Unionport Road and Morris Park Avenue
Staffed by secular clergy; first pastor (Dominic Fiorentino) of Italian extraction, educated at the archdiocesan seminary
Parochial school founded 1953
Staffed by Sisters of Saint John the Baptist

Santa Maria
1926
2350 Saint Raymond Avenue
Staffed by secular clergy of Italian extraction
Parochial school founded 1951
Staffed by Sister Apostles of the Sacred Heart

Saint Lucy
1927
833 Mace Avenue
Staffed by secular clergy of Italian extraction
Parochial school founded 1955
Staffed by Sisters of Saint Dominic, Blauvelt

Saint Theresa of the Infant Jesus
1927
2855 Theresa Avenue
Staffed by secular clergy; first pastor (Bonaventure Filetti) of Italian extraction, educated at archdiocesan seminary
Parochial school founded 1954
Staffed by Sisters of Saint Dominic of Sparkhill, New York

Saint Clare of Assisi
1929
1027 Rhinelander Avenue
Staffed by secular clergy; first pastor (Francis Cagina), born and educated in Italy
School founded 1951
Staffed by Oblates of Divine Love

STATEN ISLAND

Saint Joseph
1902
171 Saint Mary's Avenue (this is the rectory; the church itself is on Tompkins Avenue, Rosebank)
Staffed by secular clergy; first two pastors of Italian extraction; second pastor (Anthony Cattogio) educated at archdiocesan seminary
Parochial school information lacking
Staffed by Sisters of Saint Dominic of Blauvelt

Our Lady of Mount Carmel
1913
1286 Castleton Avenue, West New Brighton
Staffed by secular clergy; first pastor (Louis Riccio) of Italian extraction; beginning in 1929 became the mission of the neighboring parish of Blessed Sacrament

Saint Rita
1921
281 Bradley Avenue
Staffed by secular; first pastor (Emanuel Toverna) of Italian extraction; in 1937 staffed by Pious Society of Saint Paul of Alba, Italy; later returned to archdiocesan clergy
Parochial school founded 1922
Staffed by Sisters of the Roman Congregation of Saint Dominic

Assumption
1921
Brighton and Webster Avenue
Staffed by secular clergy; first pastor (Carmelo Crisci) educated and ordained in Italy
Parochial school information lacking

Saint Roch
1922
602-608 Richmond Avenue, Port Richmond
Staffed by secular clergy; first pastor (Catello Terrone) educated
Salerno
Parochial school foundation information lacking
Staffed by Sisters of Saint John the Baptist

Saint Michael and Saint Clement
1922
211-213 Harbor Road; on Van Pelt Avenue from 1922 to 1927
Staffed by secular clergy; first pastor (Emil E. Molinelli) of Italian extraction, educated at archdiocesan seminary

Our Lady of Pity
1923
1616 Richmond Avenue, Graniteville; begin in 1870 as mission of
Saint Joseph's on Amboy Road; in 1920 became mission of Our lady
of Mount Carmel; in 1923 elevated to a separate parish and met at 30
Summer Avenue; church at 1382 Richmond Avenue erected in 1924
Staffed by secular clergy; first rector (Cyrus Falco) of Italian extraction;
staffed by Pious Society of Saint Paul of Alba beginning in 1937; since
returned to archdiocesan clergy

Saint Benedicta
1925
Now closed; began as a mission of Our Lady of Mount Carmel; in
1924 building erected at Market and State Streets, West New Brighton
Staffed by archdiocesan clergy; fist pastor (Bonaventure J. Filetti) of
Italian extraction, educated at archdiocesan seminary

Holy Rosary
1927
203 Sand Lane
Staffed by secular clergy; first pastor (Dominic Epifanio) educated in Italy
Parochial school founded 1955

Christ the King
1928
192 Park Avenue
Staffed by secular clergy; originally a mission of Saint Mary the Assumption in Port Richmond; incorporated separately in 1929; first pastor (Cyrus Falco) of Italian extraction; from 1932 to 1939 again
administered by Saint Mary's; in 1939 a pastor with a non-Italian
name (Cornelius J. Hayes) appointed; now a chapel of Saint Mary's.

Appendix 3

Donations to Catholic Charities of the Archdiocese of New York Manhattan, Various Years, 1923-1930

Parish	1923	1924	1925	1929	1930
Cathedral	34,537.17	41,933.11	37,650.49	56,530.57	46,917.94
St. Agnes	12,176.82	14,000.00	12,794.97	16,583.90	13,824.97
St. Albert	551.17	665.00	605.24	619.65	418.00
St. Aloysius	8,109.05	6,729.10	4,329.25	2,207.35	1,668.75
All Saints	6,585.05	7,716.06	6,978.91	4,830.75	4,022.50
St. Alphonsus	2,583.10	2,669.15	2,193.00	1,558.70	1,321.55
St. Ambrose	2,833.10	4,305.00	3,307.25	2,005.03	1,547.70
St. Andrew	1,436.25	1,959.87	2,203.45	2,736.19	2,763.16
St. Ann (12th St.)	2,227.83	2,765.04	4,746.47	5,061.22	7,562.70
St. Ann (110th St.)	919.27	789.91	1,002.02	353.86	369.40
Annunciation	9,544.00	10,257.50	11,005.50	11,050.00	9,839.94
St. Anthony of Padua	3,142.76	3,270.60	2,960.25	3,455.85	2,532.90
Ascension	12,710.80	14,878.20	15,488.05	17,905.70	17,673.73
Assumption	2,234.00	2,522.00	1,898.75	1,064.00	891.25
St. Benedict the Moor	800.00	1,013.00	920.75	302.00	314.00
St. Bernard	10,056.51	8,553.05	10,095.69	7,942.18	6,270.19
Blessed Sacrament	15,039.00	14,577.00	15,263.30	12,620.60	12,271.75
St. Boniface	3,325.25	3,278.50	2,611.50	2,786.75	2,180.95
St. Brigid	694.55	735.00	634.25	580.00	557.40
St. Catherine of Genoa	5,637.68	9,199.75	7,453.55	8,022.85	6,581.54
St. Catherine of Sienna	2,000.00	4,311.85	3,321.18	2,287.25	1,801.78
St. Cecilia	3,886.50	4,125.00	3,314.00	3,006.25	2,590.00
St. Charles Borromeo	6,598.72	4,755.24	2,500.00	621.38	549.59
St. Clare	551.60	739.63	687.50	425.60	285.80
St. Clemens Mary	600.00	472.50	657.25	563.60	350.55
St. Columba	5,129.57	8,065.38	9,655.00	6,243.98	4,752.53
Corpus Christi	4,731.50	5,642.30	5,916.90	5,320.00	4,518.60
Ss. Cyril & Methodius	363.13	365.30	246.05	200.00	305.45
St. Cyril	482.75	408.50	453.50	309.25	205.00
St. Elizabeth	4,122.65	4,922.32	5,309.32	6,729.74	5,306.00
St. Eliz. of Hungary	156.75	169.50	256.45	558.00	442.30

Parish	1923	1924	1925	1929	1930
Epiphany	4,270.25	3,320.56	3,546.50	3,423.00	2,888.50
St. Francis de Sales	8,300.00	8,715.50	8,507.00	12,559.85	12,703.81
St. Francis of Assisi	22,990.06	3,416.30	3,795.78	5,537.76	5,411.34
St. Francis Xavier	6,779.50	8,850.90	8,257.65	6,816.52	5,874.01
St. Gabriel	8,362.25	9,994.55	7,824.05	7,005.00	4,249.20
St. George (Wash. St.)	n/a	n/a	50.00	60.00	85.00
St. George (7th St.)	155.00	165.00	66.50	n/a	n/a
Good Shepherd	4,979.85	5,108.00	5,108.00	6,121.63	5,336.00
St. Gregory the Great	11,111.35	12,066.50	12,748.25	15,732.00	17,290.00
Guardian Angel	1,723.75	2,024.50	1,666.00	2,421.25	1,899.39
Holy Cross	5,455.94	6,806.35	5,527.55	3,135.00	3,027.00
Holy Family	n/a	n/a	n/a	414.35	219.00
Holy Innocents	1,843.75	2,102.00	1,826.50	1,814.60	1,688.00
Holy Name of Jesus	16,005.00	16,441.50	3,023.25	17,184.86	16,582.59
Holy Rosary	1,156.75	1,185.85	1,154.00	1,067.00	1,078.75
Holy Trinity	27,056.25	27,615.59	34,205.42	20,240.85	19,393.46
St. Ignatius of Loyola	28,519.25	38,822.95	42,094.45	58,126.20	58,472.25
Immaculate Conception	3,982.15	4,559.85	4,014.00	3,858.00	2,945.75
Incarnation	5,512.50	8,097.70	7,058.75	7,329.29	7,142.82
St. James	2,909.00	2,893.50	2,796.50	2,361.85	1,897.55
St. Jean Baptiste	14,196.05	12,905.62	14,511.95	14,919.83	13,904.55
St. Joachim	1,361.00	n/a	n/a	720.00	602.92
St. John Nepomucene	840.65	1,076.34	1,077.85	1,222.80	1,100.49
St. John the Baptist	1,733.00	1,722.30	1,627.51	1,486.10	1,511.00
St. John the Evangelist	8,852.15	13,299.37	11,653.50	15,401.42	15,424.43
St. John the Martyr	2,362.60	2,534.90	2,779.55	2,645.30	2,690.00
St. Joseph (6th Ave.)	12,162.00	12,700.17	11,402.07	10,300.00	11,228.40
St. Joseph (87th St.)	3,824.75	2,082.90	3,765.00	3,070.40	2,749.50
St. Joseph (125th St.)	11,079.70	12,615.29	11,454.31	6,953.91	5,520.15
St. Joseph (Wash. St.)	60.00	60.00	60.00	65.00	60.00
St. Joseph (Catherine St.)	n/a	n/a	n/a	513.00	503.38
St. Lucy	1,515.00	1,473.25	1,358.00	796.30	604.00
St. Malachy	2,221.00	3,426.50	3,118.40	6,279.90	5,336.58
St. Mark the Evangelist	900.00	750.75	1,135.46	853.00	525.00
St. Mary	1,465.50	2,240.50	2,183.25	1,684.61	1,445.00
St. Mary Magdalen	226.05	212.00	159.00	295.50	331.10
St. Matthew	3,168.25	3,096.50	3,595.15	2,418.92	1,520.50
St. Michael	7,000.00	6,629.00	5,884.50	3,524.75	2,403.00
St. Monica	6,084.84	7,347.00	6,196.47	5,665.80	4,429.15
Mary, Help of Christians	1,010.40	1,112.25	1,157.75	1,270.70	1,056.35
Most Holy Curcifix	n/a	n/a	333.60	527.61	535.70

Parish	1923	1924	1925	1929	1930
Most Holy Redeemer	1,963.75	2,353.70	1,961.30	2,239.64	1,859.18
Most Precious Blood	367.00	442.15	521.30	425.05	502.15
Nativity	1,055.00	2,125.00	2,060.00	2,601.00	2,054.00
Notre Dame	3,497.85	3,341.50	4,268.00	6,754.80	3,576.45
St. Nicholas	1,022.00	1,309.50	1,387.50	1,088.00	974.33
Our Lady of Angels	1,296.86	1,191.80	842.25	820.77	718.22
O.L. of Experanza	1,996.20	1,549.00	1,786.00	2,258.00	1,824.50
O.L. of Good Counsel	7,119.05	9,590.10	7,349.80	6,037.22	4,991.97
O.L. of Guadalupe	760.00	614.50	905.10	774.86	885.00
O.L. of Loreto	1,386.18	1,252.95	1,252.95	523.35	926.13
O.L. of Lourdes	19,541.80	19,500.25	21,325.97	21,201.90	16,935.05
O.L. of Mt. Carmel	1,019.00	1,122.54	1,091.25	893.95	546.15
O.L. of Peace	1,000.00	841.93	1,047.66	682.00	699.05
O.L. of Perpetual Help	4,150.25	4,903.11	4,618.81	5,641.95	4,428.02
O.L. of Pompei	717.44	957.72	1,064.25	n/a	518.50
O.L. of Sorrows	711.85	681.41	763.30	1,045.00	1,056.50
O.L. of the Mir. Medal	n/a	n/a	n/a	1,184.75	1,190.25
O.L. of the Rosary	1,162.00	1,534.50	1,327.00	1,417.92	728.00
O.L. of the Scapular	1,737.34	1,881.40	2,323.05	1,770.90	1,845.00
O.L. of Vilna	425.00	346.45	425.00	451.00	450.00
O.L. Queen of Martyrs	n/a	n/a	n/a	1,865.80	1,884.73
St. Patrick Old Cathedral	2,234.10	2,810.00	1,711.24	1,440.42	1,317.10
St. Paul	3,361.20	4,306.45	4,880.36	4,784.96	3,857.30
St. Paul the Apostle	16,805.59	18,216.37	15,428.06	15,821.15	13,507.39
St. Peter	4,604.00	5,308.00	5,012.33	4,724.35	2,195.53
St. Raphael	3,489.95	4,891.00	4,847.05	3,217.41	2,195.53
Resurrection	7,370.00	7,805.00	5,725.61	1,308.42	1,028.00
St. Rose	1,033.30	1,229.15	1,288.00	1,175.30	1,271.38
St. Rose of Lima	8,306.95	7,962.50	8,430.39	9,018.97	8,009.45
Sacred Heart of Jesus	9,040.18	10,684.80	9,583.50	9,067.99	7,008.61
S.H. of Jesus & Mary	1,019.00	1,528.00	300.00	986.58	1,090.28
St. Sebastian	625.05	821.05	1,006.55	380.13	397.54
St. Stanislaus	1,172.70	865.00	895.00	1,880.00	1,603.00
St. Stephen	8,953.65	9,513.00	10,431.51	10,712.56	9,505.47
St. Stephen of Hungary	862.39	528.90	500.00	649.00	636.10
St. Theresa	1,100.00	1,347.50	1,174.00	897.25	623.35
St. Thomas the Apostle	12,254.36	12,777.00	11,430.84	6,045.60	4,715.22
Transfiguration	1,126.15	1,149.35	2,498.45	3,121.80	2,999.10
St. Veronica	2,583.70	2,520.25	2,498.45	2,121.80	2,999.10
St. Vincent Ferrer	16,165.01	18,115.97	19,013.28	25,878.46	34,379.70
St. Vincent de Paul	1,892.00	2,733.00	2,820.55	2,416.75	2,121.50

Sources: Catholic Charities' annual reports, 1924, 1925, 1929, and 1930, variously titled.

Appendix 4

Gaetano Salvemini's List of
New York Italian Catholic Clergy

(In the mid-1930s anti-Fascist activist Gaetano Salvemini compiled a list of New York clergy whom he accused of being fascists. To aid in the discussion in Chapter 7, this list below reproduces the Italian names. Each entry gives the priest's name, parish, and Salvemini's reasons for considering the person a fascist.)

Gaetano Arcese, Holy Rosary. No reason given.

Victor Bassi, Our Lady of Grace. Collected gold wedding bands for Mussolini; celebrated victory over Ethiopia.

Joseph A. Caffuzzi, Our Lady of Mount Carmel (Belmont). Opened Italian school; celebrated *Te Deum* (a religious service) when Mussolini escaped assassination; member of committee to honor Italo Balbo (Italian aviator).

Francis Cagnina, Saint Clare of Assisi. "His parochial school children praised by cultural agent of the consulate general."

Anthony Cattoggio, Saint Joseph (Staten Island). Chaired committee to honor Pasquale Margarella (Fascist and head of Italian Child Welfare League).

Joseph M. Congedo, Sacred Hearts of Jesus and Mary. Organized summer camp; knighted by Victor Emmanuel III; opened Italian high school; received gold medal for spreading Italian culture; received donations from Fascists for his school; participated when Federation of Apulian Associations gave bust of Mussolini to University of Bari.

Ernesto Coppo, S.D.B., Our Lady of the Rosary (Portchester; originally at Transfiguration). Official speaker when Italian Committee of North America gave Consulate General plaque commemorating tenth anniversary of March on Rome.

Antonio Demo, P.S.S.C., Our Lady of Pompei. Shareholder in *Il Carroccio*; knighted by Victor Emmanuel III.

Daniel De Nonno, Holy Family. Mass for the Unknown Italian Soldier of World War I held in his church.

Bonaventure J. Filetti, Saint Theresa of the Infant Jesus. No reason given.

Dominic J. Firorentino, Saint Dominic. Part of committee to give bust of Mussolini to Univesity of Bari.

Severino Focacci, Our Lady of Mount Carmel (Belmont). No reason given.

Germano Formica, Our Lady of Loreto and Director of Italian Auxiliary. No reason given.

Francis J. Grassi, Saint Anthony (Commonwealth Avenue). Preached on Fascism in 1924; decorated by Fascists in 1926; honorary president of *Fascio* (local group) Podesta-Priori, Bronx; member of committee to honor Italo Balbo; part of Lictor Federation; golden anniversary celebrated by playing *Fascist Italy* (a musical piece); received congratulatory telegram from Charles Coughlin; praised defeat of Ethiopia.

Vincent Jannuzzi, P.S.S.C., Saint Joachim and Saint Joseph. Shareholder in *Il Carroccio*; subject of an article in the magazine in 1924; Fascist League celebrated Mussolini's escape from assassination at Saint Joseph; member committee to honor Italo Balbo.

Giacomo Lassandro, Our Lady of Loreto. At same church as Giuseppe Silipigni.

Gregory Liucci, O.F.M., Most Precious Blood. No reason given.

Francesco Magliocco, Our Lady of Mount Carmel (Belmont). Assistant to Giuseppe Caffuzzi; shareholder in *Il Carroccio*.

Leonardo Pavone, Sacred Hearts of Jesus and Mary. Assistant to Joseph Congedo. Pro-Hitler and anti-Semitic.

Valerian Piangiani, O.F.M., Saint Anthony of Padua (Sullivan Street). No reason given.

Giuseppe Silipigni, Our Lady of Loreto. Spoke under auspices of *Fascio* of New York in 1923; fundraiser for his school held aboard an Italian ship; spoke at a dinner honoring Francis Grassi; *Fascio* Armando Cassalini organized in his church; wrote Mussolini thanking him for his part in Lateran Pact; on Italo Balbo committee; shareholder in *Il Carroccio*.

Analdo Vanoli, P.S.S.C., Saint Joachim. Shareholder in *Il Carroccio*; participant in Birthday of Rome in 1933.

John Voghera, S.D.B., Transfiguration. No reason given.

Paul Zolin, S.D.B., Mary, Help of Christians. The Lictor Association, the Francesco Crispi *Fascio*, and the Maria Jose *Fascio* held celebrations in his auditorious; *Grido della Stirpe* (a Fascist paper) received proceeds from a fundraiser he held.

Source: Gaetano Salvemini, *Italian Fascist Activities in the United States*, ed. by Philip V. Cannistraro (New York: Center for Migration Studies, 1977), 113, 145-164.

Archives and Bibliography

Archives

The Archives of the Archdiocese of New York. Saint Joseph's Seminary, Dunwoodie, Yonkers, New York, 10704. A convenient source for the parish histories listed below. It has original (and lets researchers use microfilm) copies of episcopal correspondence. It also holds a few institutional records; the Italian Apostolate reports were the major find.

Center for Migration Studies. 209 Flagg Place, Staten Island, New York, 10304. The collections used for this monograph were files pertaining to the Scalabrinians in North America, files from the National Catholic Welfare Conference, and the Italian Americans and Religion Collection, which contains photocopies and clippings from other archives.

Church of the Nativity. 44 Second Avenue, New York, New York, 10003. The clergy at Nativity during the 1930s updated the register with information on the marriages of persons baptized at the parish.

Church of the Transfiguration. 29 Mott Street, New York, New York, 10013. Transfiguration's baptismal and marriage registers go back to 1827. The years 1880–1902 were consulted.

New York Province of the Society of Jesus. 501 East Fordham Road, Bronx, New York, 10458. Correspondence between the Fathers Provincial and the pastors and curates at the Jesuits' two Italian missions, Our Lady of Loreto and Nativity.

Our Lady of Mount Carmel. 92 South Lexington Avenue, White Plains, New York, 10602. Mount Carmel's marriage register for the years 1903, 1913, 1923, 1933, and 1943 proved most helpful, as the clergy carefully noted exactly where persons being married had been baptized.

Province of the Immaculate Conception. 147 Thompson Street, New York, New York, 10012. Archives of the Immaculate Conception Province of the Order of Friars Minor. Has mostly parish histories, newspaper clippings, and some early records of Most Precious Blood, 113 Baxter Street.

Saint Patrick's Old Cathedral. 263 Mulberry Street, New York, New York, 10012. All Catholic parishes keep their own baptismal and marriage registers. Saint Patrick's go back to 1809. This study used the baptismal register for the years 1880–1902.

Bibliography

Abbott, W. M., S.J., editor
1966   *The Documents of Vatican II*. New York: America Press.

Agnew, W. H., S.J.
1913   "Pastoral Care of Italian Children in America," *Ecclesiastical Review*, 63:256–267.

Alba, R.
1985   *Italian Americans: Into the Twilight of Ethnicity*. Englewood Cliffs, NJ: Prentice-Hall.

Anonymous
1940   "Obituary: Father Daniel J. Quinn, S.J., 1864–1940," *Woodstock Letters*, 69:359–373.

1925   *Note di Cronaca sull' Origine e Progresso della Chiesa di S. Antonio*. Naples: Tipografia Pontifica M. D'Auria.

1924   "Pastoral Care of Foreign Catholics in America," *Ecclesiastical Review*, 70:176–181.

1917   "Church of the Nativity Transferred to Our Fathers," *Woodstock Letters*, 46:411–412.

1915   "La Guida del Clero Italiano di New York," *Il Carroccio*, 76–77.

1914   "The Italian Question," *America*, 12:246.

1914   "An Italian P.E. Editorial," *America*, 11:158–159.

1913   "Diocesan Bureaux for the Care of Italian, Slav, Ruthenian, and Asian Catholics in America," *Ecclesiastical Review*, 48:221–222.

1905   "Our Church for Italians," *Woodstock Letters*, 34:448–449.

1903   "Father Nicholas Russo," *Woodstock Letters*, 31:281–285.

1892   *Annual Report of the Italian Mission of the Protestant Episcopal Church in the City of New York, 1892*. New York: Privately published.

1885   *The Italian Mission of the Protestant Episcopal Church in the City of New York Yearbook.*
           New York: Privately published.

Arrighi, A.
1895   *Sixty-Ninth Annual Report.* New York: Privately printed. This is a report of the Italian
           Evangelical Church.

Barat Settlement
1915   *The Year Book of the Barat Settlement and Day Nursery.* New York: Privately printed.

1913   *The Year Book of the Barat Settlement House.* New York: Privately printed.

Barry, C. J., O.S.B.
1953   *The Catholic Church and German Americans.* Milwaukee: Bruce Publishing Company.

Battistella, G., C.S.
1986   *Itinerant Missions: Alternative Experiences in the History of the Scalabrinians in North
           America.* New York: Center for Migration Studies (Center for Migration Studies
           Occasional Papers: Pastoral Series #6). February.

Bayor, R. H.
1993   *Fiorello La Guardia: Ethnicity and Reform.* Arlington Heights, Illinois: Harlan David-
           son.

1977   *Neighbors in Conflict: The Irish, Germans, Jews, and Italians of New York City,
           1929–1941.* Baltimore: The Johns Hopkins University Press.

Beattie, F.
1919   "The Waldensian Aid Society," *America,* 21:245–247.

1919   "The Waldensian and Protestant Episcopal Entente," *America,* 21:273–275.

Billington, R. A.
1938   *The Protestant Crusade, 1800–1860: A Study of the Origins of American Nativism.* New
           York: MacMillan.

Bisceglia, J. B.
1948   *Italian Evangelical Pioneers.* Kansas City, Missouri: Brown-White-Lowell Press, Inc.

Blake, J.
1931   "The Worm that Talked," *America,* 65:399–400.

Bodnar, J.
1985   *The Transplanted: A History of Immigrants in Urban America*. Bloomington: Indiana University Press.

Borgatti, J. L. G.
1956   *Our Lady of Mount Carmel, New York, Celebrates its Golden Jubilee, 1906–1956*. New York: Privately printed.

Brace, C. L.
1978   *The Dangerous Classes of New York and Twenty Years' Work Among Them*. Montclair, New Jersey: Patterson Smith. Reprint.

Brann, H. A.
1892   "Mr. Cahensly and the Church in the U.S." *Catholic World*, 54:568–581.

Briggs, J.
1978   *An Italian Passage: Immigrants in Three American Cities*. New Haven: Yale University Press.

Brizzolara, A., C.S.
1986   "100 Days: The Visit of Bishop Scalabrini to the United States and Its Effects on the Image of Italian Immigrants as Reflected in the American Press of 1901." Unpublished M.A. Thesis, Hunter College, City University of New York.

Brown, M. E.
1993   "Italian Immigrant Clergy and an Exception to the Rule: The Reverend Antonio Demo, Our Lady of Pompei, Greenwich Village, 1899–1933," *Church History*, 42(1):41–59

———
1992   *From Italian Villages to Greenwich Village: Our Lady of Pompei, 1892–1992*. New York: Center for Migration Studies.

———
1992   "A Case Study of the Italian Laymen and Parish Life at Our Lady of Pompei, Greenwich Village, New York City." In *Italian Americans and their Public and Private Life*. Ed. F. J. Cavaioli, *et al*. New York: American Italian Historical Association, 1993. Pp. 94–102.

———
1991   "'The Adoption of the Tactics of the Enemy': The Care of Italian Immigrant Youth in the Archdiocese of New York During the Progressive Era." In *Immigration to New York*. Ed. W. Pencak, *et al*. Philadelphia, PA: The Balch Institute Press (A New-York Historical Society Book). Pp. 109–125.

———
1988   "Competing to Care: Immigrant Aid Societies for Italians in New York Harbor in the 1920s," *Mid-America*, 71:137–151.

1987   "Italian and Italian-American Secular Clergy in the Archdiocese of New York, 1880–
        1950," *U.S. Catholic Historian*, 6(4):281–300.

1987   "The Making of Italian-American Catholics: Jesuit Work on the Lower East Side, New
        York, 1890s–1950s," *Catholic Historical Review*, 73:195–210.

Browne, H. J.
1952   *Saint Ann's on East Twelfth Street, New York City, 1852–1952*. New York: Privately
        published.

1949   *The Catholic Church and the Knights of Labor*. Washington, D.C.: Catholic University
        Press.

1946   "The 'Italian Problem' in the Catholic Church of the Untied States, 1880–1900,"
        United States Catholic Historical Society *Records and Studies*, 35:46–72.

Brumberg, J. J.
1980   *Mission for Life: The Story of the Family of Adoniram Judson, the Dramatic Events of
        the first American Foreign Mission, and the Course of Evangelical Religion in the
        Nineteenth Century*. New York: Free Press.

Bukowcyzyk, J. J.
1987   *And My Children Did Not Know Me: A History of Polish Americans*. Bloomington:
        Indiana University Press.

Caliaro M., and M. Francesconi
1977   *John Baptist Scalabrini, Apostle to Emigrants*. Translated by Alba I. Zizzamia. New
        York: Center for Migration Studies.

Carey, P. W.
1987   *People, Priests, and Prelates: Ecclesiastical Democracy and the Tensions of Trusteeism*.
        Notre Dame: University of Notre Dame Press.

Caroli, B. B.
1973   *Italian Repatriation from the United States, 1900–1914*. New York: Center for Migration
        Studies.

Christmas, G. V.
1903   "May Customs in Italy," *Catholic World*, 77:155–158.

Cirigliano, D., S.J.
1920   "Protestant Activities in our Parishes," *Woodstock Letters*, 69:229–231, 340–341.

Cohalen, F.
1983   *A Popular History of the Archdiocese of New York*. Yonkers, New York: United States Catholic Historical Society.

Cohen, M.
1993   *Workshop to Office: Two Generations of Italian Women in New York City, 1900–1950*. Ithaca: Cornell University Press.

Congedo, J. M.
1924   "Bearers of Rich Gifts," *Il Carroccio*, 20:471–473.

Conzens, K. N., *et al.*
1990   "The Invention of Ethnicity: A Perspective from the USA," *Altreitalie*, 3:37–62.

Cook, A.
1974   *Armies of the Streets: The New York City Draft Riots of 1863*. Lexington, Kentucky: University Press of Kentucky.

Cooney, J.
1984   *The American Pope: The Life and Times of Francis Cardinal Spellman*. New York: Times Books.

Corsi, E.
1935   *In the Shadow of Liberty: The Chronicle of Ellis Island*. New York: MacMillan

Cosenza, M. A.
1967   *Our Lady of Pompei in Greenwich Village*. New York: Our Lady of Pompei.

Covello, L.
1958   *The Heart is the Teacher*. New York: McGraw-Hill.

———
1967   *The Social Background of the Italo-American School Child: A Study of the Southern Italian Family Mores and Their Effects on the School Situation in Italy and America*. Lieden: E.J. Brill.

Curran, R. E., S.J.
1978   *Michael Augustine Corrigan and the Shaping of Conservative Catholicism in America, 1878–1902*. New York: Arno.

Cushing, R. J.
1954   "Italian Immigrants," *Catholic Mind*, 52:604–609.

Di Carlo, D. M.
1990   "The History of the Italian *Festa* in New York City: 1880's to the Present." Unpublished Ph.D. dissertation, New York University.

Di Giovanni, S. M.
1994   "The Apostolic Delegate and Immigration, 1892–1896," *United States Catholic Historian* 12(2):47–68. Spring.

———
1991   "Mother Cabrini: Early Years in New York," *Catholic Historical Review* 77(1):56–77. January

———
1983   "Michael Augustine Corrigan and the Italian Immigrants: The Relationship Between the Church and the Italians in the Archdiocese of New York, 1885–1902." Unpublished Ph.D. dissertation, Gregorian Pontifical University (Rome).

Diggins, J. P.
1972   *Mussolini and Fascism: The View from America*. Princeton: Princeton University Press.

Dignan, P. J.
1933   *A History of the Legal Incorporation of Catholic Church Property in the United States, 1784–1932*. Washington, D.C.: Catholic University of America Press.

Dolan, J. P.
1978   *Catholic Revivalism: The American Experience, 1830–1900*. Notre Dame, Indiana: University of Notre Dame Press.

———
1975   *The Immigrant Church: New York's Irish and German Catholics, 1815–1865*. Baltimore: The Johns Hopkins University Press.

Dolan, J. P., ed.
1987   *The American Catholic Parish: A History from 1850 to the Present*, 2 volumes. New York: Paulist Press.

DuBois, A., O.F.M. Cap.
1936   *Golden Jubilee of the Church of Our Lady Queen of Angels*. New York: Privately published.

Dunne, E. M.
1898   "Memoirs of 'Zi Pre,'" *American Ecclesiastical Review*, 49:192–203.

Ellis, J. T., ed.
1956   *Documents of American Catholic History*. Milwaukee: Bruce Publishing Co. Pp. 482–485.

———
1969   *American Catholicism*, second edition. Chicago: University of Chicago Press.

Femminella, F. X.
1961   "The Impact of Italian Migration and American Catholicism,' *American Catholic Sociological Review*, 22: 233–241.

Fidelis
1924   "Nationalism and the Catholicity of the Clergy in the United States," *Ecclesiastical Review*, 70:295–299.

Foerster, R. F.
1924   *The Italian Emigration of our Times*. Cambridge, Massachusetts: Harvard University Press (Harvard Economic Studies).

Foner, E.
1980   "Class, Ethnicity, and Radicalism in the Gilded Age: The Land League and Irish-America." In *Politics and Ideology in the Age of the Civil War*. New York: Oxford University Press. Pp. 150–200.

Formica, G.
1927   "Catholic Charities and the Immigrant," *The Voice of the Immigrant*, 4:1–2.

Franklin, L.
1900   "The Italian in America: What He Has Been, What He Shall Be," *Catholic World*, 71.

Fusco, N.
1920   "Why Do They Hate Us? Jesuitism and Italian Immigrants," *Il Carroccio*, 11:170–179.

Gannon, R. I., S.J.
1962   *The Cardinal Spellman Story*. Garden City, NY: Doubleday and Company.

Giambastiani, L.
1912   "In the Melting Pot – The Italians," *Extension*, 7:9–10, 20–21.

Greeley, A. M.
1961   "The Impact of Italian Migration and American Catholicism," *American Catholic Sociological Review*, 22:333.

Greene, V. R.
1987   *American Immigrant Leaders, 1800–1910: Marginality and Identity*. Baltimore: Johns Hopkins University Press.

Handlin, O.
1951   *The Uprooted: The Epic Story of the Great Migrations that Made the American People*. New York: Grosset and Dunlap.

_____

1958   *Al Smith and his America*. Boston: Little, Brown.

Hanley, W. A.
1948   *Golden Jubilee of Saint Philip Neri Church, 1898–1948*. New York: Allied Printing.

Hannigan, S. J.
1909   Souvenir of the Centennial Celebration of Saint Patrick's Old Cathedral, New York,
        1809–1909. New York: Privately published.

Hayes, P. J.
1923   "The Immigrant Problem," Extension, 18:13–14, 57.

1923   "The Unification of Catholic Charities," Catholic World, 117:147–150.

Hecker, I. T.
1877   "The Outlook in Italy," Catholic World, 26:1–21.

Henderson, T. M.
1979   "Immigrant Politician: Salvatore Cotillo, Progressive Ethnic," International Migration
        Review, 13:81–102.

Higham, J.
1955   Strangers in the Land: Patterns of American Nativism, 1860–1925. New Brunswick:
        Rutgers University Press.

Hillenbrand, M. J.
1935   "Has the Immigrant Kept the Faith?" America, 55:153–155.

Howard, F.
1896   "The Church and Social Reform," Catholic World, 63:286–293.

Johnson, P. E.
1978   A Shopkeeper's Millennium: Society and Revivals in Rochester, New York, 1815–1837.
        New York: Hill and Wang.

Jubilee (a Franciscan publication)
1959   "A Priest's Campaign Against Delinquency," Jubilee. November.

Kantowicz, E. R.
1983   Corporation Sole: Cardinal Mundelein and Chicago Catholicism. Notre Dame: University
        of Notre Dame Press.

1981   "Cardinal Mundelein of Chicago and the Shaping of Twentieth Century American
        Catholicism," Journal of American History, 68:52–68.

Kelley, F. C.
1915   "The Church and the Immigrant," Catholic Mind, 13:471–484.

Kelly, G. A.
1954   The Story of Saint Monica's Parish, New York City, 1879–1954. New York: Monica
        Press.

Kelly, W. R.
1924   "The Cardinal of Charities," *Il Carroccio*, 14:445–446.

Kennedy, David M.
1980   *Over Here: The First World War and American Society*. New York: Oxford University Press.

Kessner, T.
1977   *The Golden Door: Italian and Jewish Immigrant Mobility in New York City, 1880–1915*. New York: Oxford University Press.

Klein, C. R.
1988   "Jesuits and Boyhood in Victorian New York," *U.S. Catholic Historian*, 7:375–391.

Lagnese, J. C.
1931   "The Italian Catholic," *America*, 40:475–476.

La Gumina, S. J.
1979   *The Immigrants Speak: Italian Americans Tell Their Story*. New York: Center for Migration Studies.

Liptak, D., R.S.M.
1989   *Immigrants and Their Church*. New York: MacMillan (Bicentennial History of the Catholic Church in America).

———
1987   *European Immigrants and the Catholic Church in Connecticut, 1870–1920*. New York: Center for Migration Studies.

———
1979   "European Immigrants and the Catholic Church in Connecticut, 1870–1920." Ph.D., The University of Connecticut.

Lumia, J.
1960   *Golden Jubilee: Our Lady of Mount Carmel Church, Poughkeepsie, New York*. New York: Privately printed.

Lynch, B. J.
1888   "The Italians in New York," *Catholic World*, 47:67–73.

Lynch, D., S.J.
1901   "In the Italian Quarter of New York," *The Messenger of the Sacred Heart of Jesus*, 36:115–126.

Magri, F. J.
1906   *The Catholic Church in the City and Diocese of Richmond*. Richmond: Whittet and Shepperson.

Mariano, J. H.
1921   *The Italian Contribution to American Democracy.* Boston: Christopher Publishing House.

Marraro, H. R.
1949   "Italians in New York in the Eighteen-Fifties," *New York History*, 30:181–203, 276–303.

Marschall, J. P., C.S.V.
1971   "Diocesan and Religious Clergy: The History of a Relationship, 1789–1969." In *The Catholic Priest in the United States: Historical Investigations.* Ed. J. T. Ellis. Collegeville, Minnesota: Saint John's University Press. Pp. 385–421.

Marsh, M. C.
1932   "The Life and Work of the Churches in an Interstitial Area." Unpublished Ph.D. dissertation, New York University.

McAvoy, T. T., C.S.C.
1963   *The Americanist Heresy in Roman Catholicism, 1895–1900.* Notre Dame: University of Notre Dame Press.

McCadden, J., and H. McCadden.
1969   *Father Valera: Torch Bearer from Cuba.* Yonkers, New York: United States Catholic Historical Society.

McGuinness, M. M.
1985   "Response to Reform: An Historical Interpretation of the Catholic Settlement Movement, 1897–1915." Unpublished Ph.D. dissertation, Union Theological Seminary (New York).

McKeown, Elizabeth
1988   *War and Welfare: American Catholics and World War I.* New York: Garland (The Heritage of American Catholicism).

McLoughlin, P.
1919   *Father Tom: Life and Lectures of Rev. Thomas P. McLoughlin.* New York: G.P. Putnam's Sons.

McNab, J.
1977   "Bethlehem Chapel: Presbyterians and Italian Americans in New York City," *Journal of Presbyterian History*, 55:145–160.

McSorley, J., C.S.P.
1909   "In Sicily," *Catholic World*, 88:653–659, 810–819.

———
1910   "The Catholic Layman and Social Reform," *Catholic World*, 92:187–195.

1913   "The Church and the Italian Child: The Situation in New York," *Ecclesiastical Review*, 68:268–282.

McSweeney, E. F.
1908   "A New York Pastor of the Latter Half of the Nineteenth Century," American Catholic Historical Society of Philadelphia *Records and Studies*, 19:42–58.

Meehan, T. F.
1903   "Evangelizing the Italians," *The Messenger of the Sacred Heart of Jesus*, 39:16–32.

Mendezabal, Rufo, S.J.
1972   *Catalogus Defunctorum in Renata Societate Iesu ab a. 1814 ad a. 1970*. Rome: Curiam P. Gen.

Miller, J. E.
1983   "Taking Off the Gloves: The United States and the Italian Elections of 1948," *Diplomatic History*, 7:35–55.

Mize, S. Y.
1991   "Defending Roman Loyalties and Republican Values: The 1848 Italian Revolution in American Catholic Apologetics," *Church History*, 60(4):480–492.

Mosley, D. H.
1922   "The Catholic Social Worker in an Italian District," *Catholic World*, 94:618–628.

Muredach, M.
1923   "An Experiment in City Home Missions," *Extension*, 17:35–36, 62.

Mussolini, A.
1931   "Vaticano e Italia; Il Pensiero di Mussolini," *Il Carroccio*, 33:307–313.

Nativity (44 Second Avenue, Manhattan)
1971   *Church of the Nativity, New York City*. South Hackensack, New Jersey: Custombook.

New York Association for Improving the Condition of the Poor
1879   *Thirty-Sixth Annual Report of the New York Association for Improving the Conditions of the Poor*. New York: Office of the Association.

New York City Works Progress Administration
1941   "Inventory of the Church Archives in New York City: Roman Catholic Church, Archdiocese of New York." Volume Two. Typescript.

O'Brien, A. C.
1982   "Italian Youth in Conflict: Catholic Action and Fascist Italy, 1929–1931," *Catholic Historical Review*, 63:625–635.

Occhiogrosso, P.
1987   *Once a Catholic*. New York: Houghton-Mifflin.

Old Missionary, An.
1889   "Priests for Italian Immigrants," *American Ecclesiastical Review*, 20:513–516.

Orsi, R. A.
1989   "What Did Women Really Think When They Prayed To St. Jude?"*U.S. Catholic Historian*, 8(1-2):67–79.

_____
1985   *The Madonna of 115th Street: Faith and Community in Italian Harlem, 1880–1950*. New Haven: Yale University Press.

O'Shea, J. J.
1895   "After the Manner of St. Francis," *Catholic World*, 62:377–383.

O'Toole, J. M.
1991   "The Role of Bishops in American Catholic History: Myth and Reality in the Case of Cardinal William O'Connell, *Catholic Historical Review*, 77(4):595–615.

Our Lady of Loreto (303 Elizabeth Street, Manhattan)
1917   "A Short History of the Mission of Our Lady of Loreto, New York," *Woodstock Letters*, 46:171–187.

Our Lady of Mount Carmel (White Plains, New York)
1977   *Diamond Jubilee of Our Lady of Mount Carmel Parish*. New York: Privately printed.

Our Lady of Sorrows (213 Stanton Street, Manhattan)
1967   *Our Lady of Sorrows*. South Hackensack, New Jersey: Custombook.

Palmieri, A., O.S.A.
1923   "The Contribution of the Italian Catholic Clergy to the United States," In *Catholic Builders of the Nation: A Symposium on the Catholic Contribution to the Civilization of the United States*. Edited by C. E. McGuire. Boston: Continental Press, Inc. Volume 2, Pp. 128–149.

_____
1921   *Il Grave Problema Religioso Italiano negli Stati Uniti*. Florence: Librerìa Editrice Fiorentina.

_____
1920   "Il Clero Italiano negli Stati Uniti," *Vita Italiana*, 15:113–127.

_____
1918   "Italian Protestantism in the United States," *Catholic World*, 107:177–189.

Peiss, K.
1986   *Cheap Amusements: Working Women and Leisure in Turn-of-the-Century New York*. Philadelphia: Temple University Press.

Pistella, D.
1954   · *The Crowning of a Queen* Translated by Peter Rofrano. New York: Shrine of Our Lady of Mount Carmel.

Pius XI
1936   *Christian Education of Youth: Official and Complete English Text of the Encyclical Letter of His Holiness, Pope Pius XI*. Washington, DC: National Catholic Welfare Conference.

———

1931   *Catholic Action: Encyclical Letter of His Holiness, Pope Pius XI*. Washington, DC: National Catholic Welfare Conference.

Raimondo, J. J.
1979   *Saint Clare of Assisi, Bronx, New York, 1929–1979*. Pearl River, New York: Universal Graphics.

Ravitch, D.
1974   *The Great School Wars: New York City, 1805–1973: A History of the Public Schools as Battlefield of Social Change*. New York: Basic Books.

Reilly, M. P. A., O.P.
1956   "The Administration of Parish Schools in the Archdiocese of New York, 1800–1900," United States Catholic Historical Society *Records and Studies*, 44:45–83.

Reynolds, M. J.
1907   "The Italian and his Church at Home," *The Missionary Review of the World*, 20:607–610. New Series.

Riis, J. A.
1971   *How the Other Half Lives: Studies among the Tenements of New York*. New York: Dover. Reprint.

———

1904   *Children of the Tenements*. New York: MacMillan.

———

1899   "Feast-Days in Little Italy," *The Century Magazine*, 53:491–499.

Rose, P. M.
1922   *The Italians in America*. New York: George H. Doran Company.

Rosenwaike, I.
1962   *Population History of New York City*. Syracuse, New York: Syracuse University Press, 1972.

Russo, N., S.J.
1896   "The Origin and Progress of Our Italian Mission in New York," *Woodstock Letters*, 25:135–143.

Russo, N. J.
1968   "The Religious Acculturation of the Italians in New York City." Unpublilshed Ph.D. dissertation, Saint John's University (New York).

Sacred Hearts of Jesus and Mary (307 East 33rd Street, Manhattan)
1964   *Golden Jubilee, Church of the Sacred Hearts of Jesus and Mary, 1914–1964.* Hackensack, NJ: Custombook.

Saint Ann (312 East 110th Street, Manhattan)
1955   *Golden Jubilee Dinner Dance of Saint Ann's Parish, 1905–1955* (New York: Privately printed.

Saint Anthony (Commonwealth Avenue, Bronx)
1931   *Saint Anthony's, Commonwealth Avenue, the Bronx, New York City.* New York: Privately printed.

1964   *Dedication of Convent of Church of Saint Anthony . . . 1964.* New York: Privately printed, 1964.

Saint Brigid (119 Avenue B, Manhattan)
1899   *Souvenir of the Golden Jubilee of Saint Brigid's Church.* New York: Privately printed.

1889   *Souvenir of the Consecration Year of Saint Brigid's Church.* New York: Privately printed.

Saint Clare of Assisi (1027 Rhinelander Avenue)
1955   *Year Book Commemorating the Silver Jubilee of the Parish of Saint Clare of Assisi . . . 1930–1955.* New York: Privately published.

Saint Dominic (Unionport Road and Morris Park Avenue, Bronx)
1974   *Salute to Saint Dominic's.* New York: Privately printed.

Saint Joseph (5 Monroe Street, Manhattan)
1977   *Fiftieth Anniversary, Saint Joseph Church.* New York: Park Publishing Company.

Saint Joseph's (171 Saint Mary's Avenue, Staten Island)
1977   *Church of Saint Joseph, Staten Island . . . 1902-1977.* New York: Privately published.

Saint Lucy (833 Mace Avenue, Bronx)
1977   *Saint Lucy's Church, Bronx, New York.* New York: Privately printed.

Saint Rita of Cascia (448 College Avenue, Bronx)
1975   *Saint Rita of Cascia Shrine Church.* South Hackensack, New Jersey: Custombook.

Saint Roch (525 Wales Avenue, Bronx)
1949   *Golden Jubilee of Saint Roch's Parish . . . 1949.* New York: Privately printed.

Saint Vito (Mamaroneck, New York)
1961   *Church of Saint Vito, Golden Jubilee, 1911–1961.* New York: Privately printed.

Salvetti, P.
         "Una parrocchia italiana di New York e i suoi fedeli: Nostra Signora di Pompei
         (1892–1933)," *Studi Emigrazione,* 21:43–64.

Salvemini, Gaetano
1977   *Italian Fascist Activities in the United States.* Ed. Philip V. Cannistraro. New York:
         Center for Migration Studies.

Sanders, J. W.
1977   *The Education of an Urban Minority: Catholics in Chicago, 1833–1965.* New York:
         Oxford University Press.

Sassi, C., C.S.
1946   *Parrocchia della Madonna di Pompei in New York: Notizie Storiche dei Primi Cin-
         quant'anni dalla sua Fondazione, 1892–1942.* Rome: Tipografia Santa Lucia.

Scalabrini, G. B.
1968   "L'Emigrazione Italiana in America," *Studio Emigrazione,* 5:199–230. Reprint.

Scanlan, A. J.
1922   *Saint Joseph's Seminary, Dunwoodie, New York, 1896–1921.* Yonkers, New York:
         United States Catholic Historical Society.

Senner, J. H.
1896   "Immigration from Italy," *North American Review,* 162:649–657.

Sexton, P. C.
1965   *Spanish Harlem.* New York: Harper and Row.

Shaw, R.
1983   *John DuBois: Founding Father.* Yonkers, New York: United States Catholic Historical
         Society.

———
1977   *Dagger John: The Unquiet Life and Times of Archbishop John Hughes of New York.* New
         York: Paulist Press.

Shaw, S. J.
1991   *The Catholic Parish as a Way-Station of Ethnicity and Americanization: Chicago's
         Germans and Italians, 1903–1939.* Brooklyn: Carlson (Chicago Studies in the History
         of American Religion).

Shelley, T. J.
1994   "Francis Cardinal Spellman and His Seminary at Dunwoodie," *Catholic Historical Review* 80(2): 282–298. April.

———

1992   "John Cardinal Farley and Modernism in New York," *Church History*, 41:350–361.

Shipman, A. J.
1916   "Our Italian Greek Catholics." In *A Memorial of Andrew J. Shipman: His Life and Writings.* Ed. Condé B. Pallen. New York: Encyclopedia Press, Inc. Pp. 106–120.

Skerret, E.
1981   "The Irish Parish in Chicago, 1880–1930." (University of Notre Dame) Cushwa Center for the Study of American Catholicism Working Papers, Series 9, No. 2.

Smith, J. T.
1905   *The Catholic Church in New York: A History of the New York Diocese From its Establishment in 1808 to the Present Time.* New York: Locke and Hall. Two volumes.

Speranza, G. C.
1920   "Does America Americanize?" *Atlantic Monthly*, 125:263–269.

———

1918   "Heart's Allegiance," *Outlook*, 119:105–107.

Stauder, C.
1885   "Report of the Minister in Charge." In *The Italian Mission of the Protestant Episcopal Church in the City of New York Yearbook.* New York: Privately published.

Stibili, E. C.
1977   "The St. Raphael Society For the Protection of Italian Immigrants, 1887–1923." Unpublished Ph.D. dissertation, University of Notre Dame.

Sullivan, M. L., M.S.C.
1992   *Mother Cabrini: "Italian Immigrant of the Century".* New York: CMS.

Taves, A.
1983   "'External' Devotions and the Interior Life: Popular Devotional Theologies in Mid-Nineteenth Century America." (University of Notre Dame) Cushwa Center for Study of American Catholicism Working Paper Series, Series 3, Number 2.

Tessarolo, G. C.S., ed.
1962   *The Church's Magna Charta for Migrants.* New York: Saint Charles Seminary.

Testa, S. L.
1908   "'Strangers from Rome' in Greater New York," *The Missionary Review*, 31:216–218.

Thuente, C. W.
1910   "Charity in New York," *Saint Vincent de Paul Society Quarterly*, 15:164.

Tiffany, G. E.
1977   *Our Lady of Solace Parish, Seventy-Fifth Anniversary*. New York: Privately published.

Tolino, J. V.
1939   "The Future of the Italian-American Problem," *Ecclesiastical Review*, 101:221–232.

_____
1939   "The Church in America and the Italian Problem." *Ecclesiastical Review*, 100:22–32.

_____
1938   "Solving the Italian Problem," *Ecclesiastical Review*, 99:246–256.

Tomasi, S. M.
1975   *Piety and Power: The Role of the Italian Parishes in the New York Metropolitan Area, 1880–1930*. New York: Center for Migration Studies.

Tomasi, S. M., and E. C. Stibili
1992   *Italian Americans and Religion: An Annotated Bibliography*. Second edition. New York: Center for Migration Studies.

Transfiguration (29 Mott Street, Manhattan)
1977   *Transfiguration Church: A Church of Immigrants, 1827–1977*.

Tricarico, D.
1984   *The Italians of Greenwich Village: Social Structure and Transformation of an Ethnic Community*. New York: Center for Migration Studies.

_____
1980   "The Italians of Greenwich Village: The Social Structure and Transformation of an Ethnic Community." Unpublished Ph.D. dissertation, New School for Social Research (New York).

U. S. Catholic Historian
1987   *U. S. Catholic Historian* 6(4). Fall. (Special issue on Italian-American Catholicism.)

United States Department of Commerce, Bureau of the Census
1975   *Historical Statistics of the United States, Colonial Times to 1970*. Washington, DC: Government Printing Office, 1975. Two volumes.

Varacalli, J. A.
1986   "The Changing Nature of the 'Italian Problem' in the Catholic Church of the United States," *Faith and Reason*, 12(1):38–73

Vecoli, R. J.
1969   "Prelates and Peasants: Italian Immigrants and the Catholic Church," *Journal of Social History*, 2:217–267.

———

1964   "*Contadini* in Chicago: A Critique of *The Uprooted*," *Journal of American History*, 51:404–417.

———

1963   "Chicago's Italians prior to World War One: A Study of Their Social and Economic Adjustment." Unpublished Ph.D. dissertation, University of Wisconsin.

Walsh, J. C.
1919   "Ireland and Article X," *America*, 21:193–196.

———

1919   "Cross Currents at Versailles," *America*, 21:141–143.

Walsh, J. J.
1926   *Our American Cardinals*. New York: D. Appleton and Co.

Ware, C.
1965   *Greenwich Village, 1920–1930: A Comment on American Civilization in the Post-War Years*. New York: Harper. Reprint.

Waters, M. C.
1990   *Ethnic Options: Choosing Identities in America*. Berkeley: University of California Press.

White, J. M.
1989   *The Diocesan Seminary in the United States: A History from the 1780s to the Present*. Notre Dame: University of NotreDame Press.

Wiebe, R.
1967   *The Search for Order, 1877–1920*. New York: Hill and Wang.

Whyte, W. F.
1955   *Street Corner Society*, second edition. Chicago: University of Chicago Press.

Wright, F. H.
1907   "The Italian in America," *The Missionary Review of the World*, 20:196–198.

Young, A.
1888   "How to Obtain Congregational Singing," *Catholic World*, 47:721–738.

Zarrilli, J.
1928   "Some More Light on the Italian Problem," *Ecclesiastical Review*, 79:256–268.

1924   *A Prayerful Appeal to the American Hierarchy*. Two Harbors, MN: Privately printed.

1924   "A Suggestion for the Solution of the Italian Problem," *Ecclesiastical Review*, 70:70–77.

Zema, G. A., S.J.
1936   "The Italian Immigrant Problem," *America*, 55:129–130.

1953   "Jottings in Italy," *Ecclesiastical Review*, 139:95–99.

Index

Also Published by the Center for Migration Studies

REFUGEES: A CHALLENGE TO SOLIDARITY. PROCEEDINGS OF THE INTERNATIONAL ROUND TABLE ON THE QUESTION OF REFUGEES *sponsored by the Permanent Observer Mission of the Holy See to the United Nations and the Path to Peace Foundation.* 1994. Pp. 370. ISBN 0-934733-78-3.

JOHN BAPTIST SCALABRINI AND ITALIAN MIGRATION *by Lice Maria Signor.* 1994. Pp. 300. ISBN 0-934733-79-1.

A VISION UNFOLDING: THE SCALABRINIANS IN NORTH AMERICA (1888–1988) *by Alba Zizzamia.* 1989. Pp. 150. ISBN N/A.

A SCALABRINIAN MISSION AMONG POLISH IMMIGRANTS IN BOSTON, 1893–1909 *by Silvano M. Tomasi, C.S.* 1985. Pp. 25. ISBN 0-934733-01-5.

EVOLUTION OF THE MISSION OF THE SCALABRINIAN CONGREGATION *by Velasio de Paolis, C.S.* 1985. Pp. 44. ISBN 0-913256-84-6.

THE PASTORAL ACTION OF BISHOP JOHN BAPTIST SCALABRINI AND HIS MISSIONARIES AMONG IMMIGRANTS IN THE AMERICAS, 1887–1987 *by Silvano M. Tomasi, C.S.* 1984. Pp. 31. ISBN 0-913256-71-4.

JOHN BAPTIST SCALABRINI *by Marco Caliaro and Mario Francesconi, C.S. Translated by Alba Zizzamia.* 1977. Pp. 580. ISBN 0-913256-24-2.

JOHN B. SCALABRINI: AN INSIGHT INTO HIS SPIRITUALITY *by Mario Francesconi, C.S.* 1973. Pp. 106. ISBN 0-934733-44-9.

BISHOP SCALABRINI'S PLAN FOR THE PASTORAL CARE OF MIGRANTS OF ALL NATIONALITIES *by Mario Francesconi, C.S.* 1973. Pp. 38. ISBN 0-934733-24-4.

THE CHURCH'S MAGNA CHARTA FOR MIGRANTS *edited by G. Tessarolo.* 1961. Pp. 300. ISBN 0-913256-45-5.